The Sportsman Guide to UFOs: Around the World

by

John Scott Chace

The Sportsman Guide to UFOs: Around the World

Edition 1
Series 1

Book Cover Page designed by John S Chace
At Cover Creator

No part of this book may be used of reproduced in any manner whatsoever without written permission except in case of brief quotations embodied in critical articles or reviews.

All photographs in the book are in the public domain and have been referenced.
All UFO illustrations in the book are designed by John Scott Chace.

Other Books by John Scott Chace on Amazon.com

Individual Books on UFOs

"The Invasion of Earth: UFO and Extraterrestrial Contact"
"Project Blue Book, Top Secret UFO Files: The Untold Truth"
"God Extraterrestrials and Man": A Christian Perspective on UFO'
"UFOs In The Sky: Celebrities, Politicians and Military Officers"

The Regional UFO Series

"UFOs In U.S. AirSpace: Hard Evidence"
"UFOs In European AirSpace: More Evidence"
"UFOs In Central and South American AirSpace"
"UFOs In The Sky: The Upper Midwest States"
"UFOs In The Sky: The Southwest States"
"UFOs In The Sky: Mid-Atlantic States"
"UFOs In The Sky: The Southeastern States"

Copyright © 2018 John Scott Chace
All rights reserved.
ISBN: 9781790894956

The Sportsman Guide to UFOs: Around the World

Dedication

It is with honor, I dedicate this book and its contents to the following:

God Almighty, my heavenly Father and Jesus Christ for everything. Whom I believe created the Angels of heaven, people on earth and the people of different worlds according to his will.

My wife Kristin, children and grandchildren.

My father Colonel Alston Rigby Chace, Chaplain (Col. U.S.A.F.- Retired), Vietnam Veteran and his brother Colonel Frank Clinton Chace Jr. (Col. USMC-Retired / deceased), Vietnam Veteran. My mother and all my Aunts and Uncles. My sister Carey and brother James (deceased); all my cousins and their spouses who are living or deceased.

To all my business associates in the Insurance Industry who have had UFO experiences or want to know more about this phenomenon.

To all the residents, police, physicians, politicians, teachers, students, governors, mayors and military officers who came forward, to tell the truth about the UFO reality. For having courage in the face of skeptics who have never seen a UFO.

To you, the citizens around the Globe, that want to know the truth that we are not alone in this Universe.

Table of Contents

Acknowledgements viii
Introduction ix
Chapter 1: Why They Come 15
Chapter 2: Politicians and the Military 20
Chapter 3: Police confirm UFOs 27
Chapter 4: Large UFOs 30
Chapter 5: They come in Fleets 38
Chapter 6: UFOs land 44
Chapter 7: UFOs over Roads 54
Chapter 8: Near our Cars 60
Chapter 9: UFOs at Camps and Golf 66
Chapter 10: Potential Abductions 73
Chapter 11: People and Animals Injured 81
Chapter 12: Rivers and Lakes 85
Chapter 13: Traveling In The Sky 104
Chapter 14: Reservoirs, Ponds 122
Chapter 15: Beaches and Harbors 129
Chapter 16: UFOs off shore 140
Chapter 17: Photographic Evidence 152
Chapter 18: Over Hills and Mountains 157
Chapter 19: Shooting UFOs 164
Chapter 20: Near Ships and Boats 168
Chapter 21: Submerged UFOs 173
Chapter 22: Near Planes and Jets 178

Chapter 23: Windows and Occupants 181
Chapter 24: Electromagnetic Effects.......................187
Chapter 25: Near Industrial Centers 191
Chapter 26: Incredible Speeds...............................194
Chapter 27: Strange Lights and Noises 199
Chapter 28: Attracted to Dams...............................204
Chapter 29: Conclusion 208
About the Author..213
Addendum 1: The Ships "Illustrations" 214
References and Sources 225

Acknowledgements

To all the UFO researchers and newspapers identified in this book who have made this book possible. Special credit to the following;

UFO Researchers

Dr. Olavo Fontes (of APRO); Major Donald Edward Keyhoe (USMC), Jan Aldrich (Project 1947), Barry Greenwood, Bob Pratt and Phillip J. Imbrogno; Larry Fawcett; Jacque Vallee, Dr., J. Allen Hynek (Project Blue Book), Dr. James E. McDonald; Dr. Richard F. Haines; Loren E. Gross; Retired Detective Constable Gary Heseltine; Dr. Steven Greer (Sirius and Disclosure); and Stephen Bassett (Citizens Hearing).

UFO Organizations

Thanks to NICAP.org, APRO (MUFON), NUFORC, CUFOS, NARCAP and Project 1947

UFO Magazines

Thanks to the editors and contributors of The APRO Bulletin, The UFO Investigator, The Flying Saucer Review and "UFOs: A History" by Loren E. Gross and all those that contributed to the material.

Important Websites for Researchers

Project 1947| hosted by Jan Aldrich – go to: http://www.project1947.com
NICAP.org | hosted by Francis L Ridge – go to: http://www.nicap.org/index.htm
Water UFO | hosted by Carl Feindt - go to: https://www.waterufo.net
NARCAP.org | hosted by Dr. Richard Haines | http://www.narcap.org/index.html
Sirius Disclosure | hosted by Dr. Stephen Greer | http://siriusdisclosure.com
The Citizens Hearing | hosted by Stephen Bassett | http://www.citizenhearing.org
NUFORC |hosted by Peter Davenport | http://www.nuforc.org

Military / Blue Book files

National Archives: https://www.archives.gov/research/military/air-force/ufos.html (for National Archives -input the word UFO, and materials will appear as links)
Fold3.com: https://www.fold3.com/
The Black Vault: http://www.theblackvault.com/documentarchive/project-blue-book/

For my list on top recommended UFOs books on the UFO reality and coverup go to back of book.

Introduction

UFOs are not Delusions or Illusions

Becoming aware UFOs exist –
will change your Paradigm in an instant.

As one discovers the reality of UFOs, a person must understand two fundamental truths that will change their entire life's meaning and future. Knowing about these future changes will help us evolve to become a better person in life – not only for ourselves but those around us.

Let's face the facts, we base our beliefs on our cultural beliefs and experiences as to what we know to be truth and we make important decisions about our lives. If the foundation of those cultural beliefs is false, then there is a good chance our beliefs are rooted in falsehood.

An example of this is Santa Claus. Growing up we were told by our parents if we were good, Santa would ride his sleigh and deposit a gift under our tree. It was later we all learned there is no Santa Clause and we had to adapt to the new thinking that this was untrue but a beautiful story.

Regarding UFOs, there is one distinct challenge for all of us who have had to make such a change. That is, to understand those around us, who have never experienced a UFO or desire to know about UFOs.

For those of us who have seen a UFO and have been able to adapt the meaning of this to our new worldview will enlighten our mind, body, and spirit. The key here is to understand the coming change and embrace (adapt) to that change.

Paradigm Shift

When a person sees a UFO for the first time, his or her world is changed forever, this is because his former believe in the world as he or she knew it, no longer is valid.

This shift in our basic worldview (from our earlier understanding of the world) is called a Paradigm shift. Some people adapt well to these shifts, while others stubbornly attempt to hold onto false beliefs.

Humans have faced hundreds of paradigm shifts throughout history. Paradigm shifts take place in Theology, Science, Psychology, etc. The list below provides some easy to understand shifts from formerly held beliefs that were later proven false.

Early Beliefs (Old Worldviews) that were proven false

Early Belief (Old Worldview)	The Truth (New Worldview)
The Earth is Flat	The Earth is Round!
The Sun revolves around the Earth (Ptolemy geocentric model)	The Earth revolves around the Sun! (Copernicus)
We are unable to escape earth's gravity	We escape earth's gravity with enough force in rockets or gravitational elimination (anti-gravity) drives!
Man cannot split the atom	Man invented the "Atomic Bomb"!

Delusional Thinking

When we share our UFO sightings to those with an open mind or those who have seen a UFO, they will "get it." Meaning they have come to know the truth or they are open to the truth. However, when we share such stories with a non-believer (someone who is closed minded or never seen a UFO) they may believe we are "delusional."

The reality is 50% of Americans, and 80% of those in the UK have either seen a UFO or know of someone who has. So half of the U.S. population is clueless to the UFO reality – they think its poppycock!

If you are called "delusional," you need to put the term aside and speak the truth to the person. You need to stand your ground and inform them they do not understand the whole truth or the definition of "delusion."

According to *'Psychology Today'*; "Delusions are fixed, and false personal beliefs that are resistant to change in light of conflicting evidence.

Delusions are the extreme case of irrational beliefs. These beliefs are obsessive and cause emotional distress."

'Psychology Today'; states; "the delusional belief is something very important to those who hold them. That is why they are blind to counterevidence because they do not want to change their belief."

An example is to believe in someone's leadership when evidence shows they have performed poorly at the task.

'Psychology Today' points out; "Delusions exist on a continuum with irrational belief, Even some otherwise rational people appear to believe bizarre things are not true." Two questions must be answered:

1. What is it that brought the delusional idea to mind in the first place? (e.g., experience, dream, belief, vision, etc.)
2. Why is this idea not rejected when so much evidence against its truth is available to the person? (does evidence proof it's a false reality)

"Delusional reasoning can be described by an over-reliance on instinctive (rapid and non-reflective) thanking and under-reliance ion analytical thinking (deliberative, effortful)."[i]

One can see above that seeing a UFO – does not qualify as a delusional belief as radar, photographic and eyewitness evidence proved their existence and not a fantasy. Therefore the person who has labeled you this is naïve and not educated in the reality of UFOs.

The book you are about to read is aimed at the 50% of Americans who have never seen a UFO or refuse to believe in UFOs for reasons of overpowering denial. Webster's defines "Denial" in several ways;

1. From a psychological perspective; denial is a "defense mechanism" in which confrontation with reality is avoided by denying the existence of the truth.
2. Refusal to acknowledge a thing.[ii]

Illusions do not leave evidence

Merriam-Webster defines '*Illusion*' as a "misleading image presented to the vision, or perception of something objectively existing in such a way as to cause misinterpretation of its actual nature."

Another definition would be the state or fact of being intellectually deceived or misled. Another definition is an "idea or belief that is not true."

An excellent example of an illusion would be someone looking at the moon or meteor (real objects) and misinterpreting them as a UFO. The moon, meteors and stars are not UFOs. But they can look like a bright glowing UFO.

In looking at a UFO we know specific facts, some object in the sky is present, yet we have not scientifically or personally (at the time) been able to determine what it is.

What we can say is UFOs do leave in many cases evidence of their presence. An example is after landing and taking off, investigators find landing pad depressions in the mud or grass where the UFO had been.

In other cases, UFOs may leave "angel hair" behind in the trees and telephone wires.

UFOs can break off the top of tree branches as they fly over or descend into the forest floor. UFOs have been known to boil the tar on highway surfaces.

In other cases, UFOs coming into close proximity to people leave burns and scars on human flesh. Their propulsion system affects the brains of Dogs, Horses and other animals making them crazy enough to scurry around to fund shelter away from the alien crafts.

Illusions do not leave evidence of its presence as it's not real. Therefore UFOs are not illusionary.

The next time someone says you saw an illusion – you need to set them straight. These so-called friends or family members were not present to see what you saw; therefore they do not know what he or she is talking about when they mention you just saw an illusion. In fact, it may be quite the opposite, the person saying this to you may be in deep denial or closed minded to the scientific truth that UFOs exist.

If you happen to see UFO congrats!

If you have to see UFO congratulations you are now part of the 50% of Americans that know UFOs exist. Realize you just left the other 50% who are unaware of its reality or are too afraid to consider the truth. Whatever you do if those around you are part of the 50% of unbelievers, have compassion on them as they see the world through Rose colored glasses. Your glasses are now crystal clear.

The Moral of the Story

So the moral of the story is, if you see a UFO, you are not delusional and you have not experienced an illusion, as the phenomena have been proven true by Astronomers, Scientists, Military officials, Presidents, and the common man and woman.

As mentioned earlier, if someone calls you delusional, you need to set them straight as they do not understand the concept of delusional thinking or studied the proof that Aliens exist.

The second moral of the story is to embrace your change and move on to helping the world and the loved ones around you the best you can for the time you have on this planet.

Chapter 1: Why They Come

If you are reading this book, you are a sportsman and are interested in UFOs you may see while in the wild or are just curious about the types of things that attract UFOs.

As I discuss in my book "UFOs In U.S. AIRSPACE" there are specific reasons for the pilots and crews of UFOs to visit particular locations.

Excluding natural phenomenon (e.g., meteors, birds, bats, bugs, planets, and manmade aircraft), there are several reasons we see a UFO. Excluding abductions, the following provides a few of these reasons for UFO visitation:

1. UFOs are on a reconnaissance mission to nuclear or industrial plants to monitor emission levels;

2. UFOs are on a reconnaissance mission to a nearby military base to monitor the stockpiles of atomic weapons.{*Note, you can read about this in my other books*}

3. UFOs are curious about the latest design of planes flying over the Southwest including any nuclear weapons aboard;

4. UFOs are curious about firework displays during the summer months and observe large gatherings of people. The occupants study how we react and what we do;

5. UFOs are traveling over your location on the way to another mission. You just happen to see the craft on its way to their new assignment.

There are many additional reasons for UFOs to stop over your home and neighborhood. The list is longer than the topics that label each chapter of this book. However, we will explore a few of the primary reasons in this chapter.

Secret 1952 Air Force Study on UFOs
20% of all UFO sightings
are over Atomic Plans and Military Installations.

On September 25, 1952, a detailed (formerly classified) Air Force report revealed that the Los Alamos Labs (NM) and White Sands Missile Range

(NM) were just a few of the many secret military bases and atomic installations in which UFOs have been seen. In fact in the United States over 20 military bases had regular visitation from UFOs and their occupants. According to the 1,800 sightings reviewed in the 1952 study, the Air Force stated:

> "the most authoritative and detailed sightings
> came from atomic plants and military bases
> and research centers.
> 20% of all sightings involved these locations."

As far as European studies on the concentration of UFOs at bases, we know of no published report in any newspaper on the subject. We do, however, have some idea of the many countries studying the phenomenon.

National UFO Studies

In my book "The Invasion of Earth" chapter 1 is dedicated to a well-known researcher for APRO. His name is Dr. Olavo T. Fontes. Fontes provided much-needed background evidence of the UFO reality as shared to him from the Brazilian government.

Within ten years of the Brazilian study, the French group Cometa also came to the same conclusion that UFOs were real. In this book, we will discuss the various European countries who have already determined UFO reality.

As far as a backdrop, if this is news to you, (UFO Reality) you are not alone. The U.S. began a secrecy campaign to prevent public panic in 1953.

The concern was a potential of anarchy in the streets of loss of faith in our government for not being able to defend our citizens from an advanced force off world.

Though this fear by local governments appears far-fetched today, it was a concern during the cold war. The major impetus behind these fears was the American CIA. I go into the CIA's debunking campaign in my book" UFOs; in US Air Space" chapter 1.

Why They are Here

In the United States, we know UFOs visit Nuclear Missile Sites, Nuclear Reactors and Nuclear Weapons Storage Areas. These cases are well documented in several books by many authors including my own material.

Besides nuclear sites, the occupants of UFOs appear interested in studying us. You will read in the following chapters that UFOs chase our cars, planes as well as visit schools, hospitals, and Airports. Just about anywhere a human is – the occupants want to study humans in action.

The Evidence Continues to mount

It's now a fact that UFOs are real and they are piloted by beings from other worlds. The facts are based on Radar and Photographic evidence, Eyewitness testimonies, releases of actual military photographs by the Pentagon and other military forces as well as military leader stopping forward admitting the truth.

If interested in seeing some great discussions on YouTube by military officers, just visit "The Disclosure Project" and "The Citizens Hearing."

Today's Reality
Those that are ignorant to UFO reality

It is regrettable we have to deal with certain segments of the world population who have not seen a UFO or have accepted the reality. For these people, they tend to have a distorted view of the world. That is they are cocooned from reality as we know it. For those of us who have seen UFOs and realize they are real from experience and military world testimonies, these people tend to think we are delusional.

For some of us, it may be our wives or other members of our community that remain ignorant to the facts of the new world they truly live in.

We must take pity of them and listen to their comments of shame.

How many Believe in UFOs
Gallup Polls

It's a fact, as more people see UFOs the facts become clear that these extraterrestrials space craft exist. The fact that UFOs exist no longer requires proof as their presence proves beyond any doubt, such witnesses are not delusional and in fact rooted in truth.

1966 | In 1966 a Public Opinion Poll by George Gallup shared: "More than five million Americans claims to have seen a flying saucer."

"About half the US adult civilian population believe these frequently reported flying saucers, while not necessarily saucers, are real and not just a figment of the imagination." [iii]

1973 | A Gallup survey released yesterday found that 51 percent of those persons interviewed believe that unidentified flying objects, sometimes called "flying saucers," are real and not just a figment of the imagination or cases of hallucination.

Also, 11 percent in the poll said they had seen UFO, double the percentage recorded in a previous survey on the subject by Gallup in 1966. The figure then was 5 percent.

Figure 1 - Chart on UFO Belief in the U.S.

The latest survey shows that nearly half of all persons polled, or 46 percent, believe that there is intelligent life on other planets. This represents a sharp increase of 34 percent over the 1966 poll.

It is also indicated that those persons who believe in the existence of life on other planets are far more likely to believe that UFOs are real. In fact, seven in ten of those who think there is such life say. UFOs are real.[iv]

1990 | Data seemed to back up Macintyre's argument that, when it came to belief in UFOs, reason was winning out. A 1990 Gallup poll found that 27 percent of Americans believed "extraterrestrial beings have visited Earth at some time in the past." That number rose to 33 percent in 2001, before dropping back to 24 percent in 2005.

2001 | The Disclosure Project (Dr. Steven Greer) launched the eyewitness testimonies of several hundred military officers UFO accounts at the National Press Club giving a wider audience to the truth. This is now on YouTube.

2015 | According to a 2015 Ipsos poll, 45 percent of Americans believe extraterrestrials have visited the Earth.[v]

2017 | nearly half the population believes UFOs could be a sign of extraterrestrial visitation.

A Huff Post/YouGov poll reveals that 48 percent of adults in the United States are open to the idea that alien spacecraft are observing our planet — and just 35 percent outright reject the idea.

The poll was seen as vindication from the community of UFO researchers who often feel they are laughed off by government officials.[vi]

More than one in two people in the UK, Germany and the US believe there is intelligent life out there in the universe. The next time the subject comes up at the dinner table, and you hear sniggers when someone admits they believe in aliens, it is worth remembering that it is not a fringe belief to think there is intelligent life out there – it is the mainstream viewpoint across the western world.

Germans (56%) are the most likely to believe this, followed by Americans (54%) and then British people (52).

At most, a third (32% in Germany) assertively do not believe in extra-terrestrial life, although this is lower in Britain and the US. Men, across all three countries, are more likely to believe in extra-terrestrial life.

Only in Germany do a majority of women (51%) believe. The oldest people are the least likely to believe in all three countries – in Britain, for example, 45% of over-60s believe in aliens compared to 59% of 18-24s.[vii]

Conclusion

This edition of The Sportsman UFO cases, we expect this volume to be succeeded by another as we build case materials. In this book, we are looking for the genuinely outstanding examples of visitation for our reading pleasure.

Chapter 2: Politicians and the Military

Figure 2 - The US Capital - courtesy of Martin Falbisoner, CC By-SA 3.0 | [viii]

In most of my books, I discuss statements made by military leaders of UFO activity in their countries. Most of these military experts agree the UFOs seen in the sky or on the ground are spacecraft from outer space and are piloted by beings of other worlds.

In addition to military personnel, we have many politicians (mayors, Presidents, Governors) who have gone on the record that they have seen a UFO and now believe in their existence.

In the United States, we have several high-level Governors and Presidents such as Jimmie Carter, Ronald Reagan, Dwight D. Eisenhower, Richard Nixon and many others discussing the reality of these flying machines.

While these statements are hard to find we note many newspapers, of the day, rarely discussed the UFO reality as a result of the pressures being brought by the CIA.

Senator Barry Goldwater on UFOs
Senator Goldwater and Former General Becomes Believer

Hunting | Sometime after the Kenneth Arnold (UFO) sighting in 1947, a friend of Senator Barry Goldwater was a member of a five-man hunting party when they witnessed several UFOs. Interested in the matter, this man informed the Senator of the flight characteristics of these high speeds and maneuverable craft.

Among the witnesses were two Air Force pilots who also witnessed the event. Goldwater's friend asked the Senator for more information on the subject of UFOs. [ix]

Mayor Greenwood: South Carolina

Hunting | In 1949 around 5:00 pm a UFO was visible to witnesses at Greenwood, South Carolina.

The director of the tree department in Columbia, Mr. William Shields, was hunting with some friends in the countryside when a UFO was noticed in the sky. The strange craft looked to them like a "fluorescent light bulb" and hovered for at least 30 minutes in the sky in one spot.

It then "shot off through the sky at a terrific rate of speed." Shields later told the press:

> "I thought I saw things until I heard that other people had seen the object also."

The '*Greenwood Index-Journal*' had this to say among other things: "Mayor A. H. Woodle asked Johnson's Flying Service to see if they could determine what it (the UFO) was. Joe Poole, instructor, and W. C. Ashley took off in a Piper Cub rising to about 3,000 feet."

"They chased it almost directly west, passing over Abbeville and almost to the Georgia line. They sighted it all the way but seemed to make no headway against it at all, although it had seemed to be traveling slowly--almost drifting--over the airport before they took off."

"From their 3,000 feet perch the object appeared to be on their level or somewhat above it: Mr. Poole had estimated the elevation at about 6,000 feet as it passed over them. "He said it looked like smoke used in sky-writing, but it never drifted apart, although the shape varied. It seemed almost like a long ribbon of paper fluttering at times, he said."

"Mr. Ashley said that it took various shapes, and appeared at one time to be a crescent. Others this morning said they first thought it was the moon when they spotted it."

"Mr. Ashley said that the object was traveling in the same direction as the prevailing wind."[x]

The Mayor sees a UFO at Sulphur Springs: Texas

Fishing | August 5, 1952, the Sulphur Springs, News-Telegram, reported: One of the most reputable citizens of Gainesville is the authority for the latest flying saucer report. He and two companions now are convinced that something fishy is going on in the heavens.

Mr. "H.A. Latham, a grocer who has been mayor of Gainesville's 11,219 inhabitants and at present is a member of the board of education, has seen a flying saucer. So has his son, 17-year-old Jimmy Latham. And so has Latham's brother, Jack Latham of Bailey View.

"The three were fishing at a lake about 10 miles south of Gainesville last night, separated by about 100 yards, when individually but simultaneously they saw an object in the sky which caused them to holler to each other. " 'It was between 8:30 and 8:45,' the ex-mayor said.

'I've been skeptical up to now of all these flying saucers stories, but all three of us saw it at the same time.' "He described the thing as cylindrical in shape but comparable in size to the fuselage of a large airplane although not so long. "Latham says he is sure it was not an airplane or a shooting star or a reflection.

It was seen to the north, moving in an arc, first slowly then extremely rapidly to the West. He estimates it was within sight of all three for about a minute." [xi]

Vice Admiral F.S. Low (U.S. Navy) request UFO Reports from Fishing Vessels

August 12, 1955, Vice Admiral Low made a request to the 31 steamship companies that all UFO sightings in the air or on the surface of the sea be reported immediately to his headquarters on Treasure Island, San Francisco. The APRO Bulletin said that the cooperation of the owners of the fishing vessels and other private craft is desired. [xii]

Goose Hunting: South Dakota Former Counselman

November 27, 1956, around 3:00 pm goose hunters north of Chamberlain, South Dakota observed a UFO.

"To shoot or not to shoot may become the question. Is it a goose or a flying saucer? Two Mitchell goose hunters, one a former city councilman, has added testimony to the list of persons who have reported seeing flying saucers.

"C.W. Klingaman, the former councilman, is convinced of the reality of 'flying saucers' or of the 'strange objects' that have recently been spotted in some South Dakota areas."

"Klingaman told a reporter Friday that he had spotted a 'silver-colored object shaped like a balloon gondola with no balloon above if north of Chamberlain Tuesday afternoon while goose hunting."

"It just hovered at about 5,000 feet,' Klingaman stated,' then shot up at an angle into the clouds leaving a vapor trail.' He further stated that the object climbed into the wind. The UFO was spotted shortly after 3:00 pm."

> "I was just as skeptical as anybody before,'
> the former Councilman averred. '
> Now I know there is something to it.'

"There had to be a motor in it for it to leave a vapor trail Klingaman explained, and there had to be somebody in it for it to climb like that.' "A hunting companion of Klingaman's, Kenneth Dahlgren, was said to have also spotted the object."

"The Chamberlain police department stated Friday they had had no official reports of anyone spotting the object."

"Klingaman indicated that he thought the objects to be some new air force development of a radical design." [xiii]

JANAP 146D Applies to Fishing Vessels
The Joint Chiefs of Staff
Military Communications-
Electronics Board Washington, D.C., February 1959

Fishing | February 1, 1959, JANAP 146D is released to all military personnel for dissemination. JANAP is the Canadian – United States Communications Instructions for Reporting Vital Intelligence Sightings.

The Scope of the report states: "This publication is limited to the reporting of information of vital importance to the security of the United States of America and Canada and their forces, which in the opinion of the observer, requires very urgent defensive and/or investigation action by the US and/or Canadian Armed Force". The procedure contained in this publication are provided for:

1. US and Canadian merchant vessels operating under US and Canadian registry;
2. US and Canadian government and military vessels other than those operating under reporting directives;
3. Certain other US and Canadian vessels including fishing vessels;
4. Military installations receiving reports from civilian or military land- based or waterborne observers unless operating under separate reporting directives;

5. Government and civilian agencies, which may initiate reports on receipt of information from land-based, airborne or waterborne observers.

The section 201 a (1) mentions two items that would apply to fishing vessels;

1. Unidentified flying objects;
2. Hostile or unidentified submarines;
3. Individual surface vessels, submarines, or aircraft of unconventional design. Which may be interpreted as constituting a threat to the United States, Canada or their forces. [xiv]

Moose Hunting: Newfoundland
Air Force Family:
They can "turn on a dime at that speed."
Early Warning System (SAC) tracks saucers

Hunting | On February 16, 1961, an Air Force family stationed at Ernest Harmon Air Force Base, Newfoundland confirmed UFOs exist.

According to an article written in the Advance Mooseburgers are very popular at the Base when hunting season opens. The same article pointed out Mrs. Marian Thomas wife of an F-102 jet interceptor pilot is now a believer in UFOs after understanding the Early Warning Radar system for Strategic Air Command.

According to the early warning system: "the aircraft control and warning section will sight unidentified objects on their radar scopes that travel at over 2,000 miles per hour and can turn on a dime, at that speed".
The article also stated: " a friend of her husband actually saw one of the objects on the ground and can describe it in detail. [xv]

Wisconsin

A letter to Hon. Gerald Ford, Minority Leader (R - Michigan)

Fishing | 1962 around 10:30 pm according to a letter to Representative Gerald Ford, a couple observed a UFO while fishing in Wisconsin. Their story is:

"Four years ago, my husband and I were on a fishing vacation at Ox-Bow Lake, near Presque Isle, Wisconsin on the Michigan-Wisconsin border in the heart of the Northern Highland State Forest. As you know the area is densely wooded, few cottages, and an extremely large lake, shaped like an Ox's bow, with 14 islands in it. We were fishing off the pier at about 10:35 pm."

"I was looking straight out over the expanse of water and sky when suddenly appearing from the Southeast and heading Northwest, was a very bright and large sparkling attraction, headed on a straight very speedy course. It was mid-way between the horizon and what we would call straight up, and according to our thinking, it was one or two city blocks distance from us."

"As soon as I saw it, I called my husband, who looked up and saw it immediately. It stayed on a straight parallel course, parallel with the surface of the water, never dipping or falling. We both watched it for several seconds, and then it suddenly went dark, it was dark in a flash, but did not fade out of our sight because if any distance. It was just as large and bright as the end when it suddenly was nothing as when I first sighted it."

"This bright flaming phenomenon was very clear-cut in appearance and outline, was shaped like a football of sun-fish, and was very good–sized. It was shiny bright, and gaseous phosphorescent in presence, a beautiful blue, and green, a tinge of yellow, and white."

"It fanned out feathery, in flame-light appearance, in the shape of a football as I mentioned."

"I do not believe under any circumstances that we saw a natural phenomenon, or meteor or such, or that it could have been any reflections of any sort, This was on a very-controlled course, straight and had all the aspects of a controlled Flying object. We have been convinced this was an Unidentified Flying Object."

A copy of the above letter was sent to Major Hector Quintanilla, Chief of The Blue Book Project. The Air Force could not come to any conclusions based on the fact it was reported 4 years after the event. Therefore they labeled the file "Information only." [xvi]

Hunting Reserve:
President of Italy Secret Service Investigation

August 20, 1963, around 9:32 pm a near landing of a UFO took place at the hunting reserve of the Italian President outside of Rome Italy. According to Jacques Vallee, he mentions a man by the name of Luciano sent him information about the case.

According to Luciano, he was part of a secret service team under a special clearance from the Italian government. The witness was the trusted chauffeur of the Italian President, driving his official car. The site was the hunting reserve of the President, not far from Rome. A disk-shaped object resembling an upside-down saucer with a turret on top hovered at low altitude above the car. The case created quite a stir among the Intelligence services, understandably.

The report was communicated to the U.S. authorities in Washington, who never followed up with the Italians but gave assurances they had passed it on to Hynek for evaluation.

According to Jacques Vallee: "Yet Hynek has never seen the report, never heard of it! I have used this case to point out to him again that he didn't see all the reports, that there must be another study somewhere, using Blue Book as a mere front". [xvii]

Chapter 3: Police confirm UFOs

The men and women of the Police forces around the world have been protecting humans since the government agencies began hundreds of years ago. Today, the police show heroism while rushing into fires to assist babies trapped in homes and stranded cars to save a life.

Despite these heroics, when Police officers observe a UFO, there is no one present to help them cope with the trauma of seeing a spaceship with humanoid beings from other worlds. Some high publicity cases in the 1960s led to several officers losing their jobs in law enforcement when telling the truth they saw a UFO.

Sadly, the loss of their jobs should have never happened. Marriages were ruined, and careers changed. I lay the full blame on these family breakups and loss of employment at the feet of the CIA and Pentagon protocols put in place in 1953.

A police officer gives chase to UFO.

South Carolina | During the first week of January 1950, Officer Lacy Bethea, Jr, observed a disc-shaped UFO while driving on Highway 301. Sergeant Bethea said he saw some light reflection in his window. To find out where the light was coming from he pulled over, stopped the car and got out.

He then saw some strange flying object at 1,500 feet that were cruising slowly by at 100 mph. Bethea, got back into his car to chase the UFO. Suddenly the disc pulled away from the chase and disappeared. Bethea estimated the disc was 30 feet in diameter and looked like it was made from aluminum or silver steel. [xviii]

UFO was seen while Fishing:
Illinois / Michigan Police confirm object seen

Fishing | On June 10, 1961, around 3:00 am two 17-year-old boys spot a UFO while fishing at Waterford Township, Fulton County, Illinois. The object seen over treetop level was around the size of a basketball and exhibited "spikes."

The two reported the UFO to Waterford Township police officers that also saw the strange objects. In looking at the thing, it was said the UFO had a large white light moving through the sky, unlike a conventional craft. Selfridge Air Force Base was contacted and told of the report. The observer reported the UFO-changed colors from white to gold then to orange and back to white. [xix]

Updated information on the case

Some of the witnesses were police officers from several towns.
Two boys fishing around 3:00 am at North Lake, Waterford Township Fulton County saw the object and decided to leave (fled) when it began descending. Police Officers at Pontiac, Waterford, and Independence were Sgt. David Putnam, Patrolman Fred Souver, Deputy Robert MacFarlane, Richard Hubble, and Corporal Maitland Landon. The incident was reported to Selfridge Air Force Base who stated they would investigate the matter. [xx]

Updated information on the case:

According to the two boys: "The object reportedly was round and gave the appearance of having spikes. "The boys said the sphere appeared at treetop level, turning colors from white to gold to orange and back to white.

"They immediately called Waterford township police officers who confirmed the sighting. "Sgt. Dave Putnam and officer Fred St. Souber said they saw a large white light, then high in the sky. It was moving, but not as a plane would, the officers said." [xxi]

Four Policeman observe diamond formation.

Florida | On August 3, 1965, four policemen at Cocoa beach observed 5 UFOs in a diamond formation. In reviewing the Air Force file, the drawing made in the report shows a cross formation. According to the officers, the UFOs were an orange-whitish color. During the sighting, they believed they heard a 'hissing sound.' Police were alerted to the formation by calls of residents mentioning UFOs were in the sky. The formation moved, and object number two sometimes went over to object number one, then went back to its position. One of the officers said to the Miami Herald;

> "If I hadn't seen it, I never would have believed it."

The next evening (4th) one of the officers stated they saw an unidentified object that looked like a sphere with a ring around it. They watched it for several minutes as it 'bobbed back and forth.' They observers were in their patrol car outside headquarter at Cocoa beach when the object was seen overhead.

The Air Force concluded the police must have seen a mirage. The formation of UFOs appeared in the local newspaper.[xxii]

UFO flew over Patrol Car

Alabama | On February 10, 1989, during the evening a woman and her sister saw a strange, lighted object (UFO) through a window of their home in the small town of Fyffe, Alabama. The nervous ladies and notified police.

A police officer and the chief responded. As the officers drove toward the location, the UFO appeared above the trees, low on the horizon. The strange craft flew right over the patrol car.

The officers relayed the UFO was about as big as a basketball and appeared to be about 1,500 yards away, traveling at a steady speed with lights illuminating it.

The UFO was triangular in shape and had rounded corners. There was no noise coming from the craft. According to researcher Bob Pratt, this particular sighting was the beginning of a series of UFO sightings, not all of the triangles, which lasted for several weeks in the Fyffe area.[xxiii]

Updated information on the case

Police Chief Junior Garmany and Assistant Police Chief Fred Works arrived at the scene where many people reported a UFO. Works shared; "We got out of the car, and we turned off the engine and the radio." We then;

"started towards it, it (the UFO) began moving away."

Garmany said the craft was "bigger than a jumbo jet" and was covered with green, white and red lights. The UFO was flying at 300 to 400 mph. According to the 'Aiken Standard,' One Pak Grove woman said the UFO looked like a banana with the arch upright. She said there was a red light on each end and a white line between them. [xxiv]

Comment | A Jumbo Jet is over 200 feet long. This would have been a mighty big ship.

Chapter 4: Large UFOs

Big ships can range from 100 feet all the way up to mothership being about several miles in length. Motherships are rarely seen in America. However, huge motherships were observed in the following locations.

1. *The Hudson Valley* – 1980's (Connecticut and New York); - many of the ships were several hundred feet long.
2. *The Phoenix Lights* – 1997 (Phoenix Arizona); -some have said the ship was several miles in width.
3. *The Stephenville Case* – 2008 (Stephenville, Texas) – a few witnesses said the ship was at least one mile in diameter.

The big ships act more like aircraft carriers, delivering equipment, personnel and smaller flying vessels to destinations all over the globe. The main job appears to be surveillance.

Hunting: Ortonville, Minnesota

Hunting | On November 13, 1956, three Minnesota newsmen in a hunting party reported seeing a metallic round object about a block square in size at Ortonville, Minnesota. This occurred early in the morning between 1:30 and 5:15 am.

Five men called from a café at Ortonville saying they all observed s strange UFO. The object (UFO) turned cherry red and sped away near Graceville, Minnesota, but then returned and followed him to Ortonville.

Earlier in the evening, a diary driver said he saw the large object drop down to 1,000 feet a half mile away from him. The thing was 12 feet thick and flashed blue-white to orange to red. [xxv]

Man calls off Fishing Trip after UFO:
Louisiana 200 foot long UFO

Fishing | On April 25, 1957, the Shreveport press informed its readers: "An Oakdale man yesterday reported seeing a blood-red object shaped like a giant half-moon land near Lake Bistineau last spring. Barksdale Air Force Base security intelligence officers investigated the report at the time but found nothing. The story was public yesterday.

"Harry Robertson, manager of an Oakdale department store, told The Times yesterday he sighted the unidentified object while on a fishing trip to Bistineau on April 25th."

"'It looked to be about 200 feet long, bigger than a house,' said Robertson, 'and it was blood-red. I saw it land on the ground in a wooded area, and sit there two or three minutes."

"Robertson said the object came from the south, passed over the road near Ring- gold, and slowly settled to earth in a 'perfect landing.' He said it remained brightly lighted, and that he saw no windows and no activity around the object."

Figure 3 - Illustration of Half a sphere UFO

"Robertson, who was living in Ruston at the time, went to a nearby resident's home and asked him to accompany him back to the place where he had sighted the object. The man refused, he said."

"He then went into Ringgold and reported the object to a night watchman who said he also had heard a noise and, when he ran outside, saw a blinking object pass over in the sky."

"Barksdale officials, contacted by Robertson, conducted a search of the area shortly afterward and interviewed Robertson. No trace of anything was found, they said yesterday."

"Base officials said the only theory advanced concerning the object is that it could possibly have been a weather balloon filled with an inflammable gas which had been struck by lightning."

"Nothing to substantiate this theory was found, they said. The base sent out a helicopter to aid in the search."

"'What I saw that night was the same thing the people in Texas saw recently [This news story is dated 14 November 1957] said, Robertson, yesterday. "After I had told Barksdale, my wife and I decided not to say anything about it because people would think I was crazy."

"Robertson said he was driving to Bistineau about 2:30 am to go fishing, but was delayed by a 'terrible rainstorm.' When he decided to return from the lake to Ringgold, he had reached a point a few miles from the town when he saw the object coming across the road.

"'It would have passed over my car if l hadn't stopped,' he related. 'It came on and crossed over the top of a little church there and then settled in the woods about a quarter of a mile from the road.''

"Robertson said he stopped his car and that the object was about four or five hundred yards away from him at the time. He said it was 'clearly visible,' and looked like a 'big slice of watermelon.''

"I put my car in the same location I had seen it before,' he said; "'But when I returned it was gone.' "He said he was 'so upset' by seeing the object that he called off his fishing trip. He never went back to the spot after that night, he said. "Robertson made no mention of the incident until he was certain Barksdale had no objection for the information becoming public." [xxvi]

200 foot Smoke Trailing Disc: New Zealand
Tauranga Big Game Fishing Club

Fishing | On April 27, 1957, at 4:30 pm Skipper Ronald L. Matheson of Mount Maunganui, New Zealand observed a disc several hundred feet long.

"I was navigating the "Rose," a fishing boat, off Port Charles on the Coromandel Coast, I was approaching the Channel Island when I noticed an irregular trail which seemed to rise behind the Island."

"As I came abreast of Channel Island, I saw an oval, disc-shaped object from which the smoke or fumes were streaming. The UFO was traveling horizontally. Two saucers fitting together face to face would be roughly similar to its appearance, Smoke streamed away from its sides as it moved on an irregular, constantly changing course throughout the sky."

Figure 4 - Illustration of Disc with flaming tail

"As I watched the object approach me at a slight angle bearing to the left, it then tiled at a steep angle and shooting upwards, showed its circular shape clearly. It appeared as big as a florin held at arm's length."

"For at least twenty minutes, I watched these movements, while I steered the Rosa out towards the Hauraki Gulf. Not knowing the actual size of the object makes it hard to say how far it was. Smoke poured out into a widening but thinning wake astern. The smoke was a dark grayish color, and the trail remained in the sky for at least ten minutes before vanishing."

"The object appeared grayish but had been made of polished aluminum, say, it would not have reflected light, the sun being beneath and to the left of it."

> "It gave me the unmistakable impression it was
> some form of controlled flying machine,
> but its flight was so rapid that by comparison,
> a jet plane would appear ridiculously slow.
> I want to make that clear.
> The thing was being flown, or directed. Somebody was flying it."

"I must also stress that I saw this object in clear daylight and as it made so many movements in the sky-plunging, ascending swiftly and turning through every imaginable angle – I was able to get an unmistakable impression of its shape."

"It was a huge disc. Its rapid movements suggest tremendous power. Moving in horizontal flight, it appeared to cover a distance of miles in as many seconds. I consider that it was very large and may have been several hundred feet in diameter. I make this statement having seen Pan American airlines at what I believe to be approximately the same distance."

"Just before flying off, it leveled out and then moved away very rapidly in horizontal flight, passing over the mainland in the direction of Warkworth and Cape Rodney in the upper Hauraki Gulf."

"During these rapid maneuvers, I heard no sound. However, the noise my boat engine was making may have muffled any other sound."

"His employer Samuel E. Rix commented on the reliability of Mr. Matheson, and that previously was skeptical of "flying saucers" but now is assured of what he saw. NICAP commented that the object may have been having mechanical difficulties (smoke) as reported in a 1952 Peru case photograph capturing a similar smoke trail which is rarely seen in UFO sightings."[xxvii]

Fishing at St Cloud: Florida
230 feet long UFO: "The size of a 747"

Fishing | On January 6, 1974, Norm Pellegrini, Assistant Administrator of Orange County Florida accompanied by Don Logan (an ITT employee) witnessed a UFO on a pre-dawn fishing trip to St Cloud, Florida.

While driving on State Road # 523 in St Cloud, they spotted an object hovering 200 feet above a group of pine trees about 200 yards south of the road. They stopped the car and got out to watch the UFO, which at first they thought was a large helicopter. They soon realized that it was not a conventional aircraft and Logan later said it was "fabulous... something you would see in a science fiction movie".

The men watched the object for 2 or 3 minutes and described it as being as large as a 747 jet aircraft with a fin-like structure protruding from the bottom of the windowless craft.

At one point the flying object illuminated the trees below. The main described it making the sound resembling jet propulsion, which changed tone as the object maneuvered over the trees. They also reported some type of symbol on the downward protruding fin. [xxviii]

Comment | According to Boeing, the 747 ranged from 231 feet to 250 feet in Length. This UFO was at least 230 feet in length (just shy of a football field).

Davao, Philippines
Mothership and smaller Discs seen

Fishing | On May 20, 1979, The *'Kapawa News Digest'* (paper in the Eastern Visayas) reported the observation of another "mothership" spewing out smaller UFOs by the population of Bacolod, Talisay, Silay City and E.B. Magalona in the Philippines on April 19th.

Police Officers, truck drivers, fishermen, and joggers outside in the early morning watched the UFOs arrange themselves in a V-formation and fly off very fast towards Mount Silay. [xxix]

UFO Flap in Zimbabwe
By Cynthia Hind
"Several Times bigger than a Boeing 747."
400 feet to 500 feet long: Nearly two football fields long

Fishing | On September 14, 1994, Cynthia Hind writes: Between 8:50 and 9:05 pm a pyrotechnic display of some magnificence appeared in the almost clear night skies of this part of the continent.

One of the stories this evening included fishermen. In her story, she states: "By this time I had received dozens of calls and the stories made me rethink the meteor identification, particularly the calls from Lake Kariba, the largest man-made Lake in southern Africa.

This is situated in the northwest corner of Zimbabwe, and apart from firming a series of wonderful holiday resorts for local people and tourists, it also provides a lucrative fishing industry, supplying fresh fish (freshwater

The Sportsman Guide to UFOs: Around the World

bream and kapenta- a small fish not unlike a sardine, which is sundried and an excellent source of protein for the people).

There are many boats on Kariba, from small powered speedboats to large passenger pleasure craft. Many of the sightings were made on the decks of these.

One person, in charge of a radio nerve center for most of the boars on Kariba, said that the kepanta fishermen who operate at night have seen a very bright light with two side lights, traveling slowly. There was no sound. The light was orange-red with tails trailing behind. The movement was to the south- southeast.

A warden in charge at Matusandona National Park said the light was above the tree line, ad he watched it for 2 and 1/2 minutes. Steve Edwards of Kariba Bream Farm took a video of the light, but it still did not reveal its true identity.

A friend of mine, Jo Hensman, was on shore when she decided to go aboard the family sailboat. They had been having a barbeque on the beach alongside their boat when Jo borrowed her husband's powerful flashlight to go onboard.

As Jo moved towards the boat, she could suddenly see this light in the sly, it looked like a small plane, but what shook her most of all was that it was coming directly towards her. She could feel the panic rising; realizing that her flashlight was still on and then she couldn't switch it off quickly, she was sure that the object was attracted by the brilliant light in her hand. Immediately, she hid it behind her back and watched with relief as the object turned away, and, following the tree line, when off along the lakeshore.

At this stage, she could see it was enormous, several times bigger than a Boeing 747. She saw it left over some hills, and she breathed a sigh of relief.

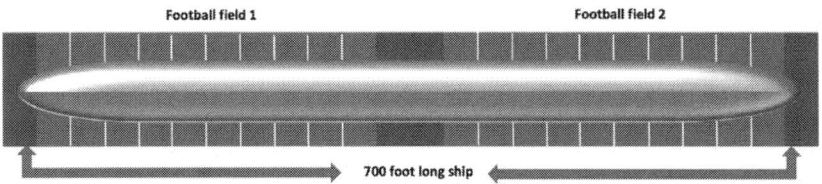

Figure 5 - Illustration of Huge Cigar ship

The story continues with another sighting on the Lake that evening. [xxx]

Fishing in Harwinton, Connecticut
The Size of a Jumbo Jet - 230 feet long
(nearly football field in size)

Fishing | On July 15, 1995, a couple driving home after fishing in the town of Harwinton, west of Hartford, Connecticut saw an ideal representative of this class of object. Several factors made this sighting exceptional:

1. More than one reputable witness
2. The large angular size of the object
3. The observation of what was likely to have been the shadow of the object, crossing the road before the object was first observed.
4. The possibility of additional independent witnesses.

According to MUFON, CT they did not report the observation, as they did not know who to report it to. The witnesses were an emergency room nurse, and her husband, a self-employed carpenter.

The wife was especially unnerved by the sighting, due at least in part to her perception that it conflicted with her religious beliefs, and a belied (unjustified by any evidence) that the object was something they weren't meant to see. She also mentioned that she had once scoffed at a friend who claimed to have a UFO sighting, angrily asking why her friend was lying, the after her observation, she felt embarrassed by her earlier position. Interviewer: " Are you religious?

She responded: Yes, a devout, practicing Catholic

Interviewer: How did you feel when you saw this object, and why did you refrain from talking about it with your husband for more than a year after it occurred?

She responded: I was raised as a Catholic and I know it says in Ezekiel... but I just never believed in any of this stuff, and it really freaked me out, and I didn't' want to talk about it. If God wanted us to know about it, he'd let us know about it.

After leaving quarry fishing, the couple was driving down a road at 20-30 miles per hour when they observed a large shadow crossing the road. The male driver looked up to see a large metallic disc over the trees to the left. The husband reported that the object hovered. The UFO did not affect their car engine and radio. The object passed slowly and smoothly over the road and perpendicular to the road. The object appeared 100 feet above the trees.

The husband said the UFO was the size of a jumbo jet. The surface of the object was said to be slightly metallic gray (Battleship gray silvery) and was faceted with all facets the size as the glass panes. The wife believed the skin of the craft was smooth.

There was no reflection of the sun; the sky or the ground was observed. There was no sound, including any roaring wind, or the sound of an object might make passing through the air.

A band of what looked like panes of dark glass (like that on a skyscraper – not mirrored, but dark smoked) crossed the upper portion of the disc roughly halfway between the rim and the top of the dome.

The bottom was visible, but they did not see any panels concealing landing gear. The husband grew up in Ohio was familiar with Blimps but said the object did not resemble a blimp.[xxxi]

Chapter 5: They come in Fleets

UFOs can be seen flying by themselves or with many other spacecraft in fleets. Fleets can range from 5 to more than 100 UFOs at a time. In one case in US History, the town of Farmington New Mexico experienced over 500 spaceships in one day. As crazy as this sounds, the local newspapers and hundreds of townspeople witnessed the event unfold over several hours.

In most of the fleet sightings I have researched, the ships all appear to be heading in one direction. The purpose of such a high concentration of airborne vehicles on display is not yet known by the common man or women. Is this to show humans they are here and there are many of them watching us? What does the military know of the purpose of such fleets?

UFO Fleet over Fielding Lake:

Fishing | On July 9, 1948, around 12:05 two men of the 72nd RCN Squadron sighted a group of unidentified objects while fishing at Fielding Lake, Washington.

The objects were described as a: "group of dots, grayish black in color numbering about 20. They were plainly visible and were either spheroid or disc-shaped. They appeared to be jockeying back and forth in the group formation, which gave the overall impression of a shotgun blast pattern".

"The objects were estimated to be at 5,000 feet or more above the terrain and were thought to be moving at speed more than 500 miles per hour. This figure reached at by seeing the things for five seconds or less. The objects were immediately below the clouds. The direction of flight was from the WNW to NSE, and the objects were definitely flying a straight course. "As the objects approached and passed, the sound sharpened into a "buzz" much like that made by a group of Jet Aircraft. No exhaust trails were visible.

The Air Force labeled this sighting as "Insects." [xxxii]

Comments | Any insects are seen at 5,000 feet have to be huge. The American population could be under attack, and that would be a "National Security."

UFOs at Springer Lake: New Mexico

Fishing | On April 25, 1949, a former Army pilot during the war writes Dr. Lincoln La Paz and explains that on the morning of April 25th at 6:30 am the two witnesses where fishing when they spotted 4 fleets of UFOs at Springer Lake, New Mexico.

Their attention was called to the objects when they heard a "high pitched whistle." They initially wondered if ducks were flying into the lake for a landing when looking up what they saw was "not ducks." What these objects were they did not know.

The objects they saw were "silvery white in color." To them they stated the objects looked like balls, "sort of like Christmas Tree Ornaments. They passed us at a very high altitude and going very fast". Being a former Army pilot, he stated these were not "jet planes" or "guided missiles."

He stated, "Whatever these "things" were they were traveling faster than sound. I know that because we were hearing the sound of the objects we had not seen and looked at others whose sound had not yet reached us." They observed these objects for over an hour. In closing the appeal to Dr. La Paz was that they had never witnessed this before and asked if anyone else had? They wanted some explanation.

The other witness added: "Dr. La Paz we haven't told many people because we are afraid they won't believe us. Do you blame us"?

Another comment he made was these objects were traveling so fast he doubted they could be picked up with field glasses. Speed was estimated at Supersonic at a height over 30,000 feet. The timeline is as follows:

Time / Heading	Number of Objects	Descriptions of Sightings
6:30 am – Due West	11	A Tight formation of 11 objects heading due west passed at high altitude. Insight only 10 seconds
6:40 am – Due West	9	10 Minutes later another group of nine objects again due west, very high altitude and traveling fast. One object left the group and headed southwest.
7:00 am – Due East	2	20 minutes later, spotted two more objects heading east. They appeared the same, as the other two groups but were farther apart than in the first two groups.
7:30 am (estimated) -South	5	The last group passed due east and heading south. They were strung out in a line going very fast and low. These objects made a "high pitched whistling sound."
	Taken from observation of eyewitness testimony of letter written to Dr. La Paz. The event occurred 4 miles Northwest of Springer, New Mexico.

The Air Force ruled this case was caused by (Birds). [xxxiii]

Comment | I almost passed up on this case when I read the Project 10073 Record card conclusion and Brief Summary. I had an odd feeling and decided to dig deeper. What this tells me is how many other reports have been inappropriately identified/classified by the Air Force?

The question for us would be what type of birds can travel at supersonic speeds and appear as silver balls? Secondly, can anyone see a flock of 11 birds moving at 30,000 feet from the ground?

Updated information on the case

According to Loren E. Gross: The correspondent claims he observed the objects for over an hour. He made a sketch that showed the objects in various formations as they zoomed overhead. The word: "zoomed" may be a good word to use since the witness remarked: "I do not believe that these objects could have been picked up or followed with field glasses; they were moving much too fast." [xxxiv]

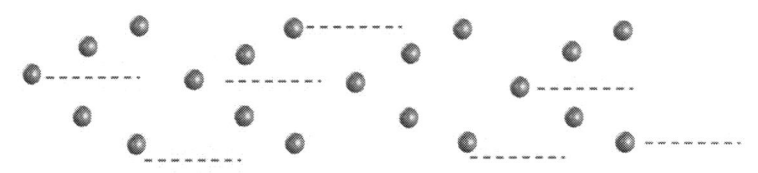

Figure 6 - Illustration - Fleet of Yellow Spheres

Two UFO Fleet's:
Oakland, California

Fishing | On August 1, 1949, at 2:30 pm a group of passengers on a commercial fishing boat approaching Golden Gate Bridge in Oakland, California reported a fleet of six objects.

While riding on a commercial fishing boat, several passengers reported six or more objects flying in formation traveling slower than a jet aircraft. These objects were oval in shape, at an estimated altitude of 1,000 feet at a distance of 10 miles.

The interviews revealed several characteristics of these objects:

1. They appeared silver in color,
2. They were oval in shape,
3. They were of solid constructions,
4. They were seen at 1,000 feet in altitude and 10,000 to 25,000 feet,
5. Their size was a penny at arms-length, which translated to 20 to 40 feet diameter objects at 10 miles,
6. There was no exhaust, no visible lights, and no effect on the clouds.
7. There were no fins, no stabilizers visible,
8. speeds were determined to be 1 and 1⁄2 to 2 times faster than a jet at times.

A stunning admittance was once the first fleet passed, a second fleet "of seven more objects exactly like the first," headed in the same direction at the same altitude.

The Air Force concluded the objects were most likely radar testing devices known as "kites" and were released from the AF Radar Installation at Treasure Island and Fort Baker. These devices are seen twice a day at 10:00 am and 4:00 pm. All six witnesses including the boat captain and a reverend were interviewed. [xxxv]

Comment | This UFO case was a big file. Many inconsistencies from the Air Force conclusion remain. At times:

1. the objects were faster than jets and at times slower than jets,
2. they appeared to be 20 to 40 feet in diameter,
3. they traveled faster than jets and at times slower than planes.

The question remains, if not "Kites" what did they see?

UFO fleet at Marrowbone Lake: Tennessee

Fishing | On March 29, 1950, around 7:00 am two Nashville Real Estate Salesmen (Mr. D.C. Whiteside and Mr. H. T. Williams) were fishing at Marrowbone Lake, 18 miles from Nashville, Tennessee when they observed a fleet of UFOs.

The observers believed the objects numbered between 6 and 12 dark objects at an altitude of 200 to 300 feet altitude. The objects flew into an opening above the lake through a break in the hills at the southeast end and circled behind the hills on the west side, all while losing altitude steadily.

The objects were black, round, heavy in appearance, about five feet long. The observers stated they appeared to look like 300-pound bombs and made a noise like wind blowing through the trees. No motors were visible. According to the news article, Mr. Williams said: "I was baiting my hook… when I looked up, they were splitting the air open right above my head. They were 200 to 300 feet high traveling at least 500 miles an hour". He further said:

> **"I don't know what to think…**
> **if I'd been by myself, I'd have said I saw things".**
> **"It's strange, but a man knows what he sees."**

The men reported the incident to Kames W. Davis, Lake Superintendent who said: "They were scared…one of them told me it made his hair stand on end."

The objects were reasonably close together and turned together at least 500 miles an hour. The newspaper clipping related that a spokesman at Stewart Air Force Base, Smyrna, Tennessee said the objects could not have been jet-propelled planes because of the description of the objects and weather conditions at the time.

The Chief communicator of the CAA (now FAA) said most planes flying over Nashville fly at a high altitude. "I don't know what to say about it...The Air Force has been attempting to disprove reports of saucers, but they are keeping their fingers crossed".

The Air Force classified this sighting as "Unidentified." [xxxvi]

Comment | Speaking from experience the sensation of "making one's hair stand on end" is a real sensation that sweeps the body. On the one hand, we are fascinated with the unknown. On the other, we are scared of what we do not know. Like walking along a path and seeing a giant snake.

UFO fleet at Prescott:
Arizona Dr. James McDonald Investigates

Fishing | On May 21, 1953, three men observe a fleet of discs while fishing in Prescott. Dr. McDonald writes Richard Olson and states the following: "I spoke by phone yesterday with two men up at Prescott who had been witnesses in an interesting sighting back in 1953. I ran across the reference to it in Dick Hall's book and succeeded in locating two of the three witnesses."

On the afternoon of 5/21/53, two of the men were up at Chino Valley, when one of them, a postal employee, looked up from his fishing, saw eight disc-like objects overhead, and, after studying them several minutes, took the risk of calling friend's attention to them.

They watched the objects milling around erratically for another five minutes, and then the third witness, a private pilot with about four year's flying experience, happened to come by, and they asked him to give them his opinion.

The three of them watched the eight objects for a length of time that was given in the contemporary account that appeared in the Arizona Republic as about 'one hour.'

The two men I talked to thought it was rather less than that, but that the objects were there for several tens of minutes before suddenly forming into a line and streaking off to the south at a velocity far greater than any aircraft the witnesses had ever seen.

The objects appeared to be very high, were disc-like, and would occasionally tip and reveal a side-view that suggested they tapered somewhat at the top. They would form in lines, and sometimes two or three would zip off from the line and 'dogfight each other for a minutes or so,' and then return to the line.

The two men said they'd never seen anything quite like it before or since. One of them was subsequently interviewed by the Air Force, and he is still annoyed at their effort to convince him that what he saw was some kind of an illusion."

The witnesses were: Ray Temple, a Post-Office employee; Ed Olson, occupation unknown, and Bill Beers, President of the Prescott Sportsman's Club and a pilot for 20 years. [xxxvii]

Chapter 6: UFOs land

Landings of UFOs with crewmembers have to be an incredible experience. Only one time in my life did I watch a UFO attempt to land near my car in the late evening in Connecticut.

I think the landing would have happened if the couple next to me in their car had not abandoned the area in such a panic. The vehicle in which the visitors came was unlike a disc or egg ship but more of a squared off Bell "Huey" carriage without a tail section and upper blades. The UFO had yellow interior lights and a silver body at night with lights.

A passenger on a plane in Australia captured the image of a UFO that appeared while in flight which then flew perpendicular to the airplane. Looking at this picture one can see an area near where the feet would be that juts out. This appears to be the same craft I saw in Connecticut.

Crashing into the Trees

Hunting | In March 1945 a man out hunting observed an elongated object flying very slowly, tilted toward the earth at Belfast, Maine.

The UFO crashed into some trees at the end of a clearing. The enormous craft seemed undamaged as it rested briefly on the ground, then lifted again with a humming sound, started to spin, released a shower of fine silvery threads, and rose straight up, disappearing in seconds. [xxxviii]

Rock Hunting (Geologists) and Roswell Crash
A Dying Archaeologist

Hunting Rocks | Late 1940's | After viewing the Unsolved Mysteries TV show in the fall of 1989 that featured the Roswell incident, a former nurse at the St. Petersburg (Florida) Community Hospital named Mary Ann Gardner called the show to relate a story that was told to her in 1975 by a terminally ill cancer patient who was in her charge at the time.

Up until the time that she saw the Unsolved Mysteries show, the startled nurse had considered the dying woman's story as nothing more than a medication-induced flight of fancy, but the woman's story bore enough resemblances to the story on Unsolved Mysteries that she decided to call the show with it.

According to the dying woman (Gardner cannot recall her name after so many years), she was a friend of someone who was part of a group which was out rock hunting or looking for fossils. The woman related that she was not supposed to be with them but went along anyway.

Gardner referred to the group as archaeologists but based upon the available testimony, they would more likely have been geologists or paleontologists interested in rocks or fossils, not archaeologists who are interested in artifacts. Whether they were professionals amateurs or students cannot be ascertained from what is currently known.

Also unknown is the time frame of the story, but Gardner sensed that it must have happened in the late 1940s because the woman did say that she was a student at that time. The woman appeared to be in her 70s in 1975, which would mean that she would have been in her 40s if it occurred in the 1940s.

To continue as the group was exploring the landscape, they came upon a crashed craft of unknown type with bodies lying about. "They were little people!" She described them as being small in stature with "big heads and slanted eyes" and wearing shiny flight suits.

While the group was examining the bodies, units of the U.S. military arrived on the scene, secured the area and swore everyone to secrecy-- Echoes of the Barney Barnett story. Even as the woman was telling the story in 1975, according to Gardner, she kept looking around apprehensively to see if anyone was listening.

"They said that they can find you," she whispered to Gardner." Who can find you?" the nurse replied." The government!. So, please, please don't tell anyone that I told you." The terror that the woman still displayed given her condition and the passage of so many years, made a lasting impression on Gardner.

The location of the crash scene according to Gardner's best recollection of what the woman had said, was Mexico. Whether or not the dying woman meant New, Mexico instead of Mexico is unknown, but Gardner is sure that the woman did, in fact, say" Mexico," which brings to mind another UFO crash/retrieval that allegedly occurred in Mexico just across the border from Del Rio, Texas, in December 1950.

The crash supposedly resulting in a jurisdictional dispute between the United States and Mexican governments with the United States winning out and sending military units into Mexico to recover the vehicle and bodies. xxxix

Bernina Mountains, Italy

Hiking | July 31, 1952, around 9:30 am Giampiero Monguzzi (an engineer), and his wife was climbing in the Bernina Mountains when they observed a landed craft on a glacier. Having his camera, he took seven photographs of the craft.

The photographs show the object on the ground, then taking off, another tilting. One photo has a person (humanoid) where what looks like space or diving suit with a helmet. Both the suit and the craft appeared in the picture as silver like. [xl]

Three Hairy Being:
France (Real or Imagination?)

Fishing | October 17, 1954, during the evening at Reims (Marne) France, a man observed a Cigar shaped ship and three hairy beings.

"An unidentified man, returning from fishing along the canal at Reims, saw a bright light resting on the grass near the canal. As he approached, he saw it came from a cigar-shaped object about 26 feet long and 7 feet high. From one end came 'phosphorescent' lights, which reflected on the metallic hull of the object.

A door appeared from which emerged three hairy beings, about 3 feet 9 inches tall, walking 'crab-wise,' or sideways. Then an even smaller being a little more than a yard high appeared, whose lower legs appeared transparent.

The witness tried to approach closer, but the entities rushed back inside the object at surprising speed, just as the witness was paralyzed by a red beam of light, which turned yellow, coming from a porthole.

The object then took off and flew rapidly towards Tinquex. The witness then recovered his freedom of movement." [xli]

Parde River: Brazil
10 to 15-foot diameter Craft lands
near Fisherman Entities grab soil samples

Fishing | November 4, 1954, Jose Alves, a resident of Pontal, Sao Paulo was fishing in the Parde River when he was approached by a silver craft. He observed the thing approach and hover six feet above the ground. The object came a few feet from where he was sitting and described it as two washbowls placed on top of one another face to face.

The object had a diameter of 10 to 15 feet. It was then he saw three little men come out, each 3 feet tall with dark skin. Each little person had a white skintight suit with skullcaps over the head. According to Alves, they did not notice him as they collected grass, leaves, and herbs. One collected water from the nearby stream. He then said they boarded the craft and it took off. [xlii]

The update to this in the Air Force Files states:

"He watched, transfixed, as it closed in with a wobbling motion and landed. It was so near he could have touched it, he said". The little men came out of "window-like opening in the side of the small object." The little man that took the water sample from the river placed it in a "shiny metal tube." [xliii]

Brazilian Fisherman sees Two Beings
Two beings of human appearance."

Fishing | May 14, 1960, around 4:00 am a fisherman spotted two humanoid beings near a spaceship in Paracuru, Brazil. (4:00 am). According to Brazilian newspapers:

"...A fisherman, Raimundo Ursulino dos Santos, was leaving his residence to go to town about eight kilometers away. He spotted two disc-shaped objects on a sandy hill of a nearby beach. The strange machines were aluminum in color, and as he approached the beach, Raimundo sighted two beings of human appearance outside the airships, talking with each other. They were small and very pallid.

One of them was dressed in a blue suit, and there was a kind of translucent glass-like helmet on their heads. Then one of them saw Raimundo who had stopped, not believing what he was seeing. The fisherman was too frightened to obey. He turned back and ran away as rapidly as possible, yelling for help. When he came back with other men, they found only the marks on the sand at the places the two discs had landed. [xliv]

Comment | Note that the APRO bulletin listed the above encounter as well as another nine cases happening that evening over Brazil, some witnessed by over 10 people while it hovered over the Sea. In one example,

"A fishing boat with three people aboard was moving through the quiet sea, far from the coast. The sky was clear and cloudless; anything moving across the sky should be spotted easily from a long distance. Suddenly the attention of the fisherman was called to a strange looking dark object that was coming down on the boat, out of nowhere."

"It stopped at 300 feet about the boat and became motionless, emitting a strong blue glow, which illuminated the boat. There was no sound. It hovered for 3 minutes and then moved away toward Paracuru."

It was then at 7:00 pm, more than 100 excited citizens at Paracuru watched the appearance of a strange disc-shaped craft over the town. Flying about 600 feet above the ground, at low speed, the "noiseless" object maneuvered over the town's main part in several directions. Once it event stopped in mid- air close to the towns church – in a strange titled position. It was oval shaped, almost circular, about 60 feet in diameter, and showed a smooth, polished dark gray surface. There was a strong bluish light on top of it. [xlv]

Natal, Africa Craft Landed

Hunting | June 25, 1960, around 11:30 am farmers, 24 miles from Uitenhage, Natal, Africa observed a UFO land in Sunlands.

Mr. Carl Coetzee, a citrus farmer, and his son, Christofel, 18, saw the object when they were out hunting on their farm at 11:30 am.

Watching the object, which appeared about 30 feet long, Mr. Coetzee and his son saw it 'hovering' in one place before moving in an easterly direction before it got into a range of hills, a mile away. Other farmers also saw the object and a search was made.'

"One of the witnesses wrote Mr. Bayman [correspondent for England's Flying Saucer Review] as follows: 'When I saw the object for the first time, it was stationary. It did not at first approach me...there was a slight up and down movement.'"

At this stage, the object was in a vertical position. From this movement it turned on its back and when in a horizontal position it moved off in an easterly direction. I would say that a darker object at its nose was a second appendage. As it appeared to me, height was more or less 200 and about 250-300 yards from me."' [xlvi]

UFO descends to the forest floor

Fishing | May 16, 1979; near Baependi, Minas Gerais State, Brazil Arlindo Gabriel dos Santos was hunting with two friends in a forest near Baependi, Minas Gerais State, Brazil around 10:30 a.m. when he became separated from the others. Sr. dos Santos next saw an object descend towards the ground in a clearing.

He approached to within 180 meters and saw that the object was shaped like a "telephone booth" about 1 meter in height. He had been carrying his Kodak camera with him and was able to take a snapshot of the object before it abruptly disappeared in plain sight. He walked to where the craft had been and then saw another object swiftly descend.

This next object was shaped like a toy top, and a little larger than the previous object. It had a small propeller like apparatus on top and a long pointy protrusion on the bottom. As he tried to photograph this second object he heard a whooshing sound and the craft was quickly enveloped in smoke.

He got closer to the smoke, and then he noticed yet a third craft descending overhead. This one was barrel-shaped and about one meter tall. It balanced above the ground before landing. It too had a large propeller at one end and was covered with red stripes. This object suddenly vanished when he tried to approach.

He finally saw a massive white, egg-shaped object descend to the ground. The ovoid craft had a pointy top and fin-like protrusions on each side. Next, to the fins, Arlindo could see several windows. While it descended it produced a horrific noise like a choking motor, and as it neared the ground it put out four, leg-like landing pods.

Arlindo approached and tried to take another photograph, but there was a sudden flash that temporarily blinded him and left his eyes irritated. Frightened, he dropped the camera and ran, but was only able to get about 10 meters before he became frozen in place, unable to move. He said it felt like someone had grabbed him from behind.

Behind him he noticed two men wearing helmets with visors and gloves. Behind their transparent visors, he could see human faces. They grabbed him, each taking one arm. He begged them to let him go in the name of God, but he received the answer, "In the name of God, we are all brothers, we don't harm anybody." The voice seemed to originate from a box like an apparatus on their backs. He was taken towards the landed object.

As he got near it, he could feel an intense cold surrounding it. Another helmeted figure stood by a ladder extending from the craft, looking from side to side. The man asked Arlindo if he had seen something, which sounded to him like a "Zurca."

Arlindo thought he could have been referring to one of the previous smaller aerial craft. That man then extended a gloved hand and pulled Arlindo inside the craft through a square-shaped doorway.

The atmosphere inside the craft was pleasant and cool, and there was a smell like "baby powder" in the air. Other men were sitting around on seats in the room. He described them as human-like wearing dark, tight-fitting outfits.

The men had large slanted eyes, thin noses, and large mouths and they seemed to operate some type of unknown machinery. The men stood up and began conversing among themselves in a strange language.

Suddenly from another room, a heavyset woman emerged. She wore a white uniform, gloves, but no helmet. The witness described her as good looking, tanned, with long light fine hair. The woman and one of the men then took him into a corridor. He then entered a room where he saw a square-shaped object in the middle.

The man pushed a button on the wall, and the object rose up. The object resembled a large piece of marble. The woman then took out a long wand-like object and pointed it at the object. On the UFO, the witness then saw an image of the planet Earth and other planets.

At this point, the man then removed his helmet, and the witness could see that he had very short light-colored hair. When Arlindo left the craft, he was told to cover his eyes and not to look at the object left. He followed these instructions and did not see the UFO departed. [xlvii]

UFO Lands in New Jersey

Fishing | September 5, 1964, Ward Campbell's two sons had been on an all- day fishing trip Saturday, September 5, at a lake near the property of Frank Sergi in Glassboro. When Mr. Campbell picked them up about 5:20 pm., they related the story that two men had emerged from the woods at about 7:30 to 7:45 pm the night before.

They claimed they had investigated and found markings on the ground, which they showed to the boys. The unidentified men then went on their way; continuing efforts to trace them have so far been unsuccessful.

Mr. Campbell went quickly to the scene, made notes and gathered physical evidence. He was instrumental in having the local police, state police, and finally, Air Force personnel from McGuire Air Force Base investigate the incident.

"Upon going to the scene, it was readily apparent that a very unnatural scene was evident in this naturally wooded clearing, Mr. Campbell told NICAP.

"Immediately evident was the crater in the ground, the Scorched earth surrounding it the broken tree limbs and partially uprooted tree, the two obvious holes of the three [NICAP Note: A fourth similar hole concealed by undergrowth was subsequently found by tree experts], and the white chemical and metal bits in and surrounding the crater."

(Mr. Campbell gathered some of the small metal bits, which he is having analyzed by a local laboratory. NICAP will publish the analysis report as soon as it is available).

The environment of the imprints was a small round clearing about 20 feet wide and 35-40 feet in a heavily wooded oak forest on the property of Frank Sergi. The ground surface in the clear that is composed of moss, oak leaves, white sand and small bushes from a few inches to about a foot in height. The sand was generally loose, and not hard packed, but there was no evidence of any crater footprints or trampling of smaller bushes.

Preliminary results of the metal analysis, Mr. Campbell said, indicate a high percentage of tin as a constituent of the melted metal.

On the night the marking was found, Dr. Pagano learned Mrs. Freda Dufala saw a globular red object hovering over the wooded area not far from the clearing. Three nights later, Irene Ritter and Carol Smith told police they saw a bright orange-yellow spherical object descends and apparently land. Emitting a red glow underneath. It made a dull muffled "thumping sound." After a few seconds, it rose just above the treetops, moved horizontally in a westerly direction, then landed a second time in a wooded area. (Official Police report).

The Air Force labeled the New Jersey case a Hoax. However, a former US Forestry Technician and tree experts disagreed in this report.
"Mr. C Zulli's findings included these observations: "The tree bent if it were a hoax, would have required heavy machinery or the combined weight of ten men plus...The root system was sprung by a downward exerted pressure.

There was a scar or bruise of recent origin at the very base of this trunk...if it were a hoax it would have had to be done by a powerful piece of machinery and a smooth metal cylinder. Any known type of tool did not inflict it. Also, see further information in the UFO Investigator as to the tree leaves being burned – they would need a "magnesium torch" for destroying the leaves. [xlviii]

Fishing: Brazil
"Little Man gives fisherman special Metal."

Fishing | August 1965 a man by the name of Jose da Rio was fishing in early August in Brazil when he saw a UFO. A tiny man about 28 inches came up the fisherman and had large luminous eyes. Speaking perfect Portuguese the little man gave Jose a piece of "unearthly metal." The little visitor told Jose he had come from another world and to offer proof gave Jose the metal.

According to the news article, the metal was being analyzed. The employer of Jose was quoted as saying he is a "simple, honest man." [xlix]

Comment | I have not seen any reports of the analysis of this metal in other statements. It is well known in the UFO research groups that since the 1940's fragments and pieces of crafts have been recovered and analyzed in some cases the levels of purity of materials reviewed were not able to be made on earth at that time with current technologies.

100 Miles east of Las Vegas
UFO near the ground

Fishing | August 1965 around 3:00 am two men fishing 100 miles east of Las Vegas observed a UFO descend to the ground.

The two were looking up at the stars when suddenly one of them started slowly moving to the right, then it came straight down, very slowly, when it neared the ground it went to the left and slowly went alongside the lake. The object was very bright and had lots of colors: blue, green and orange. We had binoculars and took a turn watching it for five minutes, and then it went behind a low mountain and seemed to land there.

About an hour later we saw an enormous explosion which looked as if it could be an atomic blast, this seemed to be about 10 miles away, due east which would be near Pierces Ferry, very remote country.

The observer stated precisely two weeks later in the same spot, the two observed three more UFOs. Two were silver, and one was like the first seen two weeks earlier. The objects followed the same path as before and appeared to land on the same spot as before.

A Teletype was prepared for WPAFB (OH), Luke AFB (AZ), CSAF and OSAF Washington (DC) and the University of Colorado. According to the information the objects appeared 150 feet off the ground and appeared to raise dust from the desert. [1]

Wild Boar Hunting

Hunting | On August 5, 2006 - At around 11:00 pm., while night hunting for wild boar, three men in Bonaire, Georgia came upon a stand of oak trees alongside a field where they had just run their dogs, and saw some lights coming from the woods. They decided to investigate and walked into the woods approximately 60 yards before they heard a loud whooshing sound. Their dogs then tucked their tails and began whining. When the men tried to get a closer look, the lights dimmed, and another whooshing sound was heard. The men then saw two small green "midgets" run from behind a tree toward what appeared to be a large "concrete mixer" with lights on it. Later on, after waiting a while and drinking a beer, the men ran back up the hill with their dogs.

The light and the object had gone, and there was an eerie silence throughout the woods so that even the insects were completely quiet. The next day, the men returned to the spot and found nothing out of the ordinary. Later that next evening one of the men went to feed his dogs and found that "Judo," his best hunting dog, was sick and would not eat anything. He claims the dog died later that week without any apparent reason. [li]

Chapter 7: UFOs over Roads

UFOs frequent our highways and roads. Researchers suspect that UFO pilot may use roads as a way to track humans to their cities and towns to where we live all over the world.

It's easy to see at the end of each road is usually some destination whether a town or some other building or residence.

In many of the UFO cases, we note UFO swooping down over cars as they travel along highways. We also notice UFOs resting in the middle of the road (like a runway) as they make repairs before unsuspecting adults show up in their automobiles.

Furthermore, many stories show passenger cars will occasionally travel under a UFO as it hovers over a roadway (assuming the car engine does not conk out from electromagnetic effects).

Hairstylist went fishing and was stunned: New Jersey

Fishing | On August 14, 1957, several individuals went fishing and had an encounter with a UFO at White Lake New Jersey. In a letter to Dr. Stringfield, Mrs. Chester Ehrie made her usual visit to the beauty salon. Her regular hairdresser was a fellow named Drago who always did a good job, but on this particular afternoon he made a bad mistake and singed her hair. He apologized profusely and explained that wasn't himself.

He said his poor performance stunned from nervousness over an event that took place in the morning of August 14th. While en route to White Lake for a day of fishing, something shocking happened.

On the road between Blairstown and Stillwater, Mr. Drago encountered a big object blocking his way. The thing was big, in fact, big enough to fill the entire windshield. The shape was like a giant saucer, and it was either resting on the road or was hovering just above it. Frighten by sight, Mr. Drago did a quick U-turn and sped away. Mrs. Ehrie knew UFO buff Stefan Santesson and informed him of the incident. [lii]

White Oaks, New Mexico
Electromagnetic Effects on Car lights

Hunting | November 9, 1957, according to the APRO Bulletin, "Three women and a teenage college student, returning to Alamogordo from a hunting camp at 7:20 pm observed a large, brilliant rapidly-moving light which approached their car and apparently caused the lighting system to fail.

The incident took place near the last foothill coming from White Oaks onto U.S. Highway 54. The lights went out on the approach, and all occupants left the car to get a better look, then the light sped off." [liii]

Moscow – Returning from a Fishing trip
An engineer sees 80-foot diameter UFO

Fishing | June 4, 1958, a news report stated:

"Dr. B. Muratov and his son, an engineering student at Moscow University, were returning from a fishing trip on the Aral Sea. They were near the town of Chimbay, Karakalpak when they both suddenly noticed a strange aerial object approaching them at a low altitude from the northeast.

Thinking it was an aircraft of some sort, they continued to watch it as it passed about 300 feet above them. Only then did the Muratovs' realize that it was not a plane, but rather a shiny, disc-shaped flying object about 80 feet in diameter which glowed red on one side and 'emanated a melodious chiming sound ---zing-zing-zing, almost like a voice ... ' At the top of this mysterious object was a sort of protrusion 'which looked like a short antenna.'

The Muratovs' estimated its speed at 'no more than 300 kilometers an hour.' When they told local fishermen of the strange experience, they were surprised to learn that a similar object had been seen in the area about two years earlier." [liv]

Rabbit Hunting: Lampasas: Texas
Six glowing objects – Chase Richardson

Hunting | December 20, 1958, between 12:30 and 2:30 am (Sunday Morning) a young couple was hunting for rabbits when they observed several UFOs near Spivey-Tapp Road near School Creek, Texas.

According to the couple, they spotted six blue-white lights, approximately four times the size of a headlight on a car, hanging about 75 feet in the air. The views were a quarter of a mile from the road.

"We didn't pay much attention to them, but after noticing them for a while, they began moving around so that sometimes they looked like a string up and down, sometimes they would blend into one light and sometimes they would dance crazily without a pattern."

"The light would jump and race and blink on an off," said Mrs. Richardson. "We watched them for a while, and suddenly two of them broke loose from the rest and approached us very rapidly."

"They came within about 150 feet out our car and then stopped and sank slowly into the ground. Shortly afterward two lights came up through a pasture, skimming the treetops and although they were out of range of a 22 caliber rifle, the lit up the interior of the car", Mrs. Richardson stated.
The article continues with them seeing the same lights on January 24th. [lv]

Updated information on the case:

The APRO Bulletin added more information to this story. According to the above article, Mrs. Richardson wrecked the automobile after being chased by the UFO. She received cuts and bruises from the car crash.

On January 24th they decided to go back to the see the light and pulled off the road to watch. According to them: "We hadn't been there but just a few minutes when we spotted a huge light about 20 miles north and to the east of us. The light hop-scotched across the mountain and in nothing flat it was directly east of us. Without slackening speed the light made a right angle turn and headed directly for us", Franklin said.

I was driving, said Mrs. Richardson, and I started the car and was trying to get out of there".

"I looked over my shoulder and saw the light to the right and in back of us, real close." I was trying to get away from it and trying to watch the road and the light at the same time when we approached a curve, and I hit the brakes.

"The loose gravel made the braking car swerve to the right, and it bounced off a tree and crosses to the left side of the road and hit another tree."
"The car was severely damaged, and Mrs. Richardson suffered cuts and bruises and had been in bed much of this week."

"I brought my wife into the hospital early Sunday morning for treatment, and when she was okay, I hunted up patrolman, and we went back to the wreck," Franklin said."

"When we got back there I saw two of the lights, but neither one was close enough to get a good look at it," he said.

The Richardsons described the lights as "blue-white, very similar to the mercury vapor lights used in some street lighting. There were no direct rays, and there was nothing solid around the lights – just the brightness without reflection or rays. [lvi]

Returning from Hunting:
Near Reno, Nevada

Hunting | On November 17, 1959, around 9:22 am three people observed an unusual craft 20 miles west of Reno, Nevada. According to the newspaper:

"'If I didn't have two others with me, I'd sworn I was crazy,' said Ronald Rinehart, Sparks businessman after spotting some 'peculiar' aircraft over the Verdi road about 20 miles west of Reno."

"He was returning from a hunting trip at Dog Valley with his sister-in-law and daughter this morning around 9:30 o'clock when they stopped to watch two slow-moving helicopters pass overhead."

"Suddenly, we spotted three other objects,' Rinehart said. " 'They're parachutes,' my sister-in-law said. " 'No they're not,' I said. "'They're going too fast to be parachutes. And they're flying in formation.' "Rinehart said he rushed to his car and pulled out an unloaded gun equipped with a high power scope."

'But before I could get the sight set, they were gone. That fast,' he added." "'I'm telling you,' Rinehart said, 'I never saw anything like this. These "things" were flat on the bottom and cone-shaped on top and kind of silvery white. I bet they were about 5,000 feet up.'" [lvii]

Crater Lake National Park, Oregon

Fishing | August 21, 1960, around 10:45 pm Thomas Page, Bob Rodolph and "Jim," all experienced a UFO encounter in Oregon approximately 10 miles before the junction of Highways 230 and 97 while traveling east on Highway 230.

Mr. Page relates the details: "During the summer of 1960, two of my college roommates and I had decided to go to Canada to see my sister and do some fishing. On the way to Canada, we stopped at Crater Lake, Oregon for dinner.

After dinner, we decided to travel through the night to get to Canada sooner. We were to take turns driving. I took the first turn and was driving out of Crater Lake. The vehicle I was driving was a 1955 Ford Pickup with a camper on the back.

"A short time later I found myself on a straight road with several dips. There was little or no traffic, and it was about 11:30 at night. As I was driving, I noticed a car in front of me, or what I thought was a car. The lighting on the

back of the car was strange. Both red taillights were out, and there was a white light on the left side of the vehicle."

"The car was traveling at the same speed I was, so I decided to increase the speed of the truck to get closer to the vehicle and see what kind of light it had. As I increased the speed of the truck the light dimmed and went straight up in the air."

"I just could not believe what I saw and in a few brief moments decided not to tell my roommates sleeping in the camper. Just after I saw the light go up into the air, I came over a small hill. As I started down, I saw the light again, or one just like it."

"I stopped the truck, got out and went to the back of the camper to get my sleeping roommates up to see this thing. One of my roommates, Bob got up, and we got into the truck and watched the light. I did not Bob what had happened, and he thought the light was a car stopped on the wrong side of the road. I turned the truck lights off to get a better look at the light. We then tried to get closer, but as the truck moved forward, the light backed up, keeping the same distance from us.

"My other roommate, Jim, knocked on the truck window [It must have been the small window between the camper and the cab]. I stopped the truck, and he got up front with us. We noticed that the light was very bright but did not hurt our eyes.

When looking at each other, we noticed that our faces were not illuminated and our heads did not make shadows on the back of the truck. We thought this was strange because we estimated the light to be close, maybe 20 to 50 yards away.

"We also noticed some colors on the end of one of the rays corning from the [See footnote again]. The light then dimmed and went out. We next saw a very dim white light that took the shape of an upside down cereal bowl that was as wide as the road. Bob noticed a little red light above the bowl-shaped light, but we could see no connection. The dim bowl-shaped light, or whatever it was, was new to us and caused a considerable amount of apprehension.

"I had turned the truck engine off to listen for a sound. We were facing downhill, so I started to roll the truck closer for a better look, but the bright light came on again and moved slowly away from us. At this time I noticed the light in the side rear view mirror.

At first, I was confused as to why I could see it in the mirror. Then I realized there was another one behind us. And I stopped the truck and got out. Behind us was another light. We guessed the distance to be about 50 yards. I walked to the back of the camper and watched the light. Bob and Jim had gotten out of the truck on the other side. None of us could hear any sound.

"I was frightened, but also frustrated at not understanding what was going on. I started running toward the light to get closer to see what it was. As I started toward the light, it started moving towards me. Jim yelled at me to stop, which I did because now I was more frightened than frustrated. The light was still moving towards me, so I raised my hands, not knowing what else to do. The light dimmed, reversed direction and went back up and over the hill out of sight. This light was not seen again.

"The light in front of the truck was still there. We got back in the truck and watched the light for a short time and then noticed a car in the distance coming toward us. I turned the lights of the truck back on, and both Jim and Bob went out on the road to flag the car down. "The light in front of us moved upwards, and the car passed under it, but did not stop. The light moved to the right and disappeared over some trees. We got back in the truck and left the area." [lviii]

Returning from Fishing, Hidalgo: Illinois
"It was as big as a house."

Fishing | August 4, 1973, during the evening Bill McMorris and his son were on their way home from an evening of fishing near Hidalgo, Illinois. Coming north on Route 130 through the hollows south of Greenup they saw the object across the top of a farmhouse owned by Walter Gabel.

"It was as big as a house," McMorris, publisher of the Greenup newspaper, said. It was at least three-fourths of a mile away and seemed to be coming down, he said.

He lost sight of it when he went down into a dip in the road, and when he came up the other side of the hill, "the object was gone." He too said it was evenly illuminated, no one spot any brighter than any other. [lix]

Chapter 8: Near our Cars

UFOs follow cars all over the globe. However, in America, this trend appears to have more cases than I have studied elsewhere. It is not known why extraterrestrials in UFOs want to come close to our vehicles. It seems in most cases, they want to observe who are in the cars. In some cases, the UFOs just fly by the cars and in others cases, make the UFO stop to interview the occupants of the automobile.

Lake of the Woods, Ontario: Canada

Fishing | July 1, 1949, around 10;30 am a Physician from Decatur Indiana on a fishing trip to Ontario Canada observed an Unidentified Flying Object. While driving on Highway #70 fifty to seventy miles from Ft. Francis Canada near the east side of Lake of the Woods, Canada witnessed a silvery gray, oblong object. The object was heading in a westerly direction. The UFO pursued a straight path of flight with an erratic motion comparable to that of Fan oblong object being thrown through the air.

The aerial anomaly appeared faster than an airplane. It did not hover and looked at 2,000 feet altitude. Another page in the report stated the object was "cigarette shaped with blunt, rounded edges." It gave off light similar to that of the sun reflecting from white celluloid.

The observer stated the object had no fins, left no vapor trail and heard no sound. "He observed the phenomenon for five minutes and did not believe that it was a balloon, dirigible, or any type of conventional aircraft."
The observer stated that he had definitely observed an object in the air unlike any other known to him. The physician wife corroborated her husband's statements and was unable to add any additional information.

The couple was interviewed by the Air Force on August 15, 1949. Reports were sent to the Director of Special Investigations USAF HQ Washington (DC). [lx]

UFO Fleet returning from Fishing:
Montana UFOs filmed and turned over to Air Force

Fishing | July 29, 1952, a family returning from a fishing trip in Idaho spotted several UFO's 8 miles south of Ennis, Montana.
The family saw a strange dark object in the sky around 2:00 to 3:00 pm. This object was hovering over the mountains to the right of the highway.

The main witness shared: "I slowed down and stopped the car, and as I did the UFO formed a white cloud around itself."

"The distance to the UFO was believed to be three to four miles. The clouds were at 1,000 feet above the summit of the mountains. "Shortly afterward three smaller disc-like objects came bursting out of the clouds from different angles traveling at an estimated two hundred miles an hour." Each of these objects took different directions and at the peak of the arc accelerated at a terrific speed and departed to a central point behind the clouds and disappeared. The observer used binoculars to see this unfold.

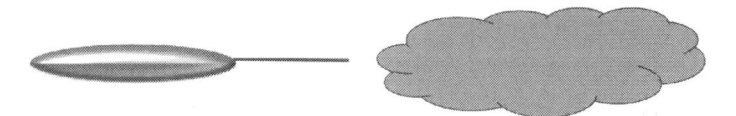

Figure 7 - Illustration of disc shooting out of a cloud

Two other cars stopped, and all 8 people watched the event. Shortly after three objects left the cloud, five others appeared on the right side of the cloud in a V formation traveling slowly, and then each of these in succession formed a small cloud around themselves. They changed formation from the V to a single file and entered the big cloud one behind the other.

The witness said; "during this time I took colored moving pictures with an 8 mm Bell and Howell Camera and still pictures with a Kodak camera." The film was turned over to a Major of the 29th Air Division at Great Falls AFB, Montana. The entire sighting lasted 30 minutes.

Witnesses confirmed the sighting to officials. One of the witnesses has a "Q" clearance (Q="Top Secret") while working with "Z" division at Sandia Base, Albuquerque, NM.

A Teletype message was sent from Great Falls AFB to ADC ENT AFB (CO), ATIC WPAFB (OH), Director of Intelligence HQ USAF Washington (DC), MATS HQ Andrews AFB (MD) and Kelly AFB (TX). [lxi]

Red Object: Galpon, Salta, Argentina

Fishing | In November 1956 an item in APRO files states: Abelardo Lopez, a dentist, tells that he and 11 other persons observed a large red UFO on Sunday at 5:00 am.

It happened while they were going fishing traveling by truck. Suddenly a bright red object came out from behind the hills ahead of them.

Then the UFO quit approaching at a distance he couldn't estimate, but it was quite far, hovering in place for a while. Dr. Lopez says that the object looked like a 'big bird fluttering.' They started the engine of the truck trying to close the distance between them and the craft, but the mysterious object moved away, suddenly disappearing at a fantastic speed in the same direction it had come.

Dr. Lopez remembers that the following day the newspaper La Gaceto (The Gazette) of Tucuman, published the report of a flying saucer which had been seen by many people in that province." [lxii]

Deer Hunting: Near Fort William, Canada

Hunting | On October 25, 1959 "Four hunters described how, on Sunday, October 25, 1959, a glowing, oval-shaped light hovered over their car for thirty miles as they drove along the Trans-Canada highway west of Fort William.

"The hunters-Douglas Robinson, Victor Arnone, Ray Disguiseppe and John Defilippo, all of Port Arthur-said they were driving back to the Lakehead after a weekend of hunting deer and partridge when they noticed a white light about forty feet above and ahead of the car.

"It was oval-shaped and kept spinning above us,' said Mr. Robinson. 'We stopped, but we didn't roll down the window to hear if it was making any noise.' He said the light stopped when the car stopped and moved again when they drove on. It was sometimes ahead of the car and sometimes behind. Finally, it veered away and disappeared." [lxiii]

Fishing Near Yukon: Missouri
"It sure gave us a spooky feeling."

Fishing | On July 5, 1961, around 9:30 pm another UFO sighting occurred while fishing near Yukon, Missouri. A press reports states:

"'An unidentified flying object was sighted last Thursday night, about four miles southeast of Yukon, by for boys, the oldest 19 years. The youths said the object was able to stop suddenly in mid-air and maintain its position, but they claimed it was not a helicopter. 'We have no idea what the thing was,'

16-year-old Ron Collins told the Houston newspapers, 'but whatever it was, it sure gave us a spooky feeling.' Collins said the object was 'stocky and sort of round, built more like a cylinder but was not a helicopter.' He said the object stopped directly over the automobile the boys were riding in, about 100 feet overhead. 'It stayed there for about a minute, and you could see the lights on front and back and sides,' he said. 'I shined my flashlight at the object, and it moved away and soon went out of sight.

The *'Republican'* shared; "Collins, who is spending the summer with his grandparents, Mr. and Mrs. C.W. Collins of Yukon, was riding in a car driven by Gary Lee Smith of Yukon. Gary's two brothers, Jimmy, 10, and Reese, 8, were in the back seat. The four boys had been fishing in Big Creek and were returning home about 9:30 Thursday night, July 6. They were traveling a dirt road, between highway 17 and 137, when Gary lee sighted the object."

"I thought it was an airplane at first,' Gary Lee said. 'But I sure changed my mind a few seconds later. We could see it flying low, and I drove faster so the car would be near the thing when it crossed the road.' When the car reached the spot, the boys stated the thing stopped directly overhead.

Collins said he and Gary Lee got out of the car to get a better look. 'When I realized a plane couldn't have stopped in mid-air and kept that position, that's when I got a queer feeling inside,' Collins said."

"A lot of things flashed through my mind. I knew it wasn't a helicopter because I've seen too many of them around St. Louis. It was bigger than a helicopter, short and stocky, like a cylinder. It had sort of a triangular lighting system. I didn't see anybody inside the thing."

"Collins and Smith said they watched it for at least a minute. 'I got my flashlight and shined it upwards,' Collins said. "I got the impression it had shiny metal of some kind on the lower side."

"The thing started moving quickly, making a loud noise, more like a Boeing 707 turbojet engine. It didn't have the whirling sound of a helicopter.' The boys said the object followed the dirt road for about a quarter of a mile then turned abruptly across a field and disappeared. Gary Lee said a few persons in that vicinity heard the noise, but nobody saw the thing." [lxiv]

Greenville: South Carolina

Fishing | On September 25, 1961, Edgar Hindman of Greer, S.C. and a fishing companion, Rev. Clark, were heading for a fishing spot at 5:05 am on 25 September 1961 when a blue flash lit up the cab of their pickup truck as they traveled on Arlington road near Greenville.

They said the tremendous flash appeared to originate at about 45 degrees elevation in the NE and made a queer noise that sounded like "spat." A city employee later corroborated the story but said he observed the object with a tapering tail as it descended below the horizon.

The Weather Bureau had not seen it, could not explain it, nor could Municipal Airport Control Tower at Greenville. [lxv]

Fishing at Richard's Bay,
150 miles north of Durban, South Africa
100 feet in Diameter Craft

Fishing | April 13, 1963, a sighting occurred north of Durban, South Africa. A Mr. Fred White told an interviewer:

"During the last Easter weekend, a friend and I motored to Richard's Bay, some 150 miles north of Durban, to do some fishing-my favorite pastime. On Saturday night (April 13) at about 10:30 pm I was fishing alone as my friend was asleep in the car, which was parked under, some trees about 500 yards away. I heard a high-pitched whine which seemed to come from the east."

"Then I spotted a very bright light of about 200 feet. The hum increased as it approached the spot where I was standing. It was then only 100 feet above me. I became alarmed and backed away as it started descending, but my only escape was to climb at a steep embankment. This I did with all possible speed."

"The object was then only 50 feet from me, and as it prepared to land, I noticed that the sand was being scattered in all directions by a strong downdraught. It was an enormous craft, undoubtedly metallic, and at least 100 feet in diameter. It glowed with a greenish light and looked for all the world like two inverted soup plates. I became paralyzed with fear but could run no farther as my knees seemed to give way."

"Of one thing I am absolutely sure, if it wasn't the same craft I had seen just two years previously it was one-identical to that in all respects."

"I noticed several oval-shaped portholes deeply recessed at regular intervals around the dome. From my vantage point, I found I could see right inside the ship. Then I noticed what seemed to be a circular control panel running along the outer wall. The floor seemed to be covered with a carpet of foam rubber strips."

"Everything inside was brilliantly illuminated, but I could not see the source of its lighting. It was then that I noticed a man had appeared at the porthole nearest to me, and he seemed to be looking directly at me. He had a fair complexion with what appeared to be smooth skin. In all, he had the same features as us."

"On his head, he wore what appeared to be a shining metallic crash helmet. I could only see him from the waist upwards, but he seemed very muscular and wore a sky-blue one-piece overall with no visible buttons, fasteners or seams- as if it had been molded to his body. He also wore gloves made of a shiny mesh."

"He never moved, but just seemed to stare at me. I did not see anybody else, although I had a strong presentiment that several others were aboard. I wondered why no one made any attempt to alight from this handsome craft, and why it should have singled me out to land virtually right in my lap."

"After a full six minutes, I heard the peculiar hum again, which increased to a slight whine as the craft lifted bodily from the beach-again scattering the sand in all directions. Once more I felt the warm air as it rose vertically, at first very slowly, but as it gained altitude, it increased in speed. As it reached a height of about 200 feet, it hovered momentarily and then moved out to sea in the direction from whence it came. Finally, it disappeared at fantastic speed."

"After waking my friend and explaining what had happened, we tried to tune in on the car's radio but could get no response on account of what seemed to be atmospheric noises blocking the station. The following day the wireless was perfect." [lxvi]

Returning from Hunting: Toledo, Ohio

Hunting | October 19, 1972, two men returning home from a hunting trip along the Ohio Turnpike said they stopped their car twice to observe a series of strange flashing red and white lights which moved about in the sky between 8:00 and 9:00 pm. According to one observer: "They moved very fast then very slow and at one point were directly over the car." [lxvii]

Chapter 9: UFOs at Camps and Golf

It has to be a scary incident to be resting at night near a Pond or lake at a summer camp with friends when a UFO descends nearby to observe the people on the shore. These type of UFO encounters are not new and have been recorded events have happened several times over the past 80 years.

Seeing them in the sky

Golfers | On August 2, 1952, six golfers at Lubbock County Club became believers when they described three UFOs being seen while playing their game. According to them, the three saucers were larger than an airplane and trailing vapor. One of the witnesses was an insurance man near Lubbock. Further residents of Lubbock said the white streak then turned into a reddish -orange color and seen by hundreds of city residents.[lxviii]

Night time Fishing: Camp of the Pines: New York

Camping | On August 9, 1956, around 1:30 am several witnesses that went fishing in New York saw a UFO. According to the '*Milwaukee Journal*.' The article starts with: "A white flash bathed the lake in the light." According to a press account:

"At about 1:30 am, Mr. and Mrs. Fred Smith of Albany and John C. Voss of Spring Valley, N.Y., all three guests at the Camp of the Pines, a lakeside resort, decided to try some night fishing.

"It was 'pitch black,' they said, so dark that they had trouble finding a white, keg-shaped buoy in front of the camp.

> "Then, suddenly, a white flash 'bathed the lake in the light.'

"It lasted for about 30 seconds, they reported and appeared to emanate from a basketball-shaped object that gave off a fiery red aura.

"The campers said that the object then took off in a northeasterly direction over Vermont, rapidly contracting in size.

"They emphasized that during the entire display there was no noise." [lxix]

Updated information on the case:

According to APRO, this same article stated; "Reverend Wilfred P. Riggs, minister of the Willsboro Congregational Church, is quoted as saying that he is convinced that "we are being observed by civilizations that are in advance of our own." [lxx]

Lake Baskatong, Ottawa, Canada

Hunting | On November 6, 1957, four friends' deer hunting in Canada was staying at a Hunting Lodge when they reported a UFO near their camp.

Their camp was Sullivan's Hunting Lodge about 100 miles north of Ottawa. That evening listening to shortwave radio, the group heard several people discussing UFOs in the vicinity. Around 9:00 pm one of the observers went outside to the outhouse when he observed a UFO hanging in the sky below the thick cloudbanks.

When calling his friends to come out and look, they laughed about "little green men." The men came out on to the porch and "sure enough, there it was."

According to the information; "to the east of south, a huge brilliantly-illuminated sphere," one eight to one-sixth the apparent diameter of the moon, was hanging a few hundred feet over the summit of a hill two or three miles away.

Below the cloud level, this object was shooting out conical beams of light fanned out from the top and bottom in all directions.

The bottom beams hit the tops of the pine trees on the hilltop, the upper beams illuminated the bottom of the cloudbanks.

According to one observer, the brightness was like "looking into a gas mantle." But its color was yellowish-white, not bluish white of a mantle.

Because of the glare, its edges were not sharply defined. For fifteen minutes it stayed still. Using binoculars did not help in determining any other details.

During the sighting "no reception" was heard on the portable radio. Another observer (Munday) tried the shortwave radio, and that too was not working. There was one exception, at one frequency a powerful signal was received. It was a rapidly modulated single tone, some like Morse code in effect, but not Morse code. Jackson believed it was in the 2.5 or 25 megacycles and not 14.286 megacycles.

According to the writer of this report, such signal was being reported all over the earth that week from pole to pole. [lxxi]

Camping Painted Rock Reservation: Montana
25-foot diameter craft

Camping | On August 9, 1964, around 12:30 am in the morning, Chief of Police James Sculley observed a UFO while camping near Painted Rock, Montana.

According to the records, Mr. Sculley and his family were at the State Creek Campground when they were awakened by their dog barking. When looking to see what the commotion was Chief Sculley observed a huge bright object hovering next to a large mountain a few miles beyond the camping site.

He mentioned: "It was like trying to look at the morning sun." The light according to Sculley, illuminated the logging road and trees on the mountain adjacent to the object.

The object projected two beams, each at a 45-degree angle from either side, which lit up a 100-foot wide area. The UFO was estimated to be 25 feet in diameter. The lights then went out, and the UFO was gone.[lxxii]

San Quentin Valley

Hunting | On August 1965 Four hunters, Manuel Waldo Romero, Ernesto Depeda, Ruben Hernandez and Adalberto Rodriguez, were hunting in the San Quentin valley near Tijuana, Mexico on the 22nd of August 1965 when they saw several UFOs.

They had made camp in the valley to be ready for the hunt early the next morning. Rodriguez was the last to go to bed, and upon getting out of the car, he saw a brilliant object in the sky.

Half joking, he singled the UFO with his flashlight and stood petrified with fear as the object approached.

At the same time, eleven other similar objects described as luminous discs appeared in the sky. Rodriguez and his companions hurriedly packed and left and reported the incident as soon as they reached Tijuana.[lxxiii]

Comment | This is quite common with people using flashlights to signal UFOs. Sometimes they will approach to see if we need help or just curiosity.

Radio Announcer sees UFO close up
Told AF: " You are doing the people of US a grave crime."

Hunting | On October 23, 1965, several witnesses observed lights in the sky around the same location at Long Prairie, Minnesota. A group that was coon hunting witnessed a flight of UFOs in the sky at the same time as James F. Townsend reported an encounter with a rocket ship in the road.

Around 7:15 am radio announcer James F. Townsend came to within 20 feet of a UFO after his car engine cut out.

While traveling on state highway 27, James Townsend's car came to a stop when an object appeared in the middle of the road. The object approximately 30 to 40 feet tall and 10 feet in diameter looked like a rocket ship resting on fins. As he approached the car engine, lights and radio cut out.

A loud Hum was heard that hurt Townsends ears. The UFO object gave off a bright metallic shine. The next thing he observed when approaching the ship was a "little creatures" or perhaps little robots that came from behind the ship. The objects had tripod arms and matchstick legs.

According to Townsend, he was fascinated with these "beings or robots" as they had no eyes or facial features but were somehow observing him. He further stated in his report he and the objects stood looking at each other for three minutes.

They then turned and went under the object, and a few seconds later the UFO started to rise slowly. After the UFO went about ¼ of a mile, the car engine started again, and the headlights came on.

He then drove to the Todd County Sheriff's department and reported what he had seen. We went back to the spot with the Sheriff and could find no evidence. Mr. Townsend then told the Air Force:

> **"I think you are doing the people of the US a grave crime not to let them known that there are things of this nature."**

His final statement was "That is what happened. I know that it is quite a wild story, but if you do not believe me, well that's your tough luck". The Air Force concluded the sighting could have been a possible sighting of the planet Venus. A Handwritten note suggested "Psychological." [lxxiv]

Updated information on the case:

The *'Flying Saucer Review'* carried further information on the above sighting. According to the observer: The UFO "was like a rocket ship. It was about 30 feet tall and about 10 feet in diameter. It was sitting on fins."

Then I saw them. They were standing in a big circle of light under the ship". He then said: "I jumped out of my car and was going to try to know one over, but then they came at me. They came right up to the car. There were three of them".

He further stated: "They may have been robots." He said: "I can't explain it because they didn't have eyes... but they were looking right at me". The entities then went back to the ship and left. The observer reported the incident to Todd County Sheriff James Bain and Long Prairie policeman Luverne Lubitz.

On the same evening on Minneapolis, at 7:00 pm at 14 years old reported seeing a sombrero-shaped machine through his 200-power telescope.

Then three other young men coon hunting in the same area reported seeing the light in the sky at the same time the rocket ship took off from the highway.[lxxv]

Mackie Lake: Ohio
They are now Believers

Fishing | On March 5, 1967, two men from Kingston, who scoffed at the idea of "Flying Saucers" are now ready to admit they are a reality, after the Experience they had on Sunday night. This is the headliner from *"The Tweed News."*

Several men had come down from Mackie Lake to the village to bring Ray McInnes home from fishing and saw strange light near the Waller Ohlman farm.

The two men were going in by snowmobile, and when they saw the strange object - they stopped and watched it. The UFO went up and down several times, hovered over the field, and moved around.

According to the two men – they had a perfect look at it and are convinced they saw a "Flying Saucer." They then headed back to camp to tell their friends. One person hearing the story mentioned the two observers "hair was still standing straight up when they got back, these young men are both family men of good reputation, so their report can be taken quite seriously.[lxxvi]

14 Hikers see UFO in Connecticut

Hiking near Camp | On July 28, 1976, 14 hikers walking along the Blueberry Mountain witnessed a UFO and reported the event to authorities. Of the witnesses, one counsel and 13 campers at Camp Delaware near Winsted said the UFO was seen at 3:45 pm.

According to the camp counselor, the UFO was about 30 feet away from the group when it appeared. Ira Lefier of New York shared "It left, and we ran." The UFO hovered for 20 seconds before it gained altitude and disappeared.

The saucer was silver colored, shaped like upside-down saucers and about the size of a car. The object made a noise similar to feedback on loudspeakers.[lxxvii]

Updated information on the case:

They heard a second whine, accompanied by a high-speed vertical ascent, and within a few seconds, the UFO had vanished by shooting straight up in the sky. The Hartford Courant following up on the above story mentioned the object frightened them away from the campground. In Leifer's words: "It left, and we ran."[lxxviii]

Comment | Thought the group did not say what feedback sounds like, having load speakers the sound could have been a "buzzing sound."

"Family trapped in UFO forcefield."
Reviewed by Dr. J Allen Hynek

Fishing | June 17, 1977, around dusk five individuals, husband and wife, their two daughters a close family friend had been camping, fishing, and swimming at Cotile Lake Louisiana when they reported a UFO.

As the sun had set, the witnesses began to break camp and go home. They were working in two groups [Mom and Dad as one and the friend and the two girls in the other]. The latter was on one of their treks to the pickup truck, which in these woods had to be parked a fair walk away, when the UFO event occurred.

Just before they reached the clearing that led to the road, they began feeling a "low-frequency vibration" in their bones. Looking upwards, they saw "the outline of a vast craft or UFO."

The UFO hovered utterly still and had points of light surrounding its shape. It appeared to have 'parking lights' on. It was huge. I would guess the size to be about 75 feet across, 50 feet high.

It was disc-shaped, but plates and sections were clearly visible. The children had been talking, but now, they too noticed the humming noise and followed my gaze upward to the UFO.

"At this very instant, the craft floated directly above us, almost. It moved immediately, yet gracefully, almost in a 'magnetic' sense of control."

"Before we could react, the middle of the craft started to glow, but I suspect that this was an illusion of a floodlight, for I looked to my side and the children were brightly illuminated."

"In their shock, mouths still open, holding the swimming gear. Before we could shield our eyes or turn away, there came from the same source several rays or beams of blue light. They were not diffused, but not unlike laser beams. They appeared to strike us at the solar plexus."

"It was an intense, electric, silver-blue, thin beam. Three to five of them...we were immediately affected. I recall hearing crackling sounds in the air, right around us. "But not loud or threatening.""

"We were trapped in what I guess was a force field, for we couldn't move, hardly at all. In a few moments, our entire bodies shown in the eerie blue 'aura.' We slowly [could force] our heads down to see our arms glowing with electric blue light. The movement was difficult, as in a dream, slow, heavy. After what seemed to be about ten seconds, all the lights vanished instantly, along with the force field."

"The craft began to glide away, over the treetops...parking lights still on. The children became frantic, but not frightened. They started shouting 'did you see that flying saucer? Did you see those lights coming down?' " The adult kept an outward calm and tried to relax the girls."

Frankly, he admitted, they seemed to take it much better than he did, and he was inwardly terrified. The girls' parents were back at the camp and saw none of this.

A friend reported the case to Dr. J. Allen Hynek, and he later visited the witnesses and spoke to all three [however a case file of Hynek's trip, if one was made, has not been located--all we know is that he credited the case enough to use it in his public talks]. [lxxix]

Hiding in plain sight

Near Golf Course | The Fullerton family got a big surprise when they spotted a vast UFO as big as a house around 7:20 pm on October 28, 1977, near the Fullerton Golf Course in Fullerton, California.

The UFO was said to be moving slowly across the sky, completely silent and oval in shape with two rows of rotating yellow lights. The UFO had a red light on top. The grandmother of the family also watched as the UFO attempted to drop behind some treetops near the ground. The family watched the UFO for five minutes.

The local authorities said the object could have been an advertising plane. However, this was ruled out as the UFO was utterly silent and near treetops.[lxxx]

Chapter 10: Potential Abductions

The Betty and Barney Hill case of New Hampshire is one of the best-documented abduction stories in America. However, there are many other great abduction cases;

1. Travis Walton – Arizona
2. Calvin Parker and Charles Hixson - Mississippi

In abduction experiences, humans are taken aboard spacecraft, against their will for examination by extraterrestrials. While in contactee cases, humans are "invited aboard." In many cases, abductions are usually caused by a shorter in stature aliens called "the grays."

Rabbit Hunting: Venezuela
9-foot diameter Craft

Hunting | December 10, 1954, two teenage boys, Jesus Gomez, and Lorenzo Flores had been out hunting rabbits at Trans-Andean Highway, between Chico & Cerro de las Tres Torres, Venezuela.

Having exhausted their ammo, they were walking back home when they saw a shiny object a short distance away from the highway. Thinking the strange UFO was a car that had gone off the road, and went to investigate.

The two boys found a flying saucer about 9 or 10 feet in diameter & hovering about 2 or 3 feet off the ground, emitting fire from the bottom. The UFO appeared like "two washbowls placed one on top of the other,"

According to the witnesses, four men came out, of the craft. Each man was about 3 feet tall. They looked "very hairy & strong." One grabbed Gomez & tried to drag him to the UFO. Flores hit the creature holding Gomez with the clubbed shotgun.

The creature's body seemed hard as a rock, & the shotgun broke, but Flores was able to get Gomez away. They ran to the nearest police station. They were bleeding & their clothing was torn. The shotgun had been a prized possession. When the police arrived on the scene, they found scorched bushes and evidence of a struggle.[lxxxi]

Updated information on the case:

Coral Lorenzen of APRO wrote: "here you'll find other detail which appeared later in other newspapers: They were arrested, as it was thought they were mad. Psychiatrists were sent to check the boys. They were hunting rabbits and had a flashlight. The spaceship gave out light, blinding flashes which lit up the nearby mountains.

The boys said: "We saw a sort of "aerial antenna" begin to emerge from the upper part of the saucer. Maybe it was a kind of human radar detector.' The boys were in perfect health and had not drunk anything…They are known in the region as people of reliability and ethical behavior."

In a second update, it was mentioned one of the boys ended up in the Hospital as a result of the incident.[lxxxii]

UFO at Blue Sea Lake Fishing Camp: Quebec
"Potential Missing Time"

Fishing | September 1961, around 11:00 pm a family spotted a UFO at the Blue Sea Lake Fishing Camp in Quebec. According to the notes given in the file, the story is told as follows:

"Back in 1961, when I was twelve years old, my family owned a fishing resort on Long Lake in Western Quebec."

"The lodge was on the shore of the lake. The back of the lodge faced the water. The front faced the lawn and the long sandy driveway. Along the driveway were a series of outbuildings: two garages, an icehouse, and a chicken coop. The coop was at least 200 feet from the lodge, down a rutted dirt path."

"Late one night, about eleven o'clock, a teenage friend and I were walking up the driveway toward the lodge, returning from locking up the chicken coop. The night was clear, with no clouds. The weather was crisp. We wore windbreakers. The path back from the coop was dark, as it was flanked with pine and cedar trees, so we had a powerful flashlight."

"We were strolling along, talking. When we rounded the curve in the drive past the garages, we found we didn't need a flashlight any longer. The entire area was glowing red."

"We stopped. Ahead of us, just past the lodge and above the lawn, a huge red and orange globe hung in the air. It didn't move, didn't make any sound. It was about 40 degrees above us, touching the tree line. It was actually in front of the tallest cedar tree in front of the lodge."

"We stood there staring for about 10 or 15 minutes. It was big enough to fit 10 regular moons inside its circumference. We didn't know what to make of it."

"Finally, I flashed my light at it and got an immediate reaction. The center became white and then yellow, then an orange-red. Glowing red rings emanated from it, like the ripple you get when you throw a stone in a calm pool."

"At that point we ran like hell back to the lodge, to tell my mother. We tumbled in, all excited, and blurted out our story. We were all in a panic, and it took a few minutes before we were coherent."

"The glow filled the kitchen windows. Mom looked out the closet window and said, 'It's nothing, don't worry about it."

"I was utterly baffled by my mother's response. Couldn't she see the thing, right there on the lawn?"

"My friend thought of sending out an adult to investigate. Our waiter/bouncer seemed like a good choice, so we scurried through the lodge trying to find him. That took another 10 minutes."

"After we found him and explained what was happening, he went out to look. He had on a white shirt. When he stepped out the door, his shirt turned red in the light from the object."

"I can't remember clearly what happened after that. I don't remember the bouncer coming back in with his report. I don't know how much longer the globe stayed there, or how it left. I don't remember going to bed, or getting up the next morning when I'm sure we would be talking about it again. How did we manage to get to sleep that night?"

"Mom never mentioned it again. I don't recall any of the guests or the staff commenting on it either. Thank God I was not alone, or I might be wondering if l saw anything. I can't understand why we didn't take pictures or call the police."

"The next day we heard a Canadian air force jet had crashed on Montreal Road near the convent. We went to see the pieces all over the road. I thought perhaps the jet had been shot down by the UFO or had crashed trying to follow it."

"I know it wasn't ball lightning. We'd had that in our cottage when I was about seven. It was a ball of fire stationery in our kitchen. Somebody screamed, "What is that?" and the object promptly disappeared up our oil stove flue."

"There was no swamp around the lodge, so it wasn't swamped gas like some people told me."

"Years passed, and we grew up and move on. I keep in touch with this friend, and we still talk about the red globe, some 30 or so years later. We don't recall anything else that happened that night after my mother looked out the window. Are we missing time?"

"I still can't understand Mom's reaction, when she looked out the window and said it was nothing. I remember talking to her about it when I was in my late teens, but it was as if it was a mystery or no big deal. I think, since she was a devout Catholic, she took it to be a sign from heaven or hell. I think she was scared to the bone but didn't want us to be frightened. She passed away some years ago. I've meant to go to find other related sightings around that time."[lxxxiii]

Possible Abduction: New South Wales: Australia

Hunting | In September 1978 two young men out hunting near lindabyne, New, South Wales reported seeing a brought spherical light on the ground some little distance away. The next night the UFO was seen again. In 1983 one of the men began to recall memories of a two-hour time lapse on one of those nights. One memory was of the two men's being floated into a room where they were placed on a table and examined by tall, white colored beings.[lxxxiv]

Fishermen Examined
The Famous Pensacola Abduction: Pascagoula: Mississippi
"Not harmed, just examined them" (Hoax or real?)

Fishing | October 11, 1973, around 7:00 pm two men claimed they were taken aboard a craft and examined by men from another world at Pascagoula, Mississippi.

The Pascagoula Incident involved two men, nineteen-year-old Calvin Parker, and forty-two-year old Charles Hickson, both of Gautier, Mississippi, were fishing in the Pascagoula River when they heard a buzzing noise behind them.

Both turned and were terrified to see a ten-foot-wide, eight-foot-high, glowing egg-shaped object with blue lights at its front hovering just above the ground about forty feet to sixty feet from the river bank. As the men, frozen with fright, watched, a door appeared in the object, and three strange beings floated just above the river towards them.

According to the men they were taken aboard the craft and given a physical examination. After the examination was completed, they were returned to the riverbank and left uninjured.

The men reported the inside of the craft was illuminated but devoid from features and furnishings. The beings were unusually clothed in that they had wrinkled skin, cone-shaped projections where the nose and ears would be, had a slit for a mouth and no eyes. The examination was painless and appeared to be suspended in mid-air when the exam was conducted.

The story continues below. According to reports Parker was hospitalized for a "nervous condition." Polygraph results showed that Hickson honestly believed he had experienced what he reported. [lxxxv]

Comment | To this day we do not know if these "others" are here to protect the earth's atmosphere or for some other reason. There is much in the UFO research literature on this case as it was carried on Television, Newspapers around the world.

Continued from Above
In the News, two men see Creatures in Pascagoula, Mississippi
Men placed under Hypnosis – "They were telling the truth."
Dr. J. Allen Hynek brought in to investigate

Fishing | October 11, 1973, in an associated press article it was reported Charles Hickson, and Calvin Parker was fishing when they observed a UFO and occupants in Pascagoula, Mississippi. The craft was described as blue in color and appeared hovering over the water. Then several reddish looking creatures floated over to the men and examined the observers.

Scientists Dr. James Harder of the University of Mississippi and Dr. J. Allen Hynek from Northwestern placed the two under hypnosis. The verdict? "They were telling the truth beyond a reasonable doubt." Civil Defense radar watcher James Thornhill at Columbia, Mississippi observed a blip on his screen a few days after the event.

The object was too fast for a helicopter. It stopped in midflight, hovered for a time and left. The sighting was three miles from the radar installation. About the same time the radar and radio communications were "jammed" for 15 to 20 minutes. A Gulfport man, John Lane of Mississippi, reported a blue colored craft landed in front of his cab on October 15, causing his car to stall and radio to go dead. He then heard a tapping on the windshield and saw the similar creatures Hickson and Parker reported.

Meanwhile in Russia, the news agency "Tass" stated their scientists were trying to determine if signals they were receiving from space were artificial or natural. The paper said: "It is not precluded that they may be sent by a technically developed civilization."[lxxxvi]

Fishing in the Bay at Pascagoula River, Mississippi
Underwater (USO) Tales from Pascagoula, Mississippi
Coast Guard chases an underwater glowing object

Fishing | November 8, 1973, Raymond Ryan (42) was fishing in the Bay of the Pascagoula River when he observed an "Underwater Glowing Object" approach his position.

Mr. Ryan reported that he attempted to reach the object several times taking swings with his oar as it began following him in four to six feet of water.

Two Coast Guardsmen were unable to capture the thing, which they termed: "unidentified, submerged, illuminating object." According to the Coast Guard report: "It appeared to be an amber light approximately four to six feet in diameter attached to some bright metal object. Moving at 4 to 6 knots.

According to Ryan, his brother and other fishermen said the object "reversed itself and darkened, then re-illuminated and returned to follow him again. The Coast Guard said: "The fishermen appeared sober and concerned about the object."

The Coast Guard chased the object for 1 hour. The Coast Guard reported it too witnessed the object: "cease illuminating, changed to a different course, and then re-illuminated itself…The object traveled on several courses while illuminating, and the men could not identify it". The report was filed in New Orleans and at Headquarters, Washington, DC.[lxxxvii]

Women abducted
Insurance Executive studies saucers

Motorists | January 6, 1976, Three women were driving on a country road near Stanford Kentucky around 11:30 pm when they encountered a UFO.

The women recalled a domed saucer appeared at treetop level then they noticed their car sped out of control for about 8 miles.

Under Hypnosis the women recalled being taken aboard the ship by humanoid beings about 4 feet high. According to their memories, they were subjected to painful physician examinations, then released. The women then took like detector tests which confirmed their stories under hypnosis.

They also all carried burn marks on the backs of their necks and suffered minor physician effects.[lxxxviii]

The case was considered not a hoax.

Heading to fish at Pelham: Georgia
Possible Abduction Case?

Fishing | August 6, 1977, around 10:30 am Tom Dawson a retired car salesman was taking a walk down to his favorite fishing pond, when suddenly a disc-shaped craft silently came into view, hovering just a few feet off the ground between nearby trees. Simultaneously, Dawson found himself unable to move and noted that his two dogs and some twenty head of cattle seemed to suffer from the same affliction.

Dawson described the object as being about 50 feet in diameter and 15 feet high, encircled by what appeared to be portholes, with a dome on top. As he watched helplessly, a ramp was extended down to the ground, and seven hairless, snow-white entities appeared.

The beings each stood about 5 feet tall, had pointed ears and noses, and while some wore a tight-fitting one-piece suit, others wore no clothing at all. They produced a high-pitched gibberish that he was unable to understand. Meanwhile, the beings placed a skullcap-looking device on his head and a hula hoop-shaped thing, which was connected to a box, around his midsection.

Dawson felt that the entities were performing some sort of medical examination upon him. Then the beings gathered some leaves and stuff, and then they returned inside the craft and were gone in the blink of an eye. At some point afterward, Dawson regained his mobility and ran uphill (estimated at 300 yards) to his trailer.

He was taken to the Mitchell County Hospital as he was having difficulty breathing and talking. A physician felt he had been very shaken by some event. In fact, he was treated for hysteria and given medicine to calm him down. Then soon afterward he was released. Dawson stated that he believed that if he had been a younger man, then the UFOnauts probably would have abducted him. [lxxxix]

Fishing at Lake Loktak, Manipur: India

Fishing | June 19, 2011, in an astounding incident, a fish farmer in Manipur experienced loss of consciousness for over 18 hours after he claimed he was hit by shockwave transmitted from an unidentified flying object.

The fish farmer was trying out his inbuilt video camera on his brand new Chinese made mobile phone when he accidentally filmed the UFO hovering over his fish farm in Bishnupur district. This is the shocking footage of an unidentified flying object, filmed by a fish farmer in Manipur. After shooting for 19 seconds, 32 years Kumam Koiremba experienced loss of consciousness.

His fish farm, located at Ngangkha Lawai, Moirang near Loktak lake. Doctor's diagnosis read 'loss of consciousness, showing signs of weakness with non-responsive motor response.' Puzzled at his claim of being hit by a UFO shockwave, he was discharged after placing him under few hours of observation. However, Kumam Koiremba still complains of weakness and exhaustion after his 'chanced encounter' with the UFO.[xc]

Chapter 11: People and Animals Injured

Though it is very exciting to see a UFO, some encounters are not friendly at all. The experience of an earth observer has much to do with the type of species of aliens he or she is encountering.

Numerous books and stories discuss the positive and negative effects of such human and alien encounters. This is not to say all encounters are negative. In fact, in many cases, the encounters are quite friendly when we are dealing with alien species that look exactly like humans.

Where we find the species to be remarkedly different (they greys, or darkling's as I call them) they experience is traumatic. The US Government has cataloged over 49 separate species visiting earth. They, however, have not shared with us, which one is hostile. It would be nice to know when to run and when to say hi. For now, your rule of thumb should be if not exactly human looking – run!

People close to a UFO may become paralyzed or severally been wounded by the occupants or the ship itself. This chapter focuses on the negative side effects of being stunned by a handheld weapon or burned by the UFO.

Boy Touches UFO, Amarillo Texas
UFO emits gas giving boy welts on hands and face

Fishing | On April 8, 1950, a newspaper reported: "Two young boys from River Road went fishing late yesterday morning, but instead of a string of perch, they came home with a flying saucer story. This flying saucer landed. One of the boys touched it.

In substance, this is a composite of what David and Charles said happened to them yesterday morning: The boys went fishing shortly before 11 o'clock yesterday morning on a creek near the southern boundary of the Convalescent Home northeast of the city.

Thinking first it was a balloon: The object was traveling from the south. As it came nearer, the object decreased in speed, and it became apparent that it wasn't a balloon.

The disk passed by only a few feet over the boys, and David shouted to Charles, "I'll bet that's one of those flying saucers, Charles, I'm going after it." Charles did not follow. David said the disk circled slowly and disappeared over a small hill to the north.

Before David could top the rise, the saucer had landed.

"It was about as big around as a regular automobile tire... and about as high as I knew maybe a foot and a half. I could see it good".

The object was rounded on the bottom and had a top part, which resembled a flat plate. "When I first saw it good," David explained, "the bottom was still, but the top was spinning around really fast, and on the top of the part that was spinning around there was a little peak that had a kind of spindle sticking out of it. The spindle was still, too. It must have been connected to the bottom part."

The object was blue-gray in color, and had no openings of any sort other than the space between the top and bottom section, according to the boys' story.

The boy said he ran toward it and dived at it.

"My fingers just barely touched it, and it felt slick, sort of like I guess a snake would. It was hot, too." The youngster went on to relate that before he could "get a hold of the thing the top began revolving faster, and it made a sort of whistling noise and took off without warming up or anything." It disappeared in a straight line into the northeast in a matter of 5 to 10 seconds, he estimated.

In the process of taking off, though, the object emitted some sort of gas or spray that turned the youngster's arms a bright red and caused small welts on his arms and face. That part of the story was borne out by the lad's father.

The object was on the ground not morethan a minute, according to Charles, who said he got no closer than 100 yards to it before it took off. "Boy, it took off just like it was on a string or something. It was on the ground for no longer than half a minute.

The article ended with this" "neither of the boys believed the alleged flying saucer are from some other plant, "I think it's something the United States is doing, don't you? He asked". [xci]

Hunting: Manosque: France

Hunting | On October 14, 1954, a man and his dog were hunting when they observed an object. The man ran away; however, the dog went for the UFO and was semi-paralyzed. The dog according to the story was hardly about to get back to his master.

This story tracks another incident in the nearby town of Valensole where a man by the name of M. Masse encountered beings that looked human. This story received a lot of attention.[xcii]

Updated information on the case:

'The anonymous witness was hunting with his dog when he saw a gray object, about four meters, and one meter high, on the ground 40 meters away. It had a dome, from which two helmeted figures emerged. The witness fled, but his dog started toward the object; but it soon retreated, walking awkwardly as if partially paralyzed."[xciii]

Fisherman drowns after seeing UFO: Venezuela

Fishing | October 6, 1961, around 11:00 pm, a Santa Rita, Venezuela fisherman drowned when he and his friends saw a UFO. According to the article, his panic-stricken friends jumped from their boats as a huge, glowing object approached.

The paper goes on to say." It was Oct. 6, 1961, about 11 pm., when the enormous UFO appeared from the north, its glow lighting up the town. As it slowly crossed Lake Maracaibo, casting its glare on the fishing boats, dozens of terrified fishermen leaped overboard. One man, Bartolome Romero, went down in the frantic swim for safety. The others made shore, unnerved by the encounter.

In Santa Rita, alarmed inhabitants watched the strange object pass slowly over the city. The UFO was visible five minutes before it vanished to the south, leaving reddish, exhaust-like trail. (This slow operation rules out any fireball or meteor answer. The source and purpose of this apparently controlled device remain unexplained.)[xciv]

Man taken to Hospital: Florida
100-foot diameter UFO

Hiking | On March 14, 1965, according to the UFO Investigator a fort Meyers Man went under treatment in a hospital for eye dame after an encounter with a cone-shaped UFO in the Everglades.

Around 1:00 to 2:00 am James W. Flynn spotted a yellow light oscillating back and forth. He drove his swamp buggy within 400 yards to investigate, then proceeded on foot. As the observer approached the thing, he noted it was brightly illuminated in the shape of a cone. He also recalled that it emitted a loud whirring noise.

He then reported at 150 feet from the object, he suddenly felt a "sledgehammer" blow and was knocked unconscious. Many hours later, when he awoke, he was partially blinded but could see a black oily looking circle on the ground where the UFO had hovered. After stopping at an Indian village for aid, Flynn made his way back to Fort Myers and entered the hospital.

The doctor treating Flynn told the press he apparently was "hit with something over the right eye." That eye was bloodshot, and both eyes are bandaged.

NICAP member Charles H. Foresman (Captain, USNR-Ret) interviewed Flynn in the hospital March 19, submitting favorable character testimony to NICAP. He found the following facts:

1. The UFO appeared to be about 100 feet in diameters at the base and 30-30 feet high
2. The first row of windows was about 12 feet from the base, the others were even spaces about it.
3. The UFO appeared shiny and metallic

Sheriff Flanders Thompson told newsmen: "Knowing Jimmy as I know him, I don't believe he would cook up a story like this."[xcv]

Chapter 12: Rivers and Lakes

UFOs will fly over and stop alongside rivers and lakes. Sportsmen and women may see a UFO at this time. The weird thing about UFOs at riverbeds and lake shores is that they sometimes land and take soil and water samples.

It appears our space buddies are concerned with the quality of our lands and water.

An Early US History UFO fishing Case
UFO at the River Bank

Fishing | In January 1920, Clark Linch said he saw a UFO descend to a river bank and then leave. Clark said it was 10:00 am when an egg-shaped object about the size of a cream can land silently about 15 feet from his river bank perch. He shared "It sat there about 15 minutes, not bothering him; and he not he bothering it.

He shared – "I wasn't in any hurry to jump up and ran over to it. – It might have killed me.

Just when I thought about going over to take a closer look at it. It took off without any sound and without turning around.

When asked why he waited so long to tell his story he shared: "You didn't talk about flying saucers back in those days." – But today more people are taking them seriously."[xcvi]

Comment | What I find interesting in so many cases is the fact just when humans are about to interact with a spaceship or some aliens, they tend to "depart." Can aliens read our minds? Do they feel threatened by human interaction? Furthermore, if so many people back in the 1910 to 1930 era did not discuss UFO's, just how many cases would there have been on the books if they had. This indicates UFOs were frequenting US Airspace for many years before 1945.

Fox Hunting:

Hunting | On July 25, 1948, according to the *'Atlanta Constitution'* newspaper, two hunters on the Yellow River in Alabama observed a UFO around 3:00 am.

Just 15 minutes earlier (2:45 am) two Eastern Aircraft pilots (Captain C.S. Chiles and John B. Whitted) observed a "wingless buck Rodgers" shaped craft over the same area. The pilots stated the object had no wings but was shooting some sort of flame from the back.

Figure 8 - Illustration of Buck Rogers type space ship

According to the Hunters, Mr. Morris, and Mr. Fail, they witnessed a bright light speeding westward. While standing around Snapping Shoals in the Yellow River, a light as bright as a room appeared. The object was seen for only a few seconds.

An Indianapolis, Indiana woman reported seeing a ball-shaped object shoot two jets of flame downward at regular intervals. This was observed 24 hours before the above pilots.[xcvii]

30 to 35-foot diameter craft, Rogue River:

Fishing | On May 24, 1949, five people fishing up the Rouge River spotted a disc near Gold Beach Oregon. Two of these observers were aeronautical engineers employed by the Ames research laboratory at Mountain View, California. The engineers approached the security officer at Ames who represented the National Advisory Committee for Aeronautics.

According to the Air Force file: "the two aeronautical experts were subsequently interrogated by Project GRUDGE (USAF) investigators." All five witnesses were questioned, and all accounts were nearly identical.

Here is one of the stories:

"While fishing with a party of friends about two and a half miles up the Rogue River from its mouth at Gold Beach, Oregon, at approximately 5:00 pm, 24 May 1949, my attention was called to an object in the sky. The UFO was to the east of my location. With the naked eye, little but glare and silvery glint could be seen. But after watching it for approximately one minute and a half, I was handed a pair of 8-power binoculars"....to look at the strange object.

"It was then possible to see that the object was roughly circular in shape and appeared to be 30 to 35 feet in diameter. It had somewhat the cross-sectional appearance of a pancake, being thicker in the center than at the edges. A small triangular fin started approximately in the middle and grew gradually higher to the rear as the object traveled. When first sighted the object was moving very slowly.

"As I watched it through the glasses, it picked up speed, and when it vanished from sight, approximately 90 seconds later, it was traveling as fast or faster than a jet plane. As far as could be seen, it had no openings or protuberances of any kind other than the fin, and there was neither sight nor sound of any driving force. It was a clear day and no clouds in the sky, and the sun was at our backs as we watched the object, which vanished in a southeasterly direction, mostly south."

Another witness stated when first seen the disc was "standing on edge" and appeared to be at 5,000 feet in altitude. The object appeared to be made of "silvery metal." A triangular fin was seen rising from amidships and extended to the trailing end of the object. There were no openings visible and no sound was heard. There appeared to be no motors, no landing gear, and no other protruding parts other than the fin described.

Air Force files "early warning radar stations in the Bay Area reported nothing unidentified on May 24, 1949" for Gold Beach, Oregon, as these stations have an insufficient range for that great a distance."

The Air Force concluded the above observers witnessed "Kites." On the Project 10073 Record, the brief comment was: "Object had no definite shape. An object appeared turning or flopping constantly and drifted lazily. Observers believed objects to be sheets of roofing paper blown about by the wind. Object reflected light. Cream Colored."[xcviii]

Comment | The shape of the craft was clearly seen "thicker in the center and thin near the center." The object had a distinct triangular fin arising amidships. This appears to be another case where the AF drove down statistics in the "unidentified" sighting categories as other researchers have commented.

One observer stated, "it had no appearance of the conventional plane but in size would be the diameter of the fuselage length of the DC-3 plane. I have fished in the general area many years and have observed various types of planes flying in this area but have never observed anything of this nature, before". They all said it appeared as a "shiny circular disk."

A DC- 3 was typically 60 feet in length. No kite I have seen is 60 feet in length. This case should have been labeled "Unidentified."

Disc at Yellowstone National Park: Wyoming

Fishing | On July 8, 1949, man and wife report their UFO sighting. The story goes as follows:

"On July 8, 1949, between the hours of 6:30 and 7:00 am, my wife and I were fishing from a rubber boat on the north end of Shoshone Lake in Yellowstone Park when I heard what sounded like the whir of duck wings."

"I said to my wife listen, what is that sound, on looking straight up over our heads, I should say 800 to 1,000 feet, there were eight objects appearing to be round, and I would say about 20 feet in diameter, and very bright metal like bright aluminum, sailing as I have sailed a lid from a can many times. They were not in a formation but reminded me of a flock of blackbirds in a group some above and some below each other."

"There was no smoke or exhaust of any kind, it was a beautiful clear morning, and the sun was shining brightly. If there had been any exhaust, we would surely have seen it. They did not sail on a level course but seemed to go up and down just like some of the smaller birds fly when in a group. They were going very fast, and if they had not been directly over our heads, we would never have heard or seen them because we were watching the water. There was no sound of a motor."

"When the disc-shaped objects were about over the center of the lake one of them turned completely over sailing in among the rest of them without coming in contact with the other objects."

"They looked the same on both sides, but I could not tell how thick they were, but judging from the diameter they are large enough to have one or more men aboard."

"Many times when I was younger I have taken a flat round lid or heavy cardboard and threw it to see what it would make. This disc object turned completely over and sailed through the air as if the air current hand changed its course. Just before the disc went out of sight the one on our right turned on its edge and sailed down and away from the rest."

"I have seen jet planes and know about their speed, but these objects were just as fast if not faster."

"I have been kidded about seeing things and having too much to drink. But the sky was clear, and the sun shone brightly. We had had a good night's rest and nothing but good clear water to drink."

"My wife and I saw these eight metal objects if we ever saw anything in our lives. My opinion is that they are controlled by some device somewhere outside of the disc itself, and there is no man aboard, even though they are large enough to carry a man. I think there is some device that keeps them from colliding with each other, and my opinion is that they belong to the United States Government, because if they did not, the U.S. Government would soon find out where they came from."

The Air Force records show the conclusion was "Birds." Further comments on the Project 10073 Record stated: "Reflection of the sun's light off the wet bodies of birds often gives the appearance of a very large object at a much greater distance from the observer than they actually are, especially during the periods of dusk and dawn."[xcix]

Huge UFO at Maura Lake, Ontario: Canada

Fishing | In July 1951 "Mr. J Allan Smith (Commanding Officer of the Canadian Air Cadets) and his wife went to Maura Lake to spend a fishing holiday weekend with their friends, Mr. and Mrs. G. Leighton Thompson and another couple.

"According to Mr. Smith's account, early in the morning, at about 6:00 am., he and Mr. Thompson had gone to get the boat ready to go fishing. There was just a slight mist on the lake at that time. Suddenly, they noticed a large object, shaped like a flattened top, hovering over an island on the lake at a maximum distance of 7/11 miles away from their camp.

It was so huge that from the observation point it seemed to cover the whole end of the lake. It appeared to be solid, with definite shape and had a dull lead-like finish. The apparent size of the object at arm's length was estimated as that of a half-dollar; the angle of elevation from the horizon was stated to be five degrees."

"The object did not suddenly appear, and apparently it had already been hovering over the island before it was seen. During the sighting, which lasted some two minutes, the object made no movement from its position, nor did it revolve."

"After the initial shock of sighting the object, Mr. Smith ran back to the cottage to waken the other male member of the party, but by the time the other man had thrown on some outer clothing it had disappeared."

"Mr. Smith stated that he could not remember seeing the object rise and speed away --it seemed to him it just disappeared -but he admitted his back could have been turned at the moment of departure."

"Mr. G.L. Thompson's report was made out separately, without any consultation with Mr. Smith, so that we should have an exact version of what each man saw. His report was consistent with Mr. Smith's in most details."

"As he remembers it, the object appeared to be bright, like silver, flat to disc-shaped and making no movement except upon take-off, when it traveled faster than a jet plane. He estimated the apparent size as that of a silver dollar held at arm's length: the distance was thought to be '1/4 to 1 mile away, over the water."

The "windows" were actually "dark markings" of undetermined identity. The lower part with "spike" is an uncertain feature because it merged with the skyline of the island. [c]

160 foot long UFO: Lake Meade: Nevada

Fishing | April 2, 1952, between 9:00 and 10:00 am three individuals fishing at Lake Meade, Nevada spotted a UFO. One of the observers was an Air Force M. Sgt from Lockbourne AFB (OH).

The object was described as "silver in color, very large." Master Sgt Smith stated the UFO was that of a B-36 without wings. The UFO remained in sight for one hour. After one hour it suddenly vanished.

The observer's attention to the object came into view when a flight of F-86's flew overhead at 9:00 am around 15,000 feet, which were leaving vapor trails. The object appeared considerably higher than the vapor trails left by the planes.

A Teletype message was sent to ADC Ent AFB (CO), ATIC WPAFB (OH), HQ USAF Washington (DC) and Strategic Air Command at Offutt AFB (NE). The report was sent from March AFB (CA).

The Air Force could not come to a conclusion based on "insufficient data for evaluation."[ci]

Comment | A B-36 had a length of 160 feet. I am surprised the Air Force did not try to assume this was a weather balloon of some sort traveling in the upper atmosphere. This would have been ruled out, as it remained fixed for one hour. Most balloons are seen anywhere from several minutes to four minutes as they travel across the sky.

Patuxent River: Maryland

Fishing | June 21, 1952, Two Air Force officers from Andrews AFB were fishing in the Patuxent River when they witnessed a UFO. The Security Squadron officers reported the object to proper channels. The UFO was described as a greenish – white tear shaped craft traveling from NE to SW and passed from 40 degrees to 5 degrees before disappearing. No sound was heard during the sighting.

A Teletype message went to Ent AFB (CO), ATIC Wright Patterson AFB (OH) indicating facts of the sighting. The Air Force concluded the observer most likely witnessed a meteor.[cii]

Disc at Crookston: Minnesota

Fishing | On July 14, 1952, *'The Crookston Times'* reported: "Mr. and Mrs. [M.J] Long say they do not know what they saw, either.

Around 11:30 am the couple was fishing with Mr. and Mrs. John Croy of East Grand Forks on Union lake, when they heard the noise of a heavy aircraft and spotted a shiny silver object some 20,000 feet in the air, they said.

"They paid little attention to it until one of the party saw an airplane approaching from the northeast."

"We knew then the noise we had heard was from the plane,' Long said. 'We watched the saucer, or whatever it was until it suddenly took off and moved with tremendous speed over the horizon."

"Long believed the object 'must have been moving thousands of miles an hour' judging by its speed in relation with that of a fighter plane which passed over shortly after. The party noticed two more of the objects together until they suddenly disappeared."

"The objects were sighted about 11:30 am. July 14. "We were all wearing dark glasses, or we would probably not have seen them at all,' Long said. He estimated the objects were the 'size of a dishpan.'"[ciii]

Near Cambria Pines: California
"We were afraid to say anything about it."

Fishing | On July 19, 1952, around 10:55 pm "Two San Luis Obispo county men have added their eyewitness account of 'aerial objects' to the rash of 'flying saucer' stories which are currently sweeping the nation from coast to coast and have even been 'seen' on radar in Washington D.C.

"Wilbur Dean, Atascadero warehouseman employed by the California National Guard at Camp San Luis Obispo, and Sam Wright Sr., a Cayucos carpenter, also employed by the guard at the local camp, broke down this morning and admitted that they too had seen the mysterious objects last Saturday night.

"'We were afraid to say anything about it,' Dean said this morning. 'We thought everybody would think we were crazy".

"We were on a fishing trip up the coast highway,' Dean said, 'and were camped on the oceanfront about 28 miles north of Cambria Pines. 'Saturday night about 10:55 pm our dogs began barking and running up and down and awakened us.

We looked out and saw these lights flashing right straight out ahead of us just about ocean level [?]. There were seven of them. Suddenly one of them took off right straight up into the air, and five others followed [leaving behind one] about 1,000 feet apart.'

"Dean described the objects as being 'round and flat' and said they appeared to be 'very large." "They went up into the air in a spiral, corkscrew motion, trailing a flame- like exhaust,' he said. "They went really faster than a jet, even, and when they got about 2,000 feet up in the air, they just disappeared.

"'We watched the other one [the remaining object of the original seven] for about 20 minutes,' Dean concluded, 'then it took off the same way the other six did".[civ]

Fishermen see UFO

Fishing | On August 15, 1952, around 9:15 pm men in a small boat were fishing on Diamond Lake near White Cloud, Michigan when they spotted a UFO.

One observer, a 26-year-old pilot realized he was observing an unidentified flying object and yelled out to his friend. The object passed over their heads at 800 feet and 1,000 feet away. They guessed the speed of 700 miles an hour and having the fuselage size of a large aircraft.

The object was giving off a fluorescent blue-green glow. 20 other witnesses at the lake saw the same UFO. A drawing is in the Blue Book files, which shows the image of an oval shaped craft, round on the front and bottom and flat on the top.[cv]

Comment | We are not sure of the exact size of the craft however in 1950 at-large aircraft could be between 60 feet and 116 feet long depending on the design.

Smokey Balls, Mt Sterling: Ledford Lake, Kentucky

Fishing | On August 26, 1952, the Mt Sterling "Advocate" reported that Last Tuesday night around 8:00 pm a local fisherman was at Ledford Lake on the Spencer pike in Montgomery County and observed a UFO.

When he suddenly looked up, he observed two large balls of smoky, orange-colored fire swooping down on the lake. He watched the strange spectacle for about 30 seconds and said that the two things came to within 150 feet of the water and then started climbing again in a long curve, finally disappearing in the sky.

"The fisherman, who may stretch the size of the fish he catches, but is a sober and hard-working man and not given to hallucinations, said the objects, about four feet in diameter, were constantly changing shape and came down and then went up parallel to each other about five or six feet apart.

"At first he thought they might be meteors, but changed his mind when they started back up into the sky. He said they made absolutely no sound at all and appeared to be traveling a lot faster than a jet plane."

"It so happened that another person, who lives here, was fishing across the lake from him, and after the things disappeared in the sky, our fisherman remained silent, thinking that he might have been the only one to see the smoky, orange-colored balls."

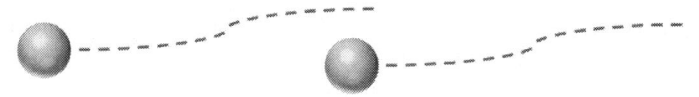

Figure 9 - Illustration of Orange Spheres together

But at that moment a voice hailed him from across the water and asked, "What in the world was that?" and he knew it was not his imagination. "The fisherman, who asked that his name not is disclosed, said that quite many night birds had been flying around the lake, diving at the water and emitting shrill cries before the things appeared, but after they disappeared not a bird could be seen, or a sound heard.

"Needless to say, the two men quickly up their fishing equipment and quietly stole away-even though it was only eight o'clock." [cvi]

UFOs at Lake Salem, Vermont

Fishing | Mid-August 1953, according to three citizens (Richard Clapper and family) they observed silver globes while fishing at Lake Salem, Derby, Vermont. The information was provided to CSI Los Angeles via a letter after the event. The story is as follows:

"We had been there for quite a while when we heard a large plane. We watched the plane until it got almost directly over us. Suddenly, three, silver globe-shaped things appeared fairly near the plane. They seemed to dart at the middle of the plane, and then they would swerve away from the plane.

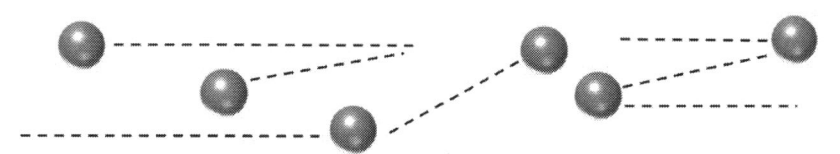

Figure 10 - Silver spheres bouncing around

They continued this performance for about two minutes, then suddenly all three of these globes seemed to fly in an upward direction with great speed, and within a matter of seconds, they had disappeared. These globes were very maneuverable, and they made turns at very sharp angles, and they were tremendously fast.

"All three of us that saw these globes had heard a lot of reports about such things, but we hadn't thought much of them. We have also heard that some people think that seeing these is just a trick of the imagination, but I don't think that all three of us would imagine these things."[cvii]

UFO at Gippsland Lakes: Australia

Fishing | January 7, 1954, around 3:30 am three men witnessed a UFO at Paynesville, Australia.

"'At 3:30 a.m. I was in a motorboat in the center of the lakes. I was with two companions. We were crossing the lakes to do some fishing. I was outside the cabin, and I noticed a brightly lit object in the sky. It was flying at about 1,000 feet-quite low, anyway-and was traveling at about the same speed as a Vampire jet fighter. The UFO came to within half a mile or so of us, and I could see it quite plainly."

"You know what a bright new ball bearing looks like? Well, if you cut one in halves, that's exactly what this thing looked like. It had a flat round bottom with a hemispherical top, which seemed to fine down to a tail at the stem. The object had no wings. It flew past us and then turned due east flying directly into the wing."

"The sun was not quite up, but it was plenty light enough to see clearly. I can't say whether it made a noise because the engine of the boat was running, and the exhaust would have drowned any noise from the object. I would say that the object at half a mile and at 1,000 feet altitude looked the size of a DC-3 airliner."

Mr. D.R. McDonald, a 54-year-old traveler, of Government Road, Paynesville, on the Gippsland Lakes, put a trunk line telephone call through to the Herald today to report a 'flying saucer,' called in this event. Mr. McDonald started his story by saying: 'I don't blame you if you think I'm a bit around the bend. I've always chucked off at these stories myself.'

"Mr. McDonald said he would make a detailed report in writing to the DCA."[cviii]

60-foot diameter Disk over Cass Lake: Minnesota
(Fishermen observe the object)

Fishing | Summer 1954 (exact date unknown) around 7:00 pm friends and family observed a large disk over their vacation home at Cass Lake, Minnesota. APRO received the information from the family. According to Loren E. Gross files very little was in the file except for the following information: "It seems a family and friends were spending some vacation time in the Minnesota woods when a UFO came into view.

According to the person making the report, a strange object went right over their cabin. At the time the witnesses' aunt was inside and noticed anything unusual except for a humming noise.

An uncle and a friend said they were out on the lake in a boat fishing when they first spotted the UFO over the trees. They saw the object leave the trees and fly over to a position close to the cabin where it slowed to a crawl, [apparently passing over the structure at this point] as if observing. After that, the UFO sped up and was lost from sight.

The object was saucer-shaped with two red lights, one bright and the other of lesser intensity. The location of the lights on the object was not indicated. The disk had no protrusions and appeared to be 60 feet in diameter. It was so big and so close its apparent size at arm's length was that of a dinner plate. There were two tall pine trees in the vicinity, and the UFO skimmed slightly above them.

Using the height of the trees as a guide, it was estimated that the UFO dropped as low as 60 feet above the ground. Estimated duration of the sighting was one minute."[cix]

UFO at Rio Santa Lucia: Argentina
10 meters in diameter

Fishing | December 7, 1954, Senor Sarandi D'Alvora witnessed a UFO with friends while fishing and relaxing at the Isla Del Francis, Rio Santa Lucia in Argentina.

His story is as follows:

"I went with three friends on December 7th to Francis Island where we have a small house. We planned to spend the night and the next day on the Island fishing and swimming, etc."

"At about 9:30 my friends were preparing a roast a little distance from the house. Suddenly crossing the trees in the direction of the river they saw a luminous object ascending at great velocity. We were discussing the episode when the object appeared again traveling at great speed but this time descending from north to south as if to land on the extreme south end of the island, Because of the trees we could not see if it actually came down.

We decided to investigate, and the strangeness and the anxiety were enormous."

"We entered a boat and commenced to row (deciding not to use the motor) south towards the throat of the Santa Lucia River known as the 'Paso de Bote.' We advanced some 300 meters when they're on the water some 25 meters from the coast we saw a great object. It had an elliptical form some 10 meters in diameter and 1.8 meters high at its central cone."

"It looked like gray metal, sometimes bluish or with yellowish tones. The outer border appeared to have an uninterrupted line of exhaust ports or something similar from which when flying issued a bright bluish haze that made its movement easy to see."

"We were aware of the press descriptions of these strange objects, in which generally the upper part is semi-spherical. This one did not have such a characteristic but was a cone not truncated in its vertice [sic vertical?]."

"When we were some 60 meters from the object one of my friends committed the error of starting the motor running when the flying disc changed its displacement very slightly (almost imperceptible) and then rose in an oblique trajectory at fantastic speed, passing over us at very few feet altitude."

"Our shock, surprise, fear, etc., continued until it was out of sight. We decided to advance to where the object had sat on the water where we encountered a curious thing; the water was hot."

"As a result of the visit there were no fish in the area the next day, but we saw many dead ones (between 200 and 300)."[cx]

Lake Imba-Numa Tokyo: Japan

November 10, 1957, around 5:55 pm American engineer Wilfred S. Hardy at Tokyo Engineer Supply Center, observed a "mysterious, glowing spaceship over Lake Imba-numa on the Boso Peninsula about 50 miles from Tokyo.

Hardy, 52, his wife and a Japanese boat boy saw the glowing, cigar-shaped object which appeared to be between 200 and 500 feet long when it suddenly lit up the entire lake.

Hardy said it was speeding at about 600 to 800 miles per hour into the south, maintaining a level course, and radiating colors like the northern lights.

Hardy mentioned the object was giving off a purplish-red trail. The body of the object had an "artificial glow, but the spectrum like reds, greens, yellows, and blues surrounding its airfoil was bring created for its flight.

"What we saw had all the physical aspects of a spaceship. However, I wasn't close enough to see any details as aerials or windows. He further stated:

> "I'm convinced. It wasn't any sort of optical illusion or sun reflection...and it wasn't Sputnik because it was too large and too long".[cxi]

Lake Placid: New York

Fishing | August 8, 1958, a woman writes Dr. J Allen Hynek of her UFO sighting:

"In 1958 my late mother visited my late husband and me to recuperate from a virus. The month was August. She was with the FAA, and there had been numerous news accounts of UFOs being sighted at that time.

"Late one afternoon, about 4:00 pm I sighted my husband returning from up the lake, where he had been fishing. He was some distance, but we had a red boat, and it was then the only one that color on the Lake Placid.

"We went outdoors to see what he had caught."

"As we stepped out on the grass and looked at the lake, movement from the direction beyond Signal Hill caught our eyes. A mighty wind was blowing from the south. A large, seemingly elongated, a flattened blimp-like vehicle was flying against that wind at great speed. The sky was cloudless-and a vivid blue."

We ran the length of our property, down to Saranac Avenue-approximately 110 feet-and watched it continue on course perhaps three times the height of Signal Hill until it vanished through the undulation of terrain.

"Our then next-door neighbor was preparing dinner for her husband. She had seen our running and wondered if an accident had occurred, never thinking to look in the direction we had been gazing (to his rear). It was aluminum (?) colored and appeared to be metal."

There were red somethings on it-lights or a recessed deck (?). We could see no evidence of landing gear or wings or tail fins. She was very excited, as was the writer, and said she was going to tell the FAA what her experiences had been on her return to New York. Whatever happened to her account I have no idea. My then neighbor scoffed it off as a 'weather balloon,' but we knew it was not one. It was the largest airborne craft one could see in broad daylight. We heard no sound."[cxii]

Green Lake: Pontiac Michigan

Fishing | August 29, 1960, a woman reported a UFO at Pontiac Michigan while fishing at Green Lake. According to the file, the UFO was heading south to the north yet reversed itself several times. The observer reported the incident to the Civil Air Patrol, who relayed it to Detroit ARTCC and on the Senior Director, Chicago ADS.

The Air Force could not come to a conclusion based on "insufficient data for evaluation."[cxiii]

Figure 11 - Illustration of egg craft "reversing direction"

Orbiting Sphere UFOs at Manso River, Brazil

Fishing | August 19, 1962, According to the testimony of Antonio Rocha, employed at Mail Department in Diamantina, was fishing on the bank of the Manso River at 4:00 pm August 19th. At that location, he had a clear view of Rivalino Silva's house. Rocha noticed two ball-shaped objects flying in circles low over Rivalino's property. Later, it was assumed this event had something to do with subsequent events.

In the '*APRO Bulletin*,' Mr. Rocha said to Lieutenant Lisboa: "I sighted two strange ball-shaped objects in the sky. They were flying in circles over Rivalino's house. They came very low and were gone a few minutes later". The story becomes more credible when a Physician reported similar object two months earlier.

"Doctor Giovani Pereira, a physician, living at Diamantine, went to the police to report the sighting of a disc-shaped object over his own house two month before. He had a night call from a patient and was driving back in his car."

"When closing the car door to go inside his home, he suddenly sighted a brilliant object, shaped like a disc, hovering low over his house. He stopped and watch it for several minutes, then it moved away at high speed after crossing over the sleeping town. He said he had kept the sighting secret because he had kept the sighting secret because he knew nobody would believe him."[cxiv]

Fishing at Yankeetown, Indiana
30 to 45-foot saucer: Indiana (Hoax?)

Fishing | On June 14, 1964, two separate UFO reports were made from the Huntington, Indiana area. It began with two youths fishing southeast of Yankeetown, Indiana who observed a UFO at treetop level.

According to the report, the UFO came to within 200 feet of the witnesses the veered away. The UFO made no sound and appeared to be 10 or 15 yards in diameter and glowing. The witnesses watched the UFO for 10 minutes.

Around 9:00 pm a farmer Charles Englebrecht stated a glowing object landed a few miles northwest of Dale City, then left leaving the smell of Sulphur. The UFO left behind a burned spot on the ground and a half-inch deep depression.

The Air Force investigator retrieved a small piece of metal, and under Jewelers glass said the surface appeared: "grooved.... Like walnut". The witness mentioned he was watching TV at the time when the lights and TV began to flicker. He ran to the door to see what was causing the interruption and witnessed the glowing basketball object land 50 feet away.

As he moved forward to get closer, he felt something like an electrical shock and was unable to move forward.

In another unconfirmed report broadcast by a local radio announcer stated the object hit a farmhouse in the vicinity, causing television set to blow up.

According to the US Air Force Files, Bill Powers from Northwestern University was brought in with a conclusion the sighting was an attempted hoax.[cxv]

Fishing at Echo Lake: New York
20 to 40-foot diameter UFO, the story carried on WHSF-TV

Fishing | On July 29, 1964, around 10:30 four 16-18-year-old boys fishing at Echo Lake (north of Binghampton) New York observed a UFO.

The object was described as 20 to 40 feet in diameter and came down on the lake, and the moved off rapidly. They were said to have a whirling appearance and glowed as the UFO moved from east to west.

The observation was for over several minutes. According to the US Air Force files the object had a ring around the cone. The story was carried on TV news WHSF from July 29-31st.

On the 30th a 26-year-old woman reported a large cylindrical object, silver moving south at a high rate of speed. No sound was heard, and it had no wings or lights on the UFO. That same day 8 separate reports were filed by people in the Binghampton area.

On the 31st another person reported a round silver UFO hovering in a field near Endicott. Watching the thing for several minutes, he observed no tail or wings and no markings. It departed quickly and made no noise.

1st Lt Thomas P. Schellinger, USAF completed the report. The report was sent to AFSC Wright Patterson AFB (OH).

The Air Force provided several conclusions of this sighting. They believed the cause was either a "B-26, meteors and/or Satellites".

The detailed Binghampton file suggests that the sightings beginning June 1964 began with a farmer in Newark Valley that a saucer landed and spoke with several spacemen.

Then in July, the five children at Kirkwood observed a ship (UFO) on the ground. The Air Force believed the deluge of reports came after the Sun-Bulletin and WHBF-TV provided the stories, which to them were unfounded. Finally, the Air Force stated; FAA personnel and the Weather Bureau at Broome County Airport reported no unusual activity from July 28 to August 3.[cxvi]

Green Lake: Wisconsin

Near the Lake | April 27, 1967, at around 10:00 pm, two men were heading to house north of Green Lake, Wisconsin.

As they drove they observed an object in the sky that glowed and changed from red to white to orange. The UFO was moving very slowly to the north and very near the ground.

They got to the house and used their binoculars and could determine the thing was ¾'s of a mile away. It hovered over the ground and tilted from side to side very slowly and was moving north towards a small wooded hill.

Through the binoculars, the object was clearly outlined and distinct. When it got to the woods "it stopped." Then it tilted toward the north and went down into the woods. It flooded the area where it was with white light. The lighted area could clearly be seen without binoculars.

It finally came up out of the woods and went over the hill. They then said: "We got into my car and went north to the top of the hill. We could still see it traveling north at the top level, but it was now quite far.

The object made no sound. The Air Force Classified this as "Venus."[cxvii]

Hunting Trip: Apalachicola National Forest

Hunting | In January 1973, Clarence Bizet, a resident of Tallahassee, Florida, and former newspaperman were on a hunting trip in the Apalachicola National Forest when a companion spotted a light over Hitchcock Lake. Bizet said; "It was the brightest light I ever saw."

The hunters described the object as "flickering" like that of a heartbeat.

"The light hovered over the treetops, then moved off quickly." Bizet was able to follow it with the help of his field glasses for a short time but then lost it. A moment later both men looked behind them, and it was hovering over the treetops again but higher up this time. Bizet observed the UFO with binoculars and described the craft as having flickering blue and green lights and much more distant than one would realize at first.

That same night came a second report from Mayor Curley Messer of nearby Carrabelle. He claims to have seen strange lights in the same area, thereby giving supporting data to the previous sighting.[cxviii]

Fishing Lake Michigan
"Hovering above the water."

Fishing | On July 5, 1965, a night fisherman on Lake Michigan reported a flying saucer was seen hovering over the water at about 200 feet.

The observer writes the Air Force for an explanation. The letter states: "We were fishing on Lake Michigan off the shore of St. Ignace, We never reported this because no one would believe us. What we saw was saucer-shaped hovering over the water at about 200 feet.

It gave off a bright, brilliant light, Visibility was about 15 feet, the temperature was 52% F. The Air Force could not come to a conclusion for "insufficient data for evaluation."[cxix]

Ball-shaped UFO while Fishing Snake River: Oregon
"I felt the object was actually traveling to go unnoticed."

Fishing | May 21, 1967, around 10:00 pm a former Air Force officer was fishing for catfish on the Snake River observed a UFO at 40,000 feet over Ontario, Oregon.

The object was described as a Ball-shaped Star moving and stopping. The observer seeing such object stop and start first believed he was tired. He then fixed the location of the object using the silhouette of the trees on the opposite bank of the river.

The object traveled in a lateral direction heading southeast except for four times when the thing moved up and down. He noticed during its transition that it would move a distance of 10 to 15 times its own size then stop for 2 or 7 seconds, then repeat the same activity. He said: "I felt the object was actually traveling to go unnoticed."

The witness was an Advertising salesman for the Ontario Argus Observer and had over 1,500 hours in KB-29 and KC-97 aircraft during his time with the Air Force.

The Air Force concluded the object seen was a "possible satellite." The Air Force did not confirm which satellite would have been seen or the approximate time the satellite would have been overhead at the time of the UFO sighting. AF records confirmed the Boise FAA office had no records of air traffic or balloon releases in the area at the time of the UFO event.[cxx]

Comment | This again appears to be a case of mistaken labeling. From 2011 to 2013, I witnessed similar objects traversing the skies over CT, performing similar "stops and starts" as well as making U-turns and "S" movements at that or higher altitudes. Using "Skywalk" no satellites were known to be in the area at the time.

During the 1960's flights of ECHO II and I, the satellite (technically a balloon) could make unusual movements because of atmospheric conditions interfering with its surface. However, the fact that the file did not reflect whether a satellite was passing at the time suggests this should have been labeled "Unknown," "Unidentified" or "Insufficient Data for Evaluation."

Oval shaped UFO followed boaters at Lake Monona
Fishing at Lake Monona: Wisconsin
APRO Investigation by John M. Kelley

Fishing | November 8, 1967, around 10:00 pm two people boating on Lake Monona, Dane County, Wisconsin observe a UFO.

While boating the couple spotted a lighted object approach the lake. They first thought the object was going to crash, but it then stopped and hovered about 50 to 100 feet above some trees.

The trees were near the boat landing on Winnequah Road. According to APRO the object then showed two bright beams at their boat. The couple tried to swerve their boat a few times, but the lights followed them. The couple very frightened went back to shore and ran into one of the observer's homes. The female observer cried for two hours. The male observer stated the object was oval in shape and made no sound.[cxxi]

Comment | This was not to our knowledge reported to the Air Force, it was not located in the US Air Force Project Blue Book Files for 1967.

Near Czluchow: Poland

Dogs Injured

Fishing | August 1978 a resident of Czluchow was rowing his boat on a lake when he saw a "dark oblong object" moving along the surface of the water. It bore a slight resemblance to a fishing boat, but it was moving rapidly and soundlessly without disturbing the water. A few seconds later another witness, this one on land, saw the object almost in the same instant that it vanished from the first witness' view.

The second observers saw it disappear behind the lakeside vegetation.

He called his dogs and with them went to the spot where he thought the "boat" would be landing. He had walked about 20 steps when he sighted, 20 meters from the shore, two beings in dark suits. They were heading toward the forest. When the dogs ran in their direction, the strangers turned around and looked at them. The dogs stopped in their tracks, barked and retreated in terror."

"The strangers resumed their trek, and over the next moments, the witness studied them carefully. One and a half meters tall, they were sealed in what resembled diving outfits. At the level of their eyes was a "glass plate" through which they could see. Their hips were unnaturally wide, and each had a "hump" between the back of his neck and his shoulders."

"The witness shouted at them to stop, but on hearing his voice, they fled into the trees. As the man was searching for them, a brightly luminous object floated up above the treetops 100 meters away. The UFO, rectangular-shaped with rounded corners, stopped its ascent about 30 meters above the ground. The light along its sides was blue-green, but this color shaded off into white in the middle of the object."

"The UFO flew away; leaving no traces where the witnesses estimated it would have been "parked." Nor could he find the footprints of its presumed occupants."

"The witness claimed that in the six months following the incident, the dogs' front legs became paralyzed and both of the animals had to be destroyed."[cxxii]

Chapter 13: Traveling In The Sky

UFOs are seen shooting through the air or parking themselves over people homes. The best time to see saucers is from dusk till midnight. I prefer 8:00 pm to 11:00 pm and that's enough time to see many planes, helicopters, some shooting stars, the moon, planets, meteors, and 1 or 2 UFOs if you are lucky. The number of UFOs I saw in one 2 hour sitting was six. The least was none. I felt lucky if I could at least see one and felt really excited at two UFOs.

The moral of the story is you have to be patients and have clear skies to see a UFO. The only way you will see them is if they are passing overhead going to a specific location and you are there to witness the event. Otherwise, you are inside your home watching a TV show, they pass over, and you never see it.

Chief Mechanic Pan American: Newfoundland
100-foot long craft blows a hole through the cloud
"AF hides Photographs of the larger UFO."

Fishing | On July 10, 1947, between 3:00 and 5:00 pm in the afternoon John E. Woodruff station Chief Mechanic for Pan American Airways was coming back from fishing when he witnessed a UFO in Newfoundland. He was near Stephenville Crossing coming over a hill when the object was seen.

The object was described traveling at an excessive speed in a circle. A definite trail was seen in which the object flew through a cloud and left sharp edges where it passed through. The UFO was described as a "disc." The disc left a bluish colored trail that was seen going right through the opening in the cloud.

According to the SIGN report the object was between 8,000 and 10,000 feet. The UFO was compared to that of a 54 or a Constellation plane. The UFO was described as a disk construction or wheel. The color of the exhaust was a dark bluish. The craft itself appeared "translucent."[cxxiii]

Comment | What the Air Force did not reveal was the following information not included in the report:

"At Harmon Air Field, Newfoundland, a number of people, including some airline mechanics, saw a high speed, round-like, object the apparent size of a transport plane. It glistened in the sun and left behind a trail of bluish-black smoke approximately 15 miles long while it zoomed northeast on a horizontal trajectory. The object cut through some clouds, boring a "hole," a gap, which was photographed twice by a witness using an Argus with a 50 mm F-2 lens.

The two Kodachrome were rushed to the Intelligence Chief of Staff at Newfoundland Base Command and then hurried on to American authorities".

More Information given in Loren E Gross Reports:

The following is the story given by the three principal witnesses, a J.N. Mehrman, an R. Leidy, and a J.E. Woodruff. The trio was returning from a fishing trip July 10th and was driving up a mountain road near Stephenville Crossing when they witness a UFO.

It was Woodruff who became excited first: "Look at the cut in the sky," he yelled. Mr. Mehrman glanced at the scattered clouds at 8-10,000 feet and then also detected a bluish-black vapor trail that apparently had made a knife-like cut through a cloud formation. The edges of the "cut, he described as "feathered similar to a weld, as if you cut a weld in half.

Mr. Leidy, like Mehrman, did not spot the phenomenon immediately, yet Woodruff's actions called for a look to the car they were riding in was brought to a halt so they could give their attention to the sky.

Leidy said he remembers: "It was a definite trail and caused the clouds to break open as it went through. It cut a clear path through the clouds, and you could see the trail right through the cloud, it looked to be traveling in a big circle, and it left sharp edges to the clouds."

Woodruff observed what had made the "hole. He stated: "I saw the object break out where the clouds opened, and it left its trail behind it. The object appeared to be a translucent disk-like wheel traveling at a terrific rate of speed and opened the clouds as it went through the air. The disk was traveling horizontally. It appeared to be about the size of a C-54."

The US Army Air Corps Technical Analysis Division at Wright-Patterson AFB, Ohio, was enthralled. The experts said:

"The bluish-black trail seems to indicate ordinary combustion from a turbo-jet engine, athodyd motor, or some combination of these types of power plants. The absence of noise and apparent dissolving of the clouds to form a clear path indicates a relatively large mass flow of rectangular cross-section containing a considerable amount of heat."

Intelligence agents discussed the case with the Commander of Harmon Field and received assurances no British or Canadian aircraft had been in the area at the time of the sighting. Weather records were examined, and they confirmed the witness's testimony about the sky conditions: cumulus clouds at 8-10,000 feet.

Mr. Woodruff left for Gander AFB, but military investigators tracked him down to obtain any amplification. Anxious to help, Mr. Woodruff met the investigators plane, and when questioned again, reiterated his previous statements, adding that the "hole" remained in the cloud for well over an hour and that the vapor spewed out by the UFO was a bit darker than the sky, a flat, ribbon-like, bluish-black smoke that reminded him of an exhaust gas of a diesel engine. The UFO itself he described as a "translucent disk shape" that appeared to have little depth and produced no audible sound. He was firm about these aspects.

A military analyst lamented the fact that the film was a little overexposed but conceded, as they were doing now with UFOs in general, that: "it is evident that some such phenomenon did occur."

A summation tainted with strategic considerations spelled out the belief they were not dealing with an ordinary aircraft.

It read that they concluded that a body having terrific heat or other power to split a cloud had passed through." Moreover: "It was very noticeable that the course of the phenomenon was approximately 30 degrees east of true north which could be an indication that it did not originate from a foreign country." A meteor seems to be the only thing that could give off such heat but, as the experts remarked, the low altitude and apparent horizontal course would rule it out.

Another Update: On July 9, 1947, at the same location: A Canadian constable and others in the community of Grand Falls, Newfoundland, vouched for the fact that, as one of them put it, a phosphorescent aura accompanying a barrelhead-like thing" shot past at 11:30 pm on July 9th. Four round-shaped objects flying side by side were also seen. [cxxiv]

One Final statement: The UFO incident at O'Hare Airport in 2006 also left a perfect hole in the cloud as the object rose vertically at a terrific speed above United Airlines terminal building. Also, note a constellation plane was about 116 feet long in 1947. This UFO craft was over 100 feet in diameter.

The Lubbock Lights Began

Cookout | On August 25, 1951, around 9:10 pm in Lubbock, three professors, teachers from Texas Technological College, Lubbock, Texas, we're having an informal Saturday night gathering 'in the backyard of a professor Robinson's Lubbock home on 24th Street.

It was warm and clear, so the group had decided to hold their talks outside. The three professors present were: Dr. A. G. Oberg, professor of chemical engineering; Dr. W. J. Robinson, professor of geology; and W. L. Ducker, 'professor and head of the Petroleum Engineering Department at Tech.

They were relaxing in chairs in the yard, exchanging comments about a proposed micro-meteorite project to be sponsored by Texas Tech. Dr. Oberg was staring at a particular constellation waiting for a meteor flash when he suddenly spotted some 50 lights approaching in a semi-circular formation.

Dr. Ducker responded: " ... as a 'string crescent formation from the northeast to the southeast at an 'incredible speed.' "The individual objects which made up the formation were indistinct, but gave off a glow, apparently reflected light, possibly from the city below."

The professors were surprised as they watched the "string of beads" zoom overhead, crossing the arc of the heavens in three seconds, which left no time to estimate the shape or size of the luminous dots. Understandably intrigued by the phenomenon, the professors agreed to wait and watch for any more overflights.

Approximately three minutes later a second group of 50 lights in a semi-circular formation flashed overhead. Dr. Ducker would later say:

> **"Frankly, we were astonished, and if I had not had confirming witnesses at the time, I feel sure I should have said nothing about what I saw, for it is incredible to believe they are of terrestrial origin and even more incredible to believe they are from beyond the earth.**[cxxv]

Updated information on the case:

Coming to the defense of his colleagues immediately was the head ·Of Texas Tech's Journalism Department, J. Russell Heitman, who remarked that he had sighted a similar flight of lights several nights earlier that matched the description of the phenomenon given by Dr. Ducker and the other two professors.

Monday four other witnesses came forward to offer supporting testimony to the claims of the Texas Tech professors. Three were housewives who had also been outside that evening talking in a backyard of a resident on Medlock Avenue. They said they had sighted similar lights flashing through the sky the same time as that mentioned in the newspaper. Likewise, professor Carl Hemminger, associate professor of German at Texas Tech who lived on Eighth Street, said he too had noticed the mystery lights.[cxxvi]

Wright Patterson gave Lubbock Lights "SECRET" Classification

On September 7, 1951, Wright Field heard about the excitement at Lubbock, and then it took a message from the OSI office at Carswell Air Force Base, Texas, to alert Air Force Intelligence in Ohio. At Carswell the OS! forwarded a Spot Intelligence Report to GRUDGE, which processed the information and then issued an order to Reese Air Force Base just outside Lubbock to get some men in town to begin an investigation.

Air Force Intelligence clamped a SECRET classification on the investigation.

OSI officer Howard Bossert accompanied by 1st Lt. John A. Farley, Assistant Wing Intelligence Officer, Reese Air Force Base, went directly to the editor of the Lubbock Avalanche-Journal, Charles Guy to ask specific questions on the incident.[cxxvii]

Two women interrogated over Lubbock Lights incident

On September 18, 1951, Air Force Intelligence Officer Lt. Fabley, and OSI Agent Howard Bosseat interrogated the two women. It seems that two women, a Mrs. Stella Tilsom and her friend, a Mrs. Eugenia T. Bethard, sighted a very strange object in the sky while driving along a road near Matador, Texas, a town some 70 miles north of Lubbock. The time of the sighting was 12:45 pm.

The military record had more detail than the press accounts and is quoted below:

" ... their attention was attracted by a strange aerial object drifting across U.S. Highway 70. Mrs. Tom Tilsom, who was driving, first noticed the object and it was apparently a few seconds before she drew Mrs. Bethard's attention to it.

Mrs. Tilsom stated that when she saw the object, it was drifting slowly in an easterly direction about 150 feet above the terrain and approximately 200 feet in front of their car. About the time Mrs. Bethard saw the object, it began a rapid ascent and moved away in a few seconds to the east in a circular ascent.

"The object was described by Mrs. Tilsom as being pear-shaped in appearance, (to quote 'like a yellow pear-shaped tomato') aluminum or silver in color, and that the object readily reflected the sunlight. The UFO had a port, window, door or a similar aperture, located at a point where the craft began to taper toward the smaller end. One UFO only was seen, and it moved through the air with the small end forward. She stated the sun was shining brightly with little or no wind.

"Mrs. Tilsom stopped the car and got out, and both then realized there was no noise, no sign of exhaust, no smoke, no wings were visible, nor was any visible means of propulsion observed. Mrs. Tilsom stated she could not estimate the speed of the object except that it went up rapidly in a curving angle east and in a few seconds was out of her sight. Mrs. Bethard did not get out of the car and lost sight of the object as it ascended due to her limited vision inside the car. Mrs. Tilsom was certain the object was not a balloon.

She compared the size of the object, to the best of her knowledge, as comparable to the Matador railway freight shed or perhaps larger. The Matador freight shed was examined and measured approximately 4R feet by 18 feet."

Air Force investigators made discrete inquiries and established to their satisfaction that both women were reputable citizens with excellent character and credit reputations. Officers Fabley and Hosseat then went to the scene of the sighting and recorded their impressions:

"An examination of the location described by Mrs. Tilsom was made, and it was observed that the terrain to the west of U.S. Highway 70 is rolling land for about 10 to 12 miles (estimated) to a line of foothills. The land is sparse to moderately heavily wooded by mesquite with the first 300 yards open flat terrain. The land to the east is fairly flat for approximately 20 to 30 miles, sparsely wooded and the first 1000 to 1200 yards is open terrain."[cxxviii]

Hunting Club: Mock Battles over Detroit Michigan (Exercise: Sign Post: Draws UFO's)

Hunting | July 27, 1952, in what may be an important attractant to UFOs is the aerial engagement of various air forces performing mock air battles. Well known to Military Airshows UFO appear to watch the aerial performance of our aircraft. On the heels of the famous Washington DC flyover of an unknown fleet, the following mock battle took place over Detroit Michigan on the July 27th. Canadian and US Air Force planes engaged in a mock bombing raid over Detroit.

What took place then were witnesses on the ground seeing both identified aircraft and "unidentified aircraft."

One couple at a hunting club on the Black River near Onaway reported seeing flying saucers after hearing bombers overhead. For 20 minutes the family observed a perfect formation. According to the witnesses, the formation appeared to be in an arrangement to guard a "mothership." The family believed after being told of the mock raid, perhaps they indeed witnesses bombers.

However, several other witnesses in the area observed objects that did not resemble planes. Some witnesses reported seeing craft resembling "shooting stars and glowing flying footballs." The Hall brothers using binoculars reported 14 objects which were very bright and blurred at the edges around 10:15 pm. One accountant, next door to the Hall brothers, watched an object that appeared as a large "light bulb."

In Detroit, several citizens reported objects "hovering" over the city (Not flying). The article stated: an air force observer said 250,000 Canadians and Americans took part in the nine-day test of defense equipment and personnel.[cxxix]

Updated information on the case

July 28, 1952, according to researcher Loren E Gross, Jet fighters were making high-speed runs at the bombers during the raid, and it seems many witnesses believed they saw "discs" when shiny objects swooped around the B-36s.

Since it was a bright clear day, the glare played tricks on the eye. Still one wonders about some sightings. For example, base operations at Selfridge AFB said "airmen on the ground," which one assumes should know better, reported seeing "spheres" near the bombers as the aircraft passed over Detroit. We do not have a detailed report from an airman, but we do have one from a civilian:

"Spheres' were reported seen Sunday morning by Henry C. Pottinger, 14025 Ardmore, who later telephoned Selfridge. He was fishing on Lake St. Clair.

"Pottinger and his brother-in-law, Roy E, Bertram, of Algonac, were watching the bomber flying overhead. Two of the spheres,' he said, 'appeared high above and behind the flight of bombers and started to swoop down toward them.

"'A third sphere appeared above and ahead of the flight and then dropped down to join the other two. All three passed under and slightly behind the bombers."[cxxx]

Comments | More chaos of the day over Michigan can be read in the article "Jet Bombers Bring Saucer Reports." It appears that the Bombers and aerial defense preparation by Canada and the US may have attracted the UFOs to investigate or vice versa."

UFOs over the Homestead

Scanning the Skies | On August 18, 1952, at Pampa "Five people were sitting on the front porch at 9:50 pm. Sunday when they saw two clusters of saucer-like objects. The 'saucers' were flying in two figure 8 formations with six to eight objects in each formation.

"Mr. and Mrs. John R. Gray, 211 N. Nelson; A.B. Cunningham, Mrs. Nelson's father; and Mrs. O.M. Briggs and Sue Biggs, 9, neighbors, watched them, as they flew overhead in perfect formation, going in a south-southeast direction.

"They were flying swiftly,' Mrs. Gray said, 'but they were gone before we had a chance to count them."

"Mrs. Gray described them as round, flat and bright. She admitted that all five people who saw them were 'most excited'-and, indeed, somewhat frightened."

"It was really a weird feeling to see them,' she commented." [cxxxi]

Hunting Doves: Texas

Hunting | September 14, 1952, a press report states: "Seeing is believing, says August Schmidt, Mason County (Texas) ranchman, who saw what he believed to be a flying saucer this week."

"A Dallas friend and I were hunting doves at my place,' he reported, 'when an object appeared in the sky. It was round and had tentacles protruding like those of an octopus or star. It was bathed in a bright glare."

"Asked how long it lasted, he answered, 'Just a few seconds. Then it disappeared.' "Aware of all the skepticism concerning flying saucers, he added, 'My friend saw it too."[cxxxii]

Deer Hunting: Utah
Witnesses are sworn to secrecy

Hunting | October 27, 1952, around 8:00 am MST, a civilian couple hunting for Deer at Hickman Canyon Utah observed a saucer-shaped UFO.

According to the Air Force files, the object was seen at 3,000 feet between St. John and Grantsville, Utah. The object formed like a saucer had a dark spot in the middle with two intake or exhaust pipes sticking out in the forward position.

The object was dark grey or light brown in color and sounded similar to an automobile traveling at 60 miles per hour. The UFO was observed through a 06 rifle telescope flying straight. The object was observed until it seemed to hit the mountain, called South Mountain. This was followed by a terrific crash with no explosion.

According to the file, searches in the area were unsuccessful. However, during November 2, 1952, searches a similar sound was heard, but no sighting of an object was seen.

In further notes, the witnesses (hunters) were startled as the object approached them at 3,000 feet in altitude. He then used his rifle-scope and compass to determine the object was descending at a 15-degree angle downward from the sky to earth. The two watched the object until it hit the mountain.

According to the female witness, she said the object was "spinning." The Air Force admitted to swearing both parties to secrecy until all facts were heard on the case.

A Teletype report was sent to the Commanding General at Ogden Air Material Area, Hill Air Force Base (Utah).

The Air Force concluded the object seen could have been a "guided missile." The area of the hunting was near Dugway Proving ground.[cxxxiii]

Comment | Today Dugway Proving Ground – or at least the areas near the providing grounds have become a UFO hotspot.

Pig Hunting: Near Manakau, New Zealand

Hunting | April 4, 1954, according to a Mr. W. R. F. Johnson of Auckland was returning from a pig hunting trip at Anawhata at approximately 8:35 pm., [when] he saw in the direction and above the Waitakere Mountains a disc-shaped silvery object, that was apparently moving at terrific speed. The object's course was in the direction of Manukau Harbor, it disappeared over Manukau."[cxxxiv]

Bouncing Spheres at Fishing Camp: Mississippi
FBI informs Air Force

Fishing & Camp | May 19, 1954, at 2030 hours (8:30 pm) an owner of a fishing camp observed three large objects, which appeared to be large balls of fire, flying in weaving and bobbing manner at low altitude over the water near Bay St. Louis, Mississippi.

The objects emitted a loud "humming sound" and were definitely not conventional aircraft. He observed the things for 20 minutes before calling the FBI, and there were still visible before calling the FBI in New Orleans. The observer stated he knew they were not conventional craft and that the light from the objects was plainly reflected in the water of the bay, and other persons besides him had seen the objects. The observer was a Veteran of the Air Force and was familiar with all types of conventional aircraft but had never seen anything similar to this before.

The shaped of the objects were described as stars but had a reddish-yellow glow. They appeared to be about twice as large as other stars. They had a reddish-yellow hue.

Each object appeared to be 6 to 8 feet apart for the observation point, and the third was 16 to 20 feet from the first two objects.

Other witnesses were interviewed and according to the file gave the same testimony. The Commander at Keeler FB, Mississippi requested the investigation.[cxxxv]

Box Shaped UFO: Illinois

Fishing | On September 18, 1954, during an early morning fishing expedition a Senior Electrical Base Engineer (Scott AFB), reported seeing a Rectangular Shaped UFO the size of an automobile at New Baden, Illinois. The description is as follows:

1. A rectangular box, the size of automobile squared off without bumpers;
2. The color was red and pinkish glow in the upper left-hand corner and a green and blue glow from the rest of the body with the brightness of fluorescent light;
3. No sound was heard;
4. The object appeared to be flying between trees;
5. Disappearance caused by Trees at the lake where fishing.

The observer was casting for Bass and looked up to see the object.

A Teletype message went to ADC ENT AFB (CO), ATIC WP AFB (OH), Director of Intelligence HQ Washington (DC), TTAF Gulfport (MISS), ATRC Scott AFB (IL). The Air Force could not come to a conclusion based on "insufficient data for evaluation."

The statement "possible meteor based on duration and luminous appearance." Another comment made by the Air Force was "possible cause of reflection from aircraft, although no aircraft were reported in the vicinity at that time."[cxxxvi]

Comment | In Connecticut, I witnessed several "rectangular box-shaped" UFOs in 2012. Those I saw were in my development over my home and several others near a lake that was blue or black in color. These were seen during the dusk hours and did have bluish windows.

Ragian, New Zealand

Fishing | On February 7, 1955, According to the story in the press:

"Two men fishing on the upper reaches of the Ragian Harbor late Monday night claim to have sighted a mysterious light hovering close to an aircraft that passed over them. The object was traveling south at about 5,000 feet.

"The men are Mr. W. Dryland, storekeeper, of Te Uku, and Mr. R. Moon, a farmer, also of Te Uku. They were at the harbor at about 11 p.m. when they sighted aircraft navigation lights overhead.

"Immediately they spotted a bright white light waving from side to side around the aircraft and keeping pace with it. The night was stormy, and there was much cloud, but for fully two minutes Messrs. Dryland and Moon glimpsed the aircraft and the wavering light.

"Mr. Dryland said yesterday he was astounded to read that a similar light had been seen by a National Airways CD3 crew. No N.A.C. aircraft were over Ragian at 10:30 p.m.

"A Tasman Airways spokesman said yesterday that the aircraft had both wingtip and tail-lights on. Landing lights were off but this type of aircraft has large cabin windows, and they give out a considerable diffusion of light."

"Mr. Dryland is emphatic that the light he and Mr. Moon saw was not a part of the aircraft or even a reflection of light."[cxxxvii]

UFOs over Santa Catalina Island (Seen by Fishermen): California

Fishing | July 9 and July 10, 1955, two news reports spanning two days recorded fishermen who observed discs in the sky. According to Loren Gross research, a more complete report was found in the San Bernardino paper as follows:

"The sighting of an unidentified object in the sky was described more fully by George Washington, San Bernardino accountant, and tax consultant, at his home Monday.

"Washington, whose office and home is at 503 Mountain View Avenue, sighted a round 'cylinder-like' object in the sky while cruising with his family towards Catalina Island Saturday afternoon. His radio report to the Coast Guard at long Beach brought Air Force jet interceptors blasting into the area almost immediately, apparently in hot pursuit of the object, he related.

"Washington said the chase was short-lived, as the object shot off into hazy clouds in the direction of San Diego, leaving the Jets 'far behind.'

"The accountant, who said his wife, Elise, and young daughter Maria, first sighted the object floating about 2,500 feet above the boat, described its shape as 'a round cylinder, grayish and white, turning rapidly within its own axis.'

"He said it was surrounded by a 'haze of fumes' apparently blowing out from the object. Washington observed it through binoculars for several minutes before deciding to notify the Coast Guard, who asked him to keep an eye on it until he could get planes into the air. He was underway at the time, having throttled down his engines when his wife and daughter called his attention to the object's presence. Washington said it maintained its position above him as he moved through the water.

He described the object's movement after the appearance of the planes in the following manner: It zigzagged upward with more fumes blowing out its sides and then suddenly zoomed away into the hazy clouds above to the south."

"The object's dimensions 'are very hard to determine…maybe sixty feet in diameter, which may be right or wrong,' he said. I don't believe in flying saucers and that sort of thing, but the only conclusion I can cane to is that it is something neither myself nor my wife has ever seen before."

"At the time of the sighting, the accountant in his $15,000 22-foot boat was about nine miles west of Newport, headed for Avalon Harbor, thirteen miles away." Sunday he mentioned Coast Guard officials and numerous press and radio correspondents concerning the sighting interrogated him."

"'It was fascinating,' he concluded. 'My only regret is that all that time I had my camera in the boat with me and didn't use it.'"[cxxxviii]

30 to 40-foot diameter Craft: Casper, Wyoming

Fishing | February 1956, A Mr. Raymond Boyd, a U.S. Department of the Interior employee and licensed pilot, tells of his UFO experience:

"In February 1956 my uncle, Mr. George Keil of Casper, Wyoming and I were fishing Pathfinder Lake, which is located 70 miles southwest of Casper. Time was near 12 noon, weather clear, and temperature in the '50s. We were fishing from the bank for brown trout.

"We both heard a whistling sound causing us to look straight overhead, and there were 7 objects. We observed them for about 5 seconds through about a 30-degree arc."

"Their height, I felt, was at least 8,000 feet as we could only make out that they were round objects. The center three were flying in a straight-line formation, the ones on either side of these were traveling a zig-zag course and one each side of these were traveling a straight line."

"Having had a pilot's license, I am familiar with aircraft, their flight characteristics, and limitations. These were no craft of any type I have ever heard of or seen."

The speed of the five ships flying in a straight line and the two ships flying an erratic course appeared to be more than 800 miles per hour. My uncle, George Keil, now deceased, was on the Casper police force at that time and I was employed by the Texas Oil Company in Casper, Wyoming."

Additional details not in the above narrative state that the objects appeared solid and darker than the background of the sky, and it was Boyd's guess the diameter of the UFOs was about 30-40 feet.[cxxxix]

Punto Fijo, Falcon State, Venezuela

Fishing | On September 3, 1956, Fisherman Manuel Pimentel and Jose Veraztegui y Pedro San Juan reported that during the nighttime while at their fishing chores, they have seen nothing of the Punta, luminous objects which cruise the sky in a North-South direction. The objects travel in straight lines, usually appear at 1:00 am and leave a luminous trail behind them. The observers stated that the objects do not descend as meteors do, but traveled on a well maintained, "determined path." [cxl]

Rothesay Bay: Scotland
R.A.F. Wing Commander:
" I have been ordered by the AM to say nothing."

Golfing | On April 4-5, 1957 two golfers at Rothesay stated that they had seen three circular objects in the sky. One of the observers, Mr. J. McLellan, said: "They were round and gave off a brilliant, silvery glow. They were in line and flying high and fast".

This sighting occurred over several days off Scotland when two independent Radar sets made contact with several UFOs. According to Wing Commander Walter Whitworth, C.O. at West Freugh he said:

**"I have been ordered by the Air Ministry
to say nothing about the object."**

He also said: "I am not allowed to reveal its position, course, and speed." "No mistake could have been made by the civilians operating the sets. They are fully qualified and experienced officers". The Radar sets were at Luce Bay when the object was picked up. A report was sent to London to be studied by top-level radar and intelligence officers.

Just before the Radar contact, a driver on the road near Penrith stated at 11:30 pm, he saw some object, shut off his engine and witnessed the craft above him. "It was a perfect half-moon, glowing yellow like the moon, but it had a distinct gold rim with a straight edge on top." The next day a man in Glasgow reported to discs over the city, which then disappeared suddenly.

Radar operators estimated the object was at 60,000 feet (11 miles). A balloon was launched earlier in the day; however, this was ruled out due to the size and speed of the objects.[cxli]

Hutchinson: Kansas

Hunting | November 10, 1957, according to a Wichita paper, dozens of individuals reported seeing a UFO north of Emporia, Kansas during the evening hours.

Four of these individuals were hunters in the Hutchinson area. According to the hunters, the object was moving southwest and after observing it, knew it was not an airplane. The hunter's names were John Skelton, Glen Skelton, Jim Smith, and Philip Mellor.

According to another observer, a John Warnhoff, observed the unidentified flying object in the sky when he was about 10 miles west of Emporia.

"The broker, who has been ribbing his wife about her belief in flying saucers stories, said he at first thought he might be seeing reflections thru his car windshield.

"The Wichitan said he pulled his car to a stop alongside the Kansas Turnpike and climbed out to observe the object from the ground. It was there.

"Warnhoff described the object as a 'molten mass of something.' It was as bright as I an arc light. But there were no flames, jet blasts or anything of the sort.

"In fact, the object seemed to float, according to Warnhoff, who estimated the speed of the object at about 100 miles per hour.

"There was no sound coming from the object, which compared in size to a Super-G Constellation aircraft flying at 3,000 feet.[cxlii]

Frog Hunting: Miami, Florida

Hunting | On May 17, 1958, around midnight two frog hunters Mr. Fred Cook and his son observed strange lights in the sky 10 miles west of State Road 441.

According to the news article, the observes witness an orange light coming out of the north, moving horizontally at an altitude of 500 feet. Mr. Cook told his son to take a look at the object, and his son turned the high-powered boat's spotlight on the UFO. Cook said the object then veered into a vertical position, changed to the color of an arc-welding torch and shot out of sight in moments. They were hunting for frogs along the Hillsboro Canal.

The Miami Air Defense Center was unable to shed any light on the unusual airborne object.[cxliii]

Men dedicated to Submarine Fishing

Fishing | March 28, 1959, on the Portuguese coast south of Setubal a searchlight came down from a UFO to highlight a home and the ocean surface.

"A group of about nine or ten people, including five engineers, recently spent a weekend holiday at Vila Nova de Fontes, at the mouth of the Mira River, 90 miles south of Setubal town, Portugal. One of the engineers was Luis Netto Lopes. Two other members of the party were Vasco Belmonte and Jose Rodrigues, clerks in the Vacuum Oil Company officers. They were all dedicated to submarine fishing.

"After dinner on March 28, members of the party took a walk. One of them pointed out to the rest that a certain house m the little village was somewhat more visible than the others. They then discovered the reason."

"The house was being focused on from a certain spot in the sky! A long beam of light like a powerful searchlight was directed down on to that particular house."

"Suddenly the beam of light was withdrawn. The group of friends discussed the affair for some time without coming to any satisfactory conclusion."

"Then once again a beam of light was seen focusing this time not on the house, but on something in the river. Senor Lopes said the glow fell upon a rock and illuminated it to a fantastic degree."

Afterward, the beam moved slowly across the river and vanished as soon as it reached the bank. Nevertheless, the spot in the sky from which the beam had been directed remained for a few seconds longer. Then the UFO suddenly moved at terrific speed to the west and disappeared over the Atlantic Ocean.[cxliv]

"Big Fish": Naknek, Alaska

Fishing | January 10, 1961, two fishermen one mile north of Naknek, Alaska observe a UFO. The primary witnesses were two fishermen. One aged 28 and the other 37. Names are deleted from official files.

There was a high, thin, scattered cloud layer at the time with visibility at 15 plus miles. Initial observation of UFO was at 0.30 degrees azimuth, 10 degrees elevation. When last seen the object was at 210 degrees elevation 5 degrees. The UFO reported was circular in shape but otherwise indistinct except for the glow it emitted. Glowing orange when it hovered, it brightened with a blue rim and "flashes" when moving.

Accompanied by a whistling sound, it was first sighted moving southeast, then northwest. While on the southwest course, the object stopped at various times and hovered. The general direction of travel was southeast.

Altitude was estimated at 50-300 feet. It was in view of about 90 minutes. Winds Aloft logs were not compatible with the motions of the object. No helicopters or other aircraft were in the area according to FAA Anchorage and King Salmon Air Force Station.[cxlv]

Duck Hunting: Popular Grove, Illinois

Hunting | November 8, 1961, around 7:15 am "Boyd G. Germansen, and his son saw three 'disc-shaped' objects while duck-hunting at Poplar Grove, Illinois.

The UFOs appeared 'bright as if of highly polished metal,' and were visible through broken clouds estimated to be at 4,000 feet. The discs were about one-fourth the apparent diameter of the full moon, and moved in a straight-line formation."[cxlvi]

Hunting: Cuyahoga Falls, Ohio

Hunting | November 23, 1961, according to a former Navy Airman a UFO was seen while hunting in Cuyahoga Falls, Ohio. Here is his story:

"I started from the house about 11:15 am with my bird dog to hunt. We were about 700 feet back in the field heading south when I looked up ahead and saw three small clouds.

Then I went back to hunting. I took four or five steps and thought something was peculiar, so I glanced back up at the clouds. Then I realized what it was.

The top and bottom clouds were going from west to east with the wind, but the one in the middle one was going east to west against it. Then I stopped and watched really close, as I watched the one in the middle continue to move to the west. Then the cloud seemed to disappear or form into a metallic elongated, egg-shaped~ object still moving to the west against the wind, very slowly.

Then it tilted up, the sun glinting from it until it stopped still in the air for a few seconds. Then it seemed to tilt back a little and moved up and away from me (due south). It then moved very slowly and wobbled up and down slightly.

Then from the edge of it came what seemed to be rays of light which were alternately bright like a spotlight and dark or black [On and off?]. After a few seconds of this, it tilted further back and wobbled a little more. Then it continued to move up and away from me slowly.

I looked around to see if anyone else was watching. No one was around, so I called my dog and ran for the house, watching the object over my shoulder as I went. I was calling for my wife, but I couldn't get her to come out of the house at first as I came down off a slight rise behind the house. I called her again and then went right back on the rise, but it was gone." (See drawing by witness showing the object's course and maneuvers). [cxlvii]

Bournemouth, England

Fishing | July 1962 around 1:00 am a UFO was seen while fishing at Bournemouth, England.

"The Bournemouth Evening Echo newspaper in July reported: What was happening in the sky in the early hours of today? Mr. R. J. Cable, a greengrocer, of Commercial Road, Bournemouth, would like to know, for shortly after I a.m. when fishing with a friend at Sandbanks, he noticed a light in the sky behaving most peculiarly.

"'It was moving to the east in short, sharp bursts. It would then stop and move back and forth. But it left no trail, and there was no noise. It was certainly not a falling star or a Sputnik."

"Mr. Cable and his friend watched in amazement for 20 minutes. Later today he was having to convince friends he had not been drinking or was suffering from hallucinations."[cxlviii]

Man shares how to saucer watch

Saucer Hunting | Don Campbell (Mufon observer and Motorola technician) shares several of his own UFO sightings in a 1973 article.

In 1968, he spotted three UFOs topped with yellow and orange lights, In 1972 he saw several UFOs traveling leisurely across the sky. He shared "as I looked at them about 1,000 feet away, they were about the size of a fist at the end of my arm."

In the same year (1972) a craft flew over western Mt. Pleasant. The UFO was oval and bright orange with what appeared to be three of four red portholes in each side. He shared the UFO "hovered and quivered for several second like a lite on a string." The UFO then shot off.

Don Campbell also confirmed a 100-foot ling UFO appeared over his home.[cxlix]

Comment | It appears Mr. Campbell had a very similar UFO encounters as I did in Connecticut from 2011 to 2013. A UFO over someone's house is quite unique and both surreal at the same time.

Fishing at Scorch Lake: Timmins: Ontario

Fishing | January 19, 1975, four residents reported a UFO while ice fishing at Scorch Lake, Ontario. The witnesses stated the bright object was three times the size of a star. It was traveling from west to east. The observation lasted approximately one minute and a half.

A fifth witness reported a similar object at the same time near the same location. He stated that the UFO traveled in a perfectly straight line and "simply vanished in midair."[cl]

Chapter 14: Reservoirs, Ponds

UFOs stop at Ponds, Reservoirs and fishing Holes in an attempt to observe a man in his elements (fishing). In many stories across the US, we also notice these visitors like to get out of their vehicles and as well as test water quality sources, fish species, and vegetation.

We are not sure why they care about earths condition as after 80 years of constant monitoring they have not invaded the earth – they have just shown up and looked around and monitored our pollution outputs.

Bush Pine Reservoir, New York

Fishing | On September 17, 1955, Frank and Eileen Bordes from Bronx NY were fishing on a reservoir near Bush Pine, New York when they encountered a disc. A loud splash and gurgling sound interrupted the rhythm of the lapping waves and attracted their attention. Mr. Border was disentangling fishing lines, did not see the iridescent pink mushroom shaped object which rose two feet above the water and then disappeared beneath the surface.

The APRO Bulletin tells us; "Frightened by the apparition, Mrs. Bordes asked to be rowed ashore. When on shore, they watched a gradually brightening light about 100 yards distant. Two parallel lights became visible below the first light. They seemed to come from an elongated object some 15 feet long that was partially submerged and round which there appeared to be a good deal of turbulence. Mr. and Mrs. Bordes (at his suggestion) rode along the shore to get a better look at the object and had the impression that they were being watched."

"Whenever they headed in the direction of the object, it came toward them a good clip. When they retreated, the object would gradually retreat, also. During this time the turbulence continued until the object moved off down the lake at high speeds until its lights faded into the distance." Mr. Bordes made the following observations:

> **The object reversed direction without turning, there was no light beam, and it moved faster than any boat he had ever seen.**[cli]

Two Fishermen near McColl, South Carolina

Fishing | On October 31, 1957, on Thursday evening, two fishermen on Bluff Pond near McColl were frightened by an 'egg-shaped' object that descended over the lake.

"Bowden Tyler and Buddy Jacobs reported their experience to McColl police and deputy sheriff.

"Jacobs related how that the 'big black ball-bigger than an automobile' came down as they sat on the bank."

Figure 12 - Egg craft with trail

"We had a kerosene lantern burning, and after we saw this strange thing coming down over us, we turned it off, and the floating object disappeared at an angle into the sky,' Jacobs recounts."

"He added that they relit the lantern, then a second egg-like thing, the same size as the first came down to within 50-75 yards over the lake. It seemed to follow a streak of light, he said."

"We heard a motor, which sounded like a big diesel, and it was still coming down when we ran away,' Jacobs added. Man was I scared! I was so afraid that I left a big fat catfish lying on the bank. We drove back to town without turning on the auto lights and reported to the officers."

"McColl police chief Henry Hudson verified the report and said officers visited the scene but found nothing there a few minutes afterward." [clii]

Fishing with UFOs at Canistear Reservoir

Fishing | On July 8, 1958, An interview conducted by Berthold Eric Schwarz, M.D., an expert on the psychiatric and psychic aspects of the UFO syndrome:

"John A. Collins of Glen Rock, New Jersey, age 49, has a responsible job in the world of banking. He is a lifelong outdoorsman, skilled in hunting and fishing. In his occupation he has flown all over the world and has dealt with many technically trained people, highly situated in the space-age industries. He is in excellent health and has never had any emotional disorder."

"It was one hour before sunset on July 8, 1958, the day of the All-Star game. I was fishing with a friend at Canistear Reservoir in northern New Jersey. It was bright and clear...cloud- less. There was a slight surface wind (on the water). In the south, we saw in the sky what I thought was a shooting star, a big light."

"When we first looked at it, the size was that of two thumbnails of an outstretched upper extremity. We sat in the boat talking about it. 'Do you see what l see?' Instead of disappearing it kept coming along."

"As it got closer, it was plainly visible. At first, it looked like a bar of hot steel pressed in a rolling mill, about the size of a railroad tie and uniformly cherry red in color. It was low in the sky and came directly toward us. It moved slowly."

"I had a 'Rollie' (camera) in the boat, but I was so scared I was afraid to take a picture. It was heading right for us, and we didn't want to excite it."

"We watched for ten minutes, and it was ever with us. It tilted 45 degrees, then leveled, and took another 45-degree turn. It was turning from red to bluish-white to white as it went up. There was still no sound, no hum, no vibration, no odor, nor anything. It leveled off and took a 90-degree turn."

"It was still the same color, and then it turned more than 90 degrees and was coming back toward us. When we faced the end of the bar, it was like looking into the firebox of a locomotive: cherry red in color."

"The rest of it was white, like two railroad ties attached end to end. We watched it for forty-five minutes in all. It was once less than 400 feet up, and we were afraid it was going to land on the water. Then it went faster, rose quite steeply, and rode away. My fishing partner and I had nothing to drink. I have never seen anything like it before or since."

"'When my partner got home and told his wife, she wouldn't listen. She was so scared. Once when I went to their home for dinner, about three months later, I thought I'd mention it as a conversation piece, but she wouldn't let me talk about it (confirmed by author's interview of the gentleman, whose wife interfered in the telephone conversation)."

"Shortly after the event, I told my wife, a close friend (a neighbor of the author), and a man that I do business with was in the Catskills a hundred miles north of us and had noticed the thing the same day and at approximately the same time. I learned this one week after my experience."

"Mr. Collins' trustworthiness was attested by three people have known him for many years: the author's neighbor, the author's father, and a friend who had been in the Catskills."

"Although no log-book fishing records were going back to 1958, the time of Mr. Collins' experience, interviews with Officer Clyde Conway of the Canistear Reservoir Police, Mr. Conway's wife, his daughter, and his two sons revealed several sightings of possible UFOs in that area in the past three years. No member of Officer Conway's immediate family has had any emotional or psychosomatic illness.".[cliii]

UFO after fishing:
150 miles north of Kelowna British Columbia

Fishing | In July 1963 around 1:00 am Carl Steiger, who was then a high school senior, and his older brother, George, took their Volkswagen van for a weekend of camping and fishing at Gallagher's Canyon, about 150 miles north of their home in Kelowna, British Columbia.

They parked off the road by a creek at the foot of the Canyon and fished all afternoon, then build a campfire and had their supper. They sat up watching the fire die down until about midnight and then went to bed in their sleeping bags in the van.

"George went right to sleep, but Carl was restless. He decided to go out and make himself a cup of coffee over the coals. When he sat up, he could see the new compass they had left on the hump over the engine housing. In the moonlight be could see that the arrow was moving slowly."

"As he watched it, it would go about three-quarters of the way around, from Southeast through North then down to Southwest, and back."

"He picked it up, wondering if it was being affected by the engine coil, clicked it off and on again. In his hand, it still moved around and back. To be put it down and went outside."

"He could hear the water running in the swift, shallow creek and hear a waterfall a little way upstream. Other than that, the night was still. Across the creek on the bare hillside five or six lights were wandering around at about walking speed. His first thought was that sheepherders must have been looking for lost sheep, but that hardly seemed likely at one o'clock in the morning."

"And the lights did not look like flashlights. They were white, about the size of basketballs, and they just floated along. They had no beam coming from them."

"Curious, Carl walked down to the stream and shouted across the water, 'Hey, out there!' Immediately all the lights went out. Carl started back to the van to tell George, but before he got there be was aware that it was getting brighter around him."

"Looking over his shoulder, he could see coming toward him, flying above the trees on the other side of the road, a very large bright light, larger than the van. It stopped about 75 feet away, pulsating slowly as it changed from dark green to light green. The light in a circle beneath it was so bright that Carl could see each pine needle on the ground."

"I could have read the newspaper", he says."

"After three or four minutes, the light continued on its path from southwest to northeast, following the canyon. By this time George had got up, and he watched with Carl as it moved along, illuminating the canyon wall."

"About three miles away they could see it rise to the top of Black Mountain, where there was a fire lookout tower. It spiraled to the top of the mountain, its lights clearly reflected in the windows of the tower. Then, picking up speed, it shot into the sky and was lost to sight among the stars."

"The next morning the boys broke camp and started the steep drive out of the canyon. They reached a point where the road dropped sharply on the west side, giving an unobstructed view across the valley. Just below them, they could see an apparently abandoned log house standing in a field. There was an outhouse and some rusting pieces of equipment, but the puzzling thing was a large black circle in the green grass."

"After stopping and looking at the scene through binoculars, they found a place on the narrow road to turn around and went back to get a closer look."

"As they thought, when they found the old ranch house it was empty, and there was no sign that anyone had been there for a long time. But about 150 feet from home, an eight-foot-wide ring was burned to the ground in the two-foot-tall grass, leaving an unburned circle about 30 feet across in the middle. On the edges of the ring, the grass leaned away from the burned area. This grass was very dehydrated and crumpled when the fellows kicked it."

"After Carl and George got home, they told their family and close friends about their experience, but they did not report it to any authorities."

"UFOs had been reported in the area that summer, Carl says, but he and his brother had taken no particular interest in the stories."

> They didn't talk much about what they had seen because 'at that time if you did tell many people they thought you were a little weird."[cliv]

Hunting: Scribner, Nebraska

November 19, 1967, three boys of Scribner, Nebraska reported that at 9:15 p.m. on November 19th they spotted a football-shaped object while hunting five miles south of Scribner. It was in the vicinity of Maple Creek and appeared to be about 100 feet above the ground and traveling fast. They attempted to follow it but were soon lost. One side of the object had a red glow and the other side a white glow with a bluish cast.[clv]

Mackerel Fishing: Canada

Fishing | On November 27, 1964, around 1:30 am Fishermen Alphonse Gaudet, Eric McInnis and Arnold Gaudet sighted a silver wingless object while fishing near North Cape, P.E. Island, Canada. While Mackerel Fishing near North Cape off Sea of Cow Pond they observed an object heading in a new direction at high speed.

Arnold Gaudet estimated the altitude to be 2,000 feet. The men thought it was an airplane at first until they noticed the absence of wings. They did observer orange colored fins extending all around the object which appeared to be 30 feet in diameter. It then disappeared to the east.[clvi]

Fishing at Reservoir in Oxford: Massachusetts
"I was scared."

Fishing | On May 29, 1971, around 4:00 am a shiny black "discus" that hovered, gyrated, and flipped over on its side was reported at a recreational area near Oxford, Massachusetts

There were four witnesses, a man and three teenage boys who were fishing at the edge of a reservoir. The object approached the four men and jerked from side to side "like a pendulum," and up and down like a ball. At the nearest point, the object was approximately some 250 feet from the observers.

At approximately at that point, the object flipped over on edge. In that attitude, the UFO was circular in shape, "like a pancake" with seven or eight glowing ports evenly spaced around the bottom. The object then stopped and moved back in the direction it came. This time it moved rapidly and was soon lost from sight.

The observers were four men. As the object came closer, the light took on a rectangular shape, and witnesses were able to see a dark body beneath it The body was overall, with pointed ends, and seemed to have a highly reflective skin, like metal.

After the object disappeared from view, a moving light appeared over the treetops in the same directions the object had disappeared. As it began to come closer, it suddenly speeds up, as though it was going to dive down and hit the beach where the men were standing. It slowed down, however, and came to a stop over the trees on the opposite shore.

Unsure of what the light would do next, the men decided to abandon the site and resume their fishing later in the day. They hurriedly gathered their gear and wet to their car, just as the light began to recede in the distance.

One of the observed reported to investigators "I was scared." Investigators reviewing the case confirmed there was no conventional activity in the area at the time.[clvii]

Fishing for Bull Frogs: Torrington, Connecticut
"Everybody's afraid to say something."

Fishing | April 24, 1977, on Friday evening between 7:50 to 9:50 pm a UFO hovered over Torrington's Burr Pond.

Stanley Dombrowski had been fishing for bullheads in the pond when he sighted the craft in the northwest sky. The object hovered 500 feet above the ground.

In his words: "The light on the object grew dimmer and dimmer until it flickered out." The object emitted a "beeping" sound which according to the Hartford Courant writer David Bergman "continued at a rate of two or three beeps a second." According to the observer, several other people were fishing that evening; however, they did not confer with one another.

In his words: "Everybody's afraid to say something." He also stated, the other fisherman "must have heard the sounds since it was quiet – there wasn't a ripple on the water."[clviii]

Chapter 15: Beaches and Harbors

UFOs frequent Beaches and Harbors. It is believed they show up at these places to observe humans sunbathing or watching us drive boats. If you go to YouTube can see several videos of UFOs near the ocean. In one case the UFO flies by at such a fast speed the film had to be slowed down to see the craft crossing the huge distance behind several seated persons on the beach.

Two UFOs take a dive

Fishing | On April 8, 1958, Two flat objects flashing red lights along their leading edges executed a shallow dive off Newport Beach California around 9:30 pm. A half a dozen people confirmed the sighting including Patrolman Roger Gordon.

The objects were first seen hovering around 9:30 pm. These two objects were flying at 500 feet, headed northeast. They appeared to be flat. Delta winged objects with no tail or superstructure. Six lights on the trailing edge flashed on and off in a series. One object made a right hand turned over Newport, and the other went up the Coast until it reached the vicinity of the Santa Ana River, then it turned toward Santa Ana.

Gordon called El Toro Marine Corps Air Station and gave the information to the Flight Operations officer.

Other observers disagreed of the number of lights on the objects. Three young fishermen stated the were: "sure weird, the way they darted and hovered".[clix]

French Fishermen see sphere-shaped UFO

Fishing | On June 12, 1958, during the evening fishermen at the port of Le Brusc, France saw a UFO; their report in the '*Flying Saucer Review*' goes as follows:

"Three of us, myself and two companions, had gone out to sea to drop our nets. It was 12 years ago, June 12, 1958. It was a very clear night, with a starry sky and the sea was calm. We saw a big shining dot of light in the sky, orange-colored, with a touch of red to it. It grew bigger, and then it began to descend very fast toward the sea and soon it was a great big globe, which was lying on the surface of the water.

"Just lightly touching the waves it remained there stationary for several minutes, but we had the impression that it was revolving, like a wheel turning round and round on the same place. It caused a big air displacement, for we could see the water being whipped up all around it. After that, the ball came rolling towards us, just gently brushing the water. We weren't a bit happy at the sight of this 'globular wheel' bearing down on our boat. Terrified, one of our party shouted 'It's going over us!'

"The fantastic wheel didn't, in fact, go over us but it passed very close by, making such big waves that we nearly capsized. When it was close to us we felt a very powerful heat from the thing and a strong blast of air. As it went by, we heard a faint humming from it, like the hum of a swarm of cockchafers."

"Comparing the UFO with our boat, its diameter seemed to have possibly been about four meters. Stupefied, we just watched it vanish at great speed. It moved along by leaps, now half disappearing among the waves, now skimming along on top of them. Then it did a right-hand turn and disappeared on the horizon."

"It did not give out any flash or beam of light; it was simply, a revolving ball or wheel, with no change of color."

"We lost no time in getting back to land, returning sooner than we had meant to. One of my mates said: Perhaps it's a flying saucer that has dropped down from the sky."[clx]

Comment | The "leaps" mentioned above as how the UFO traveled is recorded in several UFO case studies. It is almost as if the UFO skips along rather than float.

Life Guards report UFO: Newport Beach, California

Over a Beach | On January 2, 1959, trained observers of the Orange County Harbor Department and Newport Beach Life Guard Headquarters notified government officials of strange unidentified flying objects that hovered at high altitude over Newport Beach before breaking up into four glowing parts and speeding away.

The sighting lasted from 4:55 until 5:10 pm.

Before splitting into four parts, the object seemed to have a tail that rotated at various intervals.[clxi]

Comment | The ability of UFOs combining and separating is a phenomenon I am still studying. I have come across 10 such case studies. When this type of movement occurs, it is not like a smaller ship being dispatched from a mothership. This type of interaction is where similar shaped and sized objects "merge" for a brief period and then separate.

Three UFOs at Norma New Jersey

At the Harbor | On July 1959 around 2:00 am a woman on her son's boat at Norma, New Jersey observed three UFOs.

Mrs. Thomas McGrath was doing some work on her son's boat at boat slip at Norma harbor. She was bent down and was looking for tacks to use when she remembered there were some on the dashboard. She raised her head and at that point spotted some strange objects that were visible through the boat's windshield.

It was 2:00 am, the night sky was clear, the air warm, and the water calm. There was no moon, but the stars were visible. Mrs. McGrath emerged from the boat's cabin to get a better look. Two solid white, ovoid-shaped, objects in the sky appeared to be about twice the size of a regulation football. The UFOs were self-luminous and sharply outlined. They were also moving quite slowly. Intrigued, Mrs. McGrath hurried to the hut where she kept her things to get a pair of optical glasses. The building is only 75 feet from the boat slip, so she did not lose much time.

The glasses made the UFOs appear much larger. Mrs. McGrath noticed a red glow coming from the back of the "footballs."

Meanwhile, a third object appeared and joined the first two. Were the objects interested in the boat? The woman witness stated: "After the third object appeared, they circled over the boat in a counterclockwise direction for approximately ten minutes, then took off at an estimated airspeed of 25 mph. in a formation, two in front, one in back."[clxii]

Point Lookout: Long Island, New York

Fishing | October 5, 1960, around 9:00 pm an Air Force Sergeant and his son while fishing on the beach at Point Lookout, Long Island, NY reported a UFO.

The object sighted appeared to pass by the moon which was full, a reddish vapor trail could be seen. During the time the object resembled a falling star.

As the UFO passed over Point Lookout, it turned to the southeast passed out of sight going back towards the moon in a northeasterly direction. During the turn, the object appeared only as a bright, very fast moving star with no indications of a tail or vapor trail being present.

The turn was wide, extending almost to the southwest and western horizons before going again towards the northeast.

The observer stated the UFO appeared to be very high and moving faster than any airplane that he had ever seen. There was no noise. The UFO was visible only as continuous white light.

Figure 13 - glowing egg at night

The sergeant forgot about the event until talking with General Hall who suggested he report the case to proper Air Force investigators.

The Air Force could not arrive at a conclusion based on "insufficient data for evaluation." Further comment was this could have been a "high flying a/c."[clxiii]

Fishing at West Haven, Connecticut

Fishing | On July 8, 1961, around 9:00 pm several witnesses at West Haven observed a UFO hovering on the horizon and then after about an hour it rose up a short distance then came back down to about the same spot. As it hovered, it suddenly shot up into the sky and disappeared. In his words:

"I was fishing on the beach in West Haven with my neighbors when this event happened." Other observers were a policeman and a man from Firestone Tires in the town of Derby, Connecticut".[clxiv]

Fishing at Paterson's Groyne, North Beach, Durban

Fishing | In 1961 Mr. White had his first alleged sighting of a UFO encounter. His second was in 1963.

"About two years ago I was fishing at Paterson's Groyne, North Beach, Durban, together with my friend Henry a' Dank.

The time was 3 am. All of sudden we heard a peculiar whine, and looking up saw a bright light coming from the east. As it approached us, I noticed that it was a circular-shaped object and was slightly tilted towards us. It must have been at least 100 feet in diameter, and on top, a transparent dome could be seen.

The lower part seemed to be lit up with a greenish glow. It hovered over the sea quite close to us for fully ten minutes and then leveled itself and moved off northwards following the beach for about half a mile to the Dock area, where it circled a few times before ascending rapidly in a steep climb and disappearing down the coast.

"This fantastic experience aroused my interest, and I began to study magazines articles and made it my business to gain what knowledge I could about flying saucers."[clxv]

Fishing at Taupo: New Zealand

Fishing | On March 29, 1962, a story in England's *'Flying Saucer Review'* states: "The Hawke's Bay *'Herald-Tribune'* carried the following report in its issue of March 30:

"'A mysterious unidentified flying object was seen in the sky by a group of Hastings men on a fishing holiday in Taupo yesterday. The object was hovering over Whangamata Bay where the men were traveling on Mr. E. P. Taylor's launch "Ponui."

Mr. R.C. Bauld, a Hastings grocer who first sighted the object, said at first it resembled a parachute. But as it moved overhead, it could be seen through binoculars to be rotating in an anti-clockwise direction.

As the UFO moved over, the shape changed to that of a cross-very much like that of the new model airplanes?

"Till then, somebody suggested it might be a meteorological balloon--but the object dispelled this possibility by suddenly taking off. It took four seconds to disappear from sight, said Mr. Bauld."

"'According to the *'Herald-Tribune's* Taupo correspondent, Mr. Taylor said today he first saw the object at 11:32 a.m. It appeared to have a reflected silver light and was shaped like a parachute with an extension of the lines at the same angle from where the parachutist would hang for about a third of the length of the chute.

"'It passed over the launch and hovered for about two minutes. At first, he thought it was a weather balloon or similar lighter-than-air object. The launch was about half a mile from the Kinloch Marina home at the time, and because the launch engine was running, they could hear no noise from the object."

"At the end of the two minutes, the object appeared to revolve anti-clockwise, then suddenly move at a very high speed. By then Mr. Taylor had his binoculars focused on the object, and he held it in view for a few seconds longer than the other observers."

"'It disappeared faster than any jet aircraft on a shallow curving course slightly east of south, said Mr. Taylor. He would not like to say what it was, but it appeared to be a controlled craft of some sort."

He had never seen anything like it before over Lake Taupo.

"The party had previously watched the satellite Echo I go over. Mr. Bauld's impression was that yesterday's object was traveling at least three times as fast. All on board saw the object and were at first skeptical, but very soon mystified by the UFO."

'The party-comprising Messrs. V. Watkins, M. Lush, R.E. Goodall, and M. Dentice---as well as Mr. Bauld-had spent five days at Taupo.'"[clxvi]

UFO was seen while fishing near Keeler AFB: Mississippi 130 foot long UFO with Windows and lights

Fishing | On June 9, 1962, a 45-year-old woman was fishing off a pier at the foot of Pat Harrison Avenue in Biloxi, Mississippi when she noticed what she thought was a large airplane coming out of the east. It was to her leftover Biloxi Bay in the vicinity of Keeler AFB.

As it approached, she was curious about the lack of engine noise. The UFO crossed in front of her, zooming westward at fantastic speed. In a matter of 5-6 seconds, the UFO disappeared into some clouds.

The file indicates: the object (UFO) made no sound and was a color of soft silvery gray. She mentioned that it was the size of a C-124 fuselage but had no tail or wings.

The drawing in the file indicates either a disc or some sort of cigar shaped ship with windows. The observer mentioned the object had a line of light or lights through the center resembling windows of a passenger train at night. The middle light in the center appeared brighter than the windowed lights to the left and right which suggested to her, this was a round object.[clxvii]

Comment | The Douglas "Globemaster" C-124 was 130 feet long and had a wingspan of 174 feet. This UFO was over 100 feet long (1/3rd the size of a football field)

Same place different person: Mississippi

June 9, 1962, Technical Sergeant at the 3399th Squadron, Keesler Technical Training Center, Keesler AFB observed a UFO while fishing.

According to the AF files, the object showed the following characteristics:

1. It was oval or oblong in shape;
2. It was the size of an office desk (at the arm's length?);
3. It was phosphorescent or pale white; the speed was believed to be between 7,200 and 36,000 miles per hour;
4. It had no tail, no trail or exhaust;

5. There was no sound heard;
6. It was visualized from 4 to 5 seconds.

The object was said to be moving on a westerly course rising from three degrees above the horizon to forty-five degrees where it disappeared in a cloudbank.

The Air Force concluded the object was astronomical " a meteor."[clxviii]

Fishing Boat Skipper "Which Way" UFO sighting near Nova Scotia

Fishing | May 1963 around 8:00 pm the Skipper of a boat observed a UFO fifteen to twenty miles south of Seal Island, Nova Scotia.

"It was about eight o'clock on a Saturday evening, and it would be light for at least another hour."

"Capt. Woodrow Atwood, skipper of the fishing boat "Which Way" In out of Clark's Harbor, Cape Sable Island, was watching his compass when he noticed a light to the north which, at first glance, looked to be the size of a lit match. Suddenly it burst into a much larger blood-red light, 50 to 75 yards away and was now coming straight for his boat."

"Captain Atwood watched it for several moments, not knowing what to do as the thing came toward the vessel. He became aware of an intense heat corning from the object, so intense that he had to move away from the cabin window to get away from it as it slid by the boat. The lighted UFO climbed overhead and then floated there for about five minutes before slowly descending and drifting off in the direction of Brown's Bank."

"Captain Atwood made a hurried general call to any other vessels in the area relating his experience with the object. He was rewarded with a call back from the skipper of the Racer who informed him that his crew had called him, while he was below, to report that a 'large red ball of light' had just passed over their boat at such a low altitude that it narrowly missed Racer's spars."

"Later, William Nickerson, a crewman aboard the Which Way In, echoed his Captain's sentiments, describing the encounter as a very frightening experience and that the heat was so intense he had fully expected their vessel to be burnt before the object completed its pass."[clxix]

Silver UFO while Fishing: Nivala, Finland

Fishing | On October 4, 1963, Mr. "N.N.," a carpenter by trade from the city of Nivala, related his sighting, which took place on the evening of October 4th.

According to the report, the observer was on the shorefront near Lamujarvi in Pyhanta parish he was building a summer cottage for a cattle dealer. He was quite alone, and in the evening he went fishing. Although the sky was heavily overcast, and he assumed it was good weather for angling since the air was quite calm and the lake surface did not billow. The clouds were very low, but it did not rain.

Suddenly a thing like a washbasin or a saucer, seemingly made of stainless steel, descended out of the cloud layer. It did not do anything special. It just came down close to the surface of the lake where it hovered for some time.

The UFO then rose again, passing out of sight into the clouds. As the carpenter watched the arrival and departure, he thought that perhaps "some smart guy had built a fine airplane."

N.N. admitted, however, he experienced some apprehension since anything could have happened. The lake is isolated with the nearest neighbor some ten kilometers away.

N.N. estimated the object's size as some 20 meters in diameter and that it was stationary over the water about 200 meters away. He noted that during the time the object hovered, the lake surface just below the thing appeared to be bubbling.[clxx]

Comment | This was not to our knowledge reported to the Air Force, it was not located in the US Air Force Project Blue Book Files for 1963.

Shag Harbor Crash: Nova Scotia
First Report
Sambro: Nova Scotia
(Not in US Air Force Project Blue Book)

Crash in Harbor | On October 4, 1967, a UFO crashed into the sea at Nova Scotia, Canada - Shag Harbor. The event seen by many citizens is now known as the Shag Harbor Crash/ Retrieval Incident.

From early evening until 11:30 pm, numerous independent witnesses observed unexplained aerial activity. Near Sambro at 9:00 pm, the captain and crew of a fishing boat saw four brilliant red lights in a box formation that appeared to be on or just above the water. Occasionally one would flare up so bright that it would cause an afterimage in their eyes. The objects also were tracked on the ship's radar.

Between 11:00 and 11:30 pm, northwest of Briar Island, the captain and crew of a fishing vessel saw a brilliant white light the size of the moon. As they watched, three brilliant yellow lights emerged and formed a triangle around the larger light.

The satellite objects then moved across the sky and back at high speed. Other vessels also made observations.

Sambro is about 12 miles southwest of Halifax. During this same time interval 5 miles southwest of Weymouth, in the general direction of Briar Island, a policeman and three game wardens saw an orange-colored light just above the tree line moving silently and slowly with spark-like objects emanating from the light.

At about 11:20 pm just west of Shag Harbor, teenagers in a car saw an object flying low, flashing four lights, one after the other, in a straight line. It appeared to be slowly descending at a 45-degree angle. When next seen, the object had impacted the water's surface 200-300 yards offshore. It drifted on the surface showing a pale yellow light. Boats were sent out to rescue passengers from a presumed fallen airliner, but searchers found only dense yellow foam.[clxxi]

Near Sambro: Nova Scotia
Second Report
Air Canada Airliner confirms UFO near Shag Harbor

Fishing | The incident began during the evening of October 4, 1967. The first reports came in from southeastern Quebec shortly after 7:00 pm when pilots of an Air Canada airliner saw a large, brightly lit, a rectangular object thought to be at an altitude of about 12,000 feet, trailed by several smaller lights.

Then an explosion seemed to occur near the UFO, and the smaller lights began to veer away. The airline crew watched the display for several minutes until it moved out of sight. Within 30 minutes, witnesses on the ground reported seeing lights moving from the northeast to the southwest.

At about 9:00 pm the crew of fishing boat near Sambro, Nova Scotia, saw several red lights over the water and also detected objects on their shipboard radar. They reported the objects to the Canadian Coast Guard and the RCMP, who asked them to file a formal report when they returned to port.

More witnesses again reported odd lights in the sky around 10:00 p.m., including writer Chris Styles, who saw something strange over Halifax Harbor himself. He saw an orange, glowing, disc-shaped object moving over the water, and he ran to get a better look. He could see it was a 50-foot-diameter orange ball, making no sound as it passed overhead.

"Styles wasn't the only witness in the area at that time." Others also reported seeing the orange ball drifting in a southeasterly direction. Around 10:30 pm professional photographer Will Eisnor in Lunenburg took photos of three lights in the sky in a triangular formation. Around 11:00 pm, southwest of Weymouth, a police officer, and two game wardens observed a fireball just above the tree line.

But about half an hour later, the UFO reached Shag Harbor.[clxxii]

More on Shag Harbor Incident: Nova Scotia
Third Report

On October 4, 1967, according to the Halifax Chronicle Herald, a spokesman for the RCAF (Royal Canadian Navy and Air Force) said their department was very interested in the reports. Squadron Leaders Bain said, "the shag Harbor incident is one of the few where we may get something concrete on it."

According to many residents, a series of bright lights were seen gliding over the waters off Shag Harbor in full view. Within 20 minutes, several constables of the Royal Canadian Mounted Police were on the scene, attempting to reach a spot where the UFO submerged. The Coast Guard joined the Police and eight fishing vessels a large patch of yellowish foam and bubbling water was found, unlike anything is seen there before.

Navy divers searched the area for two days and found nothing according to press reports.

After a few days of the Shag Harbor incident, another object was seen that was 55- 60 feet long having a row of red lights flying at 500 to 600 feet in altitude. Five people who also reported interference on television receivers at the same time saw the UFO.[clxxiii]

Comment | The Shag Harbor case was not to our knowledge reported to the Air Force, it was not located in the US Air Force Project Blue Book Files for 1967. This file should be in the Air Force Files as military and police from other countries north of the U.S. were involved. It is conceivable this incident is filed in a "classified file" or another filing system in the United States."

More on Shag Harbor Incident: Nova Scotia
Diving for Evidence off Nova Scotia:
Information Kept from the Public
Fourth Report

Fishing | On October 6, 1967, Canadian Navy divers from the H.M.C.S. Granby began searching the waters and ocean bottom for evidence of the crashed vehicle. According to the records and the people, the official dive ended on the 8th with "nothing being found."

On the 11th it was reported more lights were seen hovering over the area, but nothing further gleamed.

In Richard M. Dolan's book "*UFOs and the National Security State, Chronology of a Cover-up 1941-1973"* we find, that in the 1990s, researchers Chris Styles and Don Ledger had interviewed the former Dive Team from the Canadian Naval Vessel. What they uncovered had never been told to the public:

"The searchers realized that the object had moved northeast, near a then-top secret submarine detection station run jointly by Canada and the U.S. As a flotilla of ships, positioned themselves over the submerged craft, a second underwater UFO joined the first and engaged in a repair operation. The members of the ships observed but did not interfere. Seven days later, a Soviet Submarine appeared but was escorted away. Soon after, the two UFOs moved off toward the Gulf of Maine. Emerging from the water, they ascended rapidly and flew off".[clxxiv]

Fishing for Bass at Cholla Bay, Sonora, Mexico

Fishing | On November 5, 1970, Albert Formiller of Phoenix, Arizona, was fishing for black sea bass about 9:00 p.m. when he observed a light in the sky coming from a circular saucer-shaped object. The sea was quiet. The object appeared to stop and hover about 200–300 feet above the surface of the water.

A light appeared from the bottom of the object and illuminated a broad spot of water, which Formiller estimated to be perhaps a one-half mile wide.

Formiller described the light as appearing to come from within a tube and changing from a broad floodlight to sharp spot on the water surface, apparently as the light was raised or lowered. There was no sound.

After a few minutes, a cloud seemed to form around the vehicle. Formiller does not believe exhaust gases caused this because there was no apparent "blowing" of the cloud from an exhaust.

About five minutes after illuminating the water, the searchlight was turned off, and a similar light was turned on atop the vehicle, illuminating the upper part of the milky cloud.

The vehicle then began to move in a westerly direction. It was visible for about 20 minutes in all. Other lights on the strange car gave the cloud a greenish cast. Similar reports came to the Phoenix Weekly American News from other Phoenix residents.[clxxv]

Chapter 16: UFOs off shore

UFOs have been hovering over ships and boats at Sea for hundreds of years.

UFOs are seen near lakes, ponds, rivers, reservoirs and the ocean. It is believed as far as rivers are concerned, some UFO pilots may use them as a sort of highway to their final destination.

As far as lakes and oceans, some UFOs enter the water, submerge and later rise from the water source.

It is not known if UFO pilots and crews use water was as a cover from human seeing them or are interested in the environment below the surface. There are stories of UFO taking water aboard their ships in vast quantities from the ocean as well as small samples from lakes.

It would seem to me, from those examples they both use water and study the chemical in the water sources they visit.

The object above Waterline: Sandy Point: Newfoundland

Fishing | On August 30, 1950, between 2:00 and 4:00 pm several young men were fishing south of Kippens, Newfoundland, Canada when they reported seeing a UFO above the waterline.

William Alexander, son Bill Alexander and nephew Austin Alexander, fishing in a dory boat about 1-1/2 miles offshore from Kippens, saw a black or yellowish-brown object thought to be a submarine. Their dory about 20 feet in length was 1 and ½ miles offshore when they observed a UFO to be another 1 and ½ to 2 miles off from them.

According to the Air Force Files, the UFO appeared the size of a "dory and looked like a large target balloon with either a black or brownish yellow color." The UFO was sitting 15 to 20 feet above the water and had a pole extending from its center to the water lines and was traveling north-northeast at an estimated speed of 3 to 5 miles.

The UFO was in sight for 5 minutes before it moved over the horizon. There was no smoke, exhaust noise or markings evident.

According to the file notes, another witness observed the same object from high ground on shore. This came to light when talking to other witnesses.

The AF files indicate that the Control Tower and Operations reported no aircraft in the area at the time. There were three aircraft over the field before the sighting (a B-29, and two DC-3's).

The Air Force concluded this sighting as "Unidentified."

According to research conducted by Jan Aldrich, a Helicopter search took place at 4:20 with negative results. According to him, a similar sighting occurred at Sandy Point / Indian Head.[clxxvi]

Coast Guard Sightings: Massachusetts
Spot Intelligence Report

Yachting | October 14, 1952, around 9:30 pm Captain Robert E. Metcalf reported receiving UFO sightings from the Coast Guard Life Boat Station at Rockport, Massachusetts, Gloucester, Mass, Provincetown, Mass, and the Coast Guard Cutter "Yankton" which was enrooting from Portland Maine to Provincetown, Mass. Other sightings were reported from a private yacht off Nantucket, Mass.

Five Coastguardsmen who witnessed the sighting were interviewed. According to eyewitnesses, the UFO was described as "cigar-shaped." Another witness believed the shape was "disc-shaped." No exhaust was reported however a light appeared slightly to the rear of the object. One witness reported a sphere shaped device like a baseball or a small sun and bright orange in color. Another reported a "football-shaped" object also having the small light near the rear. The color was bright yellowish.

As to speed, the interviewees reported the craft much faster than a jet aircraft. The timeline appears to be as follows:

Time	Location	Time of observation
1940 hours	Coast Guard Cutter "Yankton" – was near Portsmouth, New Hampshire at the time	3 seconds
2013 hours	Coast Guard Station, Provincetown, MA	1 minute
2020 hours	Watch Tower, Straitamouth Life Boat Station, Rockport, MA	8 seconds
2025 hours	Watch Tower, Straitamouth Life Boat Station, Rockport, MA	6 seconds

A Teletype report was sent to Director of Intelligence USAF Washington (DC), EADF Stewart AFB (NY), ATIC Wright Patterson AFB (OH), ADC ENT AFB (CO) and Hancock Field (NY). The report mentioned these two UFOs were seen at all three Coast Guard stations as well as 2 F-51 pilots over Barnes Airport and 8 men on the ground at the Airport.[clxxvii]

Bihagon: Philippines

Fishing | January 31, 1953, around 8:30 and 9:10 pm two observers in a rowboat off Bihagon Cove, Philippines saw 3 to 4 UFOs while fishing.

The objects were very bright and fast. They were described as being "disk-like in shape," about 18 inches in diameter. The bodies appeared transparent, moving in a circle and horizontal as well as "banked." No sound was heard; no trail or wake was seen. The objects appeared to be reflecting light from a shiny metal surface.

Lt. Colonel, Chief of Customs Secret Service and Harbor Police, Manila rejected the possibility of Jack-O-Lanterns or falling stars (meteors). The observers provided sworn and signed statements to OSI, USAF.

The Air Force concluded the observers saw an Astro-event (Meteor); however, the brief analysis states: "3 or 4 very bright, fast-moving, disc-like objects, 18 inches in diameter, transparent white light reflected from a shiny metal surface for 2 or 3 seconds. Objects appeared in a horizontal position moving around in a circle after 2 seconds, banked & assume a vertical position before disappearing to the NW in a flash.[clxxviii]

Updated information on the case:

According to other statements: The Observer stated: "I had a strike and in pulling in my line I happened to look up at the sky where I saw three or four very bright, luminous, round objects which seemed to travel around in a circle. They were visible for about two or three seconds. The objects appeared to be about eighteen inches in diameter and seemed to be transparent.

They suddenly turned or banked and zoomed away in a northwesterly direction. The UFOs traveled faster than a shooting star but did not leave any trail or wake. In my opinion, they were traveling at a much higher altitude than the Japanese planes which bombed CEBU at the outbreak of the last war.

"I was frightened and called them to the attention of Colonel. The Colonel stated that he had also seen the unusual objects and advised that he had never seen anything like them before in his life."

Comment | In reviewing this case I would say this is an apparent "misclassification of Facts" – this case should have been "Unidentified." The observers were in a small boat off Bihagon Cove, between Hornos and Tulian Point. [clxxix]

UFO over Ocean City: Maryland

Fishing | On July 27, 1954, around 3:00 pm in the afternoon, individuals aboard two fishing vessels reported a UFO over the Water. The object was described as a red ball or a ball or red flame. The UFO entered the water 15 miles southeast of Ocean City. The witnesses stated that they observed the object for 15 minutes and estimated the speed between 8 to 24 knots.

One witness stated the object traveled "submerged part of the time," others noted that it traveled on the surface. The UFO was observed through binoculars.

According to the Air Force files, the DIO advised that the water in question is too shallow to permit the operation of a submarine at Snorkel depth and no Naval craft of that type was in the vicinity at the time of the sighting. NACA (now NASA) at Wallops Island Virginia had launched two missiles that day, however, landed 30 miles from the sighting site.

The Air Force concluded the individuals observed were "smoking pot." According to one report that a smoke pot may not have been recovered from a naval exercise. However, this was never proven to be in fact the case.[clxxx]

Comment | The classification of this sighting was never proven to be true.

Columbia River: Oregon

Fishing | 1955 according to the witness: "The year was 1955, I was deep sea fishing a few miles South, Southwest of the Columbia River, alone in the cockpit of my trolling boat. While watching the tips of my trolling poles for strikes, I noticed a round silver object suspended in the air at about 25,000 to 30,000 feet. I continued to observe it for approximately twenty minutes.

During this time, it remained perfectly still. As I watched, suddenly it took flight as described below:

"From a suspended position, it suddenly accelerated on a Northward and upward course, then South on an upward path, thence back North on an upward direction, thence southward again, accelerating on each leg of its climb. Then it tipped on its side and flew straight up at a tremendous rate of speed until it disappeared from sight."

"The day was perfectly clear, and I observed it very clearly without obstruction to my view. I also have substantiation of the sighting of this mysterious UFO."

"While I do not claim to be an expert observer, I will say that as a commercial deep sea fisherman, I am accustomed to seeing all normal flying objects...and this was something definitely unknown and flew a distinct pattern at terrific speed."

"It is somewhat of an uneducated guess as to its height, as I judged from many planes I have seen flying over the same approximate location. By the same token, I would judge it to have been approximately 75' to 100' meters in diameter."[clxxxi]

Huge objects were seen over South Pacific

Fishing | July 6, 1955, the Seattle Daily Times reported the following: "Flying saucers take even more outlandish forms when they are seen in the South Pacific. Objects variously described as like throw nets, illuminated balls, and sausages have recently been seen in New Caledonia skies.

"The first report came a gypsum mine caretaker who saw an object which was yellow, luminous and shaped like a throwing net for fishing. It remained stationary in the sky for 20 minutes, and then made off at terrific speed.

"On the northeastern coast, a woman reported a huge sausage-shaped object over the sea. It, too, whisked away after about a half hour."[clxxxii]

Gotland Island: Baltic Sea, Sweden
25 Meters in Diameter

Fishing | August 5, 1957 Report of Mr. Akerberg, a criminal investigator of the Police Department of the city of Visby, Gotland Island in the Baltic Sea, Sweden.

"On the evening of August 5, 1957, I drove some friends of the family to my fishing cottage at Lergravsviken, 53 km. from Visby. This is on the east coast of Gotland. Before my wife and I left the cabin, we looked at the moon through binoculars."

"It was a full moon, a clear sky, no clouds and visibility were the best possible. The time was around 10 pm. My wife suddenly exclaimed: 'Take a look at the sea and see what it is that is coming there.' I rose and looked."

"I saw a saucer-like object coming towards us from a northeasterly direction, and it headed straight down towards us there on the roadside. The nearer it came, the bigger it appeared. The outline of the object when I first saw it was slightly blurred. The craft kept its straight course until it reached the shore when it veered off sharply to the south and then came 1,000 meters to the southeast."

"I was afraid at first that it would collide with the mountains on the seashore. Its size appeared to be that of a big football held at arm's length distance. When it made the turn, I saw that the craft tipped itself up on edge."

"When it was less than 300 meters away, I could plainly see the joints and boltings in the metal of its bottom. "In its sharp turn it appeared as if the craft fluttered, but immediately after that it resumed its steady flight--I should say at the speed of an ordinary airplane."

"When the craft took its southern course I noticed that the color of its lower part was silver-grey and that its form reminded me rather of the semi-sphere of a bicycle bell than a saucer. The bowl itself was shiny as stainless steel, and it rotated slowly around the lower part. I could see the glitter from the rotation. In the cupped part out on its nose, there were cutouts or notches with upward-folded edges."

"The craft had no labeled markings, no windows or apertures, but outlines of black lines running alongside were visible. In the bottom part, there was something like a tube, cherry-red with a steady light, no flames or peaks as one can notice on a motor having a silencer. Moreover, there was another light, red, not so big and not so bright as the first light; it reminded me of the backlight of a car."

"I estimated the size of the craft to be around 25 meters in diameter. It traveled without a sound, except for a clicking sound that reminded me of the noise you hear when you wind a watch. After the passage of the craft a very powerful draught came, that caused ripples on the water surface and the treetops to writhe quite vigorously."

"The craft turned to the southeast it just stood and swayed for a second or so, before it continued its flight and disappeared above the northeastern part of Fitudden Island."

"Then immediately came another craft of the same appearance, taking exactly the same course as the first one, excepting that its turn to the southeast was made considerably tighter than that of the first craft. A distance of about 1 kilometer parted the two craft. After the second craft passed, there was another draught of an air current. The last craft had only one steady light in its back with the same intensity as that given by the first." [clxxxiii]

Disc nearly Crashes: Sao Paulo: Brazil
Fragment recovered from exploding UFO over the Sea

Fishing | September 15, 1957, while fishing near the town of Ubatuba near Sao Paulo, some witnesses observed a giant UFO.

The object (a disc) was seen approaching the beach at an unbelievable speed, "an accident seemingly imminent – in other words a crash into the sea."

"At the last moment, however, when it was about to strike the water, it made a sharp turn upwards and climbed rapidly in a fantastic manner. We followed the spectacle with our eyes, startled when we the disk explode into flames."

"It disintegrated into thousands of fiery fragments, which fell sparkling with magnificent brightness, They looked like fireworks, in spite of the time of the accident – at noon. Most of the fragments fell into the sea. But many small fragments fell close to the beach, and we picked up a large amount of this material which was light as paper".

He then states: "I herewith enclose a sample of it. I don't know anyone that could be trusted to whom I might send it for analysis. I have never read about a flying saucer having been found or any fragments or parts of a saucer that had been picked up; unless it had been done by military authorities and the whole thing kept as a top-secret subject".

According to APRO Dr. Olavo T. Fontes visited the individual and obtained a fragment, which was analyzed by scientists. Evidence reviewed suggested a level of purity not obtainable at that time. A mystery remains of what it was.[clxxxiv]

Late night swimming party in Brazil
UFO appears

Swimming -Party | July 16, 1959, during the late evening in Rio De Janeiro, Brazil "a circular aerial object stopped over Avenida Atlantics, at 2740, the address of an apartment building where Sr. Osvaldo Santiago lives. Numerous people on the seashore avenue were bathed in the powerful blue-green beam of light, which emanated from the UFO.

Inside Sr. Santiago's apartment, a young genius on the piano, Assis Brazil, was being honored by a group of people when the glow of the UFO suddenly appeared. The noted Brazilian playwright, Juracy Camargo, who was on the terrace of the apartment at the time, told the press: 'The people were shaken by such an amazing and majestic apparition.'

"The apartment had been lavishly illuminated by the intense light from the object. Afterward, the UFO was seen to move out over the open sea, disappearing over Rasa Island. Witnesses in the apartment said the UFO came from the direction of Leme District at fantastic speed, giving the impression that it would collide with the building. Instead, it stopped nearby hovering in mid-air, then threw out the blue-green light.

The UFO wobbled slightly for a while, revealing an oval shape with several orange luminous markings, then sped away leaving a trail of orange-colored light.

"Numerous people on the avenue saw the UFO, but the persons in the apartment can be accepted as reliable witnesses: Joracy Camargo, noted playwright; Sr. Helio Fernandes; Sr. Augusto Menezes, his wife, and daughter; Sr. Humberto Strarnandinoli, Sra. Alice Menna Barreto de Assis Brazil; the young pianist Assis Brasil; (13), who was being honored; Lady-teacher Cinira de Menezes; Sra. Alba Assis Brasil; Sra. Nadir Camargo; Sr. Joao Carlos de Camargo Eboli; Lady-teacher Cecilia Strarnandinoli; Sra. Roseli Strarnandinoli; Sra. Tiza Santiago, and several others."[clxxxv]

Fishing off Savona, Italy

Fishing | June 3, 1961, around 6:35 am a couple of men took to the sea off Savona, Italy.

"Signor Giacomo Barra, of 9 via Fratelli Canepa, Savona, reported the following experience":

"'I went out in a motorboat with Giuseppe Pordoi, businessman, Filippo Marin, office employee, and Silvano Guardinfante, owner of the boat. When quite a reasonable distance out to sea, we shut off the engine and sat there chatting and enjoying the morning breeze. It was 6:35 am."

"Suddenly the rocking motion of the waves increased, and the boat began to roll badly. We looked around, thinking it must be due to the proximity of one of the many tankers that put into our port."

"But nothing of the sort." At a distance of a kilometer from us, the surface of the sea was bulging like an enormous ball, with long billows going out from it on all sides."

"Dumbfounded, we were still wondering what it was when, suddenly, a strange contraption rose up from the bulge of water. Perhaps it was one of the celebrated 'flying saucers,' for the lower part of it looked like a plate upside down, and the upper portion ended in a cone."

"While it was emerging from the sea, the water was thrust away all around it, as by a cushion of air. After it had emerged entirely from the sea, it stopped still for a few seconds, at the height of 10 meters or so, and then rocked slightly a few times. Then a halo formed around the base of it, and the thing shot away very fast across the sea and vanished towards the northwest."[clxxxvi]

Another Biloxi Mississippi Fishing Case
"Size of a full Moon."

Fishing | On September 21, 1962, around 7:37-7:50 pm the Captain of "Miss Lou" was anchored off Pass Christian (Gulf of Mexico – off Biloxi) when a UFO was seen. Captain S.A. Guthrie and deckhand saw 2 objects. They were described as red and black with orange streaks.

One object was as big as the Moon, and the other smaller and trailing arcing across the sky. These were "too large and too low to be stars." The objects were heading towards Florida. The UFOs were observed through binoculars. The incident was reported to the Coast Guard.

In his letter, he admits putting into port and a week later ran into two other men who admitted seeing the same things.

A Teletype message of the incident went to various bases: Thirty-second ADDIV Sage Oklahoma AF Station, CINCNORAD, COMEASTSEAAFRON, COFS USAF, SECRETARY OF THE NAVY, CNO, COMDT COGARD, COMEASTAREA, COMSIX, COMEAST, COMFAIR WING ELEVEN, CINCLANTFLT.

The Air Force concluded the object was "Unidentified."[clxxxvii]

Two UFOs while Fishing: Norway

Fishing | August 21 or 22, 1963, at 5.00 pm a fisherman reported a UFO at Kagsund, Norway. According to his testimony:

"I put out in my boat on a fishing trip to the sound called Kagsund, near Skjervoy. The weather was clear, and there was no outline of a grey object. I figured it was some sort of balloon or parachute. The Object then started to move eastward straight against the wind, and keeping the same altitude it passed over a mountaintop (2,350 feet), and a small village."

"As the object moved out over the sound, approaching me, it came lower, and I realized it was certainly no balloon or parachute. Then the thought struck me that it was a UFO."

"I now observed two objects, one large and one small. The large object had five big 'windows' on the side towards me, which were oval on top and about 6 feet high. The distance to the object was 450 feet, and it hovered about 40 to 50 feet above the water. Suddenly, what appeared to be two rails came down out of the large object, and the smaller one hooked on to these and was drawn into the larger one. The small thing was oval, about 6 by 9 feet. No flame or smoke was observed, and there was no sound.

Figure 14 - Disc with windows

"The time was by now 6.40 pm., and I must admit I was feeling nervous and afraid. For a short moment, I had looked around for other witnesses but could see no other boats. The wind had now increased, and the sea was dark, but underneath the object, the sea was calm and shiny. In one of the object's windows, I saw a green light, the beam from which was directed at me. The round light (about one foot in diameter) was changing color, light and dark green, and something seemed to be moving behind the light. I tried to lift a fish into the boat, but could not manage it. "l seemed to be paralyzed." Whether this was due to the excitement or something else, I do not know.

"I judged the large object to be about 30 feet high, and 105-120 feet long (diameter?). I could not say for sure if the object were oval or circular, as it had the same side turned towards me during the whole of my observation. It was flat underneath but had a dome on top.

"At about 6.30 pm, I was going to change my fishing location to near the 'Skjervoyskjeret' (sunken rock) and was looking west towards the island Arnoy. I suddenly saw a flame, as from a rocket, shooting out from the mountain."

"I thought the Navy was performing some kind of training mission, but if so, they would have had to be testing something new, because I saw a 6-feet wide orange-colored flame. I then saw an object which went straight up in the air, but the speed was not as fast as that of a rocket being launched! At the height of about 6,000 feet, the flame disappeared."

"The object had stopped right over a large sunken German cargo ship which was shipwrecked here in 1944, and which carried ore (metal) and quicksilver. "I watched something," "I am not too certain of this- either being drawn out of, or dumped into, the sea. Several little dark things were seen between the object and the sea surface". To me, it seemed that something was coming up out of the sea, and entering in through the bottom of the object. It hovered motionless through-out this time, which was about 10 minutes. The UFO then tilted a little to one side and started to accelerate.

Suddenly the large object's speed increased tremendously, and in one minute it had disappeared in a northerly direction out the fjord of Kvenangen.

"The color of the object was metallic, or silver-grey. The upper sketch shows the object as I saw it hovering in front of me. It was through the window on the left side, "marked X," that the little object was drawn into the larger. The second window from the right "marked Y," was the one from whence the green light beam shone."

"The second drawing represents the object as seen from below, at an angle. Here is seen a detail, which is not mentioned in the story: a series of round, funnel-like cups, which I believe must have been movable, because some of them pointed down, while some pointed in other directions. I cannot describe these in more detail, as I only saw them for a few seconds."

"I give my word that this is a true account of personal experience."
On the basis of the investigations carried out by TRONDHEIM UFO FORENJNG, Trondheim, and UFO-INFORMASJON, Oslo, it is considered that this person is reliable and that the story very likely is true. Mr. Mikalsen has agreed to his account being published."[clxxxviii]

Comment | This was not to our knowledge reported to the Air Force, it was not located in the US Air Force Project Blue Book Files for 1963.

At sea, near San Benedetto del Tronto
UFO circled the Boat

Fishing | November 3, 1978, Fisherman Antonio Pallesca caught sight of a reddish light at sea following his boat. Frightened, he drew up his nets and directed his ship towards land.

The light (whatever it was) stayed with him, first behind him, then beside him, then in front of him. As it circled around his boat, he couldn't discern it as anything but light. It left him shortly before he arrived in port. On November 7, he had another run-in with an orange glow and a dark floating object. Pallesca has been a seafarer for 30 years.[clxxxix]

Two miles off the coast of Grottammare

Fishing | November 6-7, 1978 Roberto Cichella, owner of the "Igea" fishing boat, saw a reddish flash or streak rise into the sky.

At the same instant, his ship's radar stopped functioning. He radioed Giorgio Mazzoni who was following him in his own boat. Mazzoni turned on his own radar and saw that the radar line (indicating the axis of his boat) was fragmented into seven or eight segments. Both men also refer to an area of churning sea in front of the coastal area between Silvi and Giulianova.

At 2:00 am, two miles off the coast of Grottammare, fisherman Antonio Pallesca watched a very vivid orange light with a white light "a few meters below at eye level." He watched them for about ten minutes before heading back due to storm warnings and fear of a huge, dark, floating object a few meters away from him.

Also on the 7th, Gioacchino Merlini of the "Andre Padre," in the company of his crew, noted an unprecedented triangular signal on the radar, which split up into many small rays. The signal was seemingly from 80 miles away, which, if real, would be inland over the Sibillini Mountains.[cxc]

UFO 5 miles off the coast of Italy
Italian Navy Investigates – sees UFO

Fishing | On November 9, 1978, the crew of an Italian Navy Boat, CP2018, set out to sea to investigate the unusual phenomena reported by the Adriatic fishermen.

Its captain, Nello di Valentino, saw with two other crewmen a very intense light about 1000 meters off the prow rise rapidly to an estimated height of 300-400 meters and disappear toward the east. There was some disagreement over the presence of a blue smoke trail. No Radar signal was returned.

At the precise instant of the sighting, communications with the Pescara Naval authorities were extremely disturbed. They were restored three minutes later. The idea of an emergency flare was ruled out, as was the presence of a normal submarine with the water depth being 23 meters. No traces were found in the area. Naval authorities openly conjectured about espionage as a cause of the strange sightings and interferences.[cxci]

Fishing near Gulf of Alaska

Fishing | July 5, 1979, around 2:45 am a group of men was halibut fishing south of Seward, Alaska when they reported a UFO.

A super bright object came down through the clouds and became stationary close to the water. At the same time, a target appeared on their radar at about two miles distant, a solid target.

All of a sudden the radar heading was knocked off of its setting and one of the crew had to reset it. It was a bright glowing object with a bowl-like shape, which faded out and simultaneously disappeared from the radar screen, then reappeared visually and on the radar.

The radar heading was knocked off when the object approached the boat. The UFO was only a couple of feet off the water. The incident lasted for about five minutes, and the radar was picking up a strong signal.[cxcii]

Chapter 17: Photographic Evidence

Photographic evidence is becoming more common as humans have handheld devices with cameras. In the 1950s and 1960s, humans had to rely on someone with a handheld camera to take photos of UFO spacecraft. Today, everyone has a cell phone with a camera, and if she or he thinks quickly enough, they can get a photograph of a lifetime.

As I mentioned in my many books, the best photographs by our world military's are held under lock and key and labeled "Top Secret."

These images reveal close up shots from gun cameras on jet interceptors, or film of UFOs from government video and motion censored cameras. You and I are usually unable to see these today until the files become declassified. Depending on the country, the files may not be declassified from 25 to 50 years. Even after the files are declassified the photographs are rarely released.

We have to thank the U.S. Pentagon for releasing the 2004 gun camera film from several F-18 super hornets off San Diego in 2017. What I would like to see today is the film from the Chilean government from the 1940s to 1960s of the UFOs over Naval fleets off deception island. This film was confirmed to exist, and yet we (the people of the world) have yet to see the movie.

Figure 15 - F/A = 18A US Marine Corps "Super Hornet" [cxciii]

Flying Boat Base, Port Moresby, Papua, New Guinea
Mr. Drury films object: AF removes best frames

Fishing | On August 23, 1953, Mr. T.P. Drury of the Director of Civil Aviation in Papua, New Guinea, and his family observed a UFO.

Around 11:00 am, Mr. Drury, his wife, and children were watching a native boy spearing a fish when they noticed a wisp of cloud suddenly appear in the blue sky from nowhere and start to build up rapidly into a white puff. Mrs. Drury pointed out the anomaly to Mr. Drury. The white puff grew into a cumulus.

Using his French-made movie camera, he focused on this cloud to film it.

"Suddenly an object like a silver dart shout out of the cloud, it was elongated in shaped like a bullet. It subtended about one inch at arm's length. It was metallic and flashed in the sun. It was clear-cut, shape in front but apparently truncated behind, though the tail may have been hidden by the vapor trail."

No wings or fins were visible. The UFO shot out of the cloud upward at an angle of about 45 degrees. It traveled at an immense speed, at least five times as fast as a jet plane traveling at the speed of sound.

The crazy looking craft was gone in a few seconds. "In spite of the supersonic speed and the comparative nearness of the object, there was no sound whatsoever."

The witness shared; "I was greatly concerned about the appearance of such an extraordinary aircraft in the sly, and without telling anyone, I drove straight to Jacksons Airport and checked with the Air Traffic Control. There we no unusual aircraft out, only a DC3 and the usual DD4 expected from Australia."

"I then reported the sighting to the RAAF, but they were quite unable to account for it. Later I sent them the film, which was sent all around the world but no one could explain the object, and it was pronounced "unknown."

According to the '*APRO Bulletin*,' this film was the first recorded unidentified flying object over the territory of Papua New Guinea.

When the film was returned to Mr. Drury, after being in America, the best frames were "cut out," and the remained show only the cloud and the vapor trail.[cxciv]

Fishing Lake Tiorati: New York
50 to 75-foot diameter disc reportedly photographed

Fishing | December 18, 1966, according to NICAP the Air Force has told the organization that a UFO taken by a man fishing at Lake Tiorati in New York does not support his story. Thought the photograph of a flying object was deemed "authentic" the disc was stated to be smaller than what the construction worker declared.

Around 4:30 pm at the northern end of Lake Tiorati three men had just fishing packing up their fishing gear when they noticed an object moving over the trees across the lake. Calling to his companions, he grabbed his camera and ran some 25 to 30 feet to get a clear view of the far shore.

The object was traveling from left to right in an "S" pattern who plane paralleled the ground. The motion was steady and quiet with no dramatic change in the objects altitude or attitude.

Illuminated by the setting sun, the UFO appeared to be roughly similar to a hat or inverted dish. The bottom was yellow and the top gray. No structural details were evident.

Within seconds of the two pictures were taken, the UFO passed behind a fire tower on the hill across the lake and disappeared down behind the trees.

After the UFO left, the witnesses ran down the road that circles the lake and when a nearby police facility to report the sighting. The police suggest contacting the Air Force at Stewart AFB about 16 miles away. Vincent phoned the base later that afternoon.

In its letter to Perna, the Air Force agrees the UFO is a real object rather than a photograph flaw or trick, but concluded the object is "a maximum of three feet in diameters," not the "50 to 75 feet" estimated by Perna.

The letter also says the object is "substantially nearer than the background trees," not over the trees as Perna said. Both Air Force conclusions are apparently based on the "relative clarity" of the object as it appears in the first picture.

The Air Force studied the first photograph while NICAP studied the "second" photograph. The second photograph indicated the object is at least 35 feet away from the camera. The top of the hill in the background is 2,000 feet away and in the calculation would place the object between 40 and 80 feet in diameter. [cxcv]

Comment | This incident was reported to the Air Force. The report was not located in the US Air Force Project Blue Book Files for 1967. The pictures for the event were found in the files.

Photographic Evidence of UFO: Louisiana
CBS TV Analyzes Evidence "Confirms authentic."

Fishing | January 12, 13, 1967 according to analysts for CBS, three photographs taken by a man of a fishing expedition in Louisiana are "authentic."

Major Dewey, J. Fournet (USAF retired) investigated the sighting on behalf of NICAP. Around 4:30 pm on January 12, the individual had just arrived at the camp and was unpacked his fishing gear when the object showed up. He took a photo of the thing and was so shook up he drove himself home to Baton Rouge. He then went back the next morning (January 13th) and at 9:30 am the UFO showed up again. This time he took two more pictures.

The object was a solid, light grey disc-like structure with domes on each side. One dome was slightly smaller than the other.

The witness said that he had no time for more than one photograph during the first encounter because it took the UFO only second to complete a turn and disappear quickly toward the east. The next morning, he noticed a large number of dead fish along the river and heard what sounded like a multiple of crows in some trees. It was about this time he saw the object. The UFO came straight toward him then completed a turn, rose straight up and disappeared after he took two more pictures.

Mr. Fournet reported a local TV station submitted the photos for CBS for analysis, and the network reported that two different agencies had examined them and declared them to be "authentic."[cxcvi]

Comments | I do not think hallucinations and sundogs or other phenomenon show up so frequently to get their pictures taken. This was not to our knowledge reported to the Air Force, it was not located in the US Air Force Project Blue Book Files for 1967.

South Island, New Zealand

Fishing | December 31, 1978, during the early morning hours shortly after midnight, a famous motion picture film was taken by a news crew while flying off the eastern coast of South Island, New Zealand near the town of Kaikoura.

The luminous UFO was seen by everyone on board the aircraft and was tracked by radar at the same time. It was somewhat cone-shaped, and was not a Japanese shrimp fishing boat, as claimed by debunkers.[cxcvii]

Two Campers at the Great Wall: China
"The first Photograph of UFO in China."

Camping | On August 23, 1980, around 4:08 am two campers near the Great Wall and the Historic Ming Tombs reported at UFO at 4:08 am.

"In a letter to the Peking Evening News (Beijing Wanbao), they said they saw an object, possibly ringed, that emitted white light. The object appeared to have a darker core, and was apparently revolving on an axis, they said.

"The campers, Xin Seng and Bi Jiang, said the object moved further away and then closer for half an hour, but they heard no noise.

"The newspaper printed a photograph showing a moon like an object, with what appeared to be protrusions around the middle. It hovered just above the side of a slope. The newspaper processed the film and made the print of the first photograph of a UFO in China."[cxcviii]

Chapter 18: Over Hills and Mountains

UFOs may be seen off in a remote section of towns hovering over Hills or Mountains. Several UFO cases in Connecticut have been reported where a witness sees the UFO hover, descend and sometimes land on a hilltop.

Hiking: England

Hiking | On September 24, 1956, during an afternoon hike, Messrs. B. Henser, John Boothroyd, A. J. Gingell and D. Elliot were returning to Ilkley from Bolton Abbey, Yorkshire when they spotted a UFO.

The *'Flying Saucer Review'* shared Mr. Henser's account of the story;

He said: "We were climbing up Beamsley Beacon when we saw a huge white bird in the sky. We watched this for a while and then simultaneous, Mr. Elliot, and I saw a bright round orange sphere. It hovered for about five minutes. Then it went below the ridge of the hill, very slowly and gracefully".

"We hurried on to see if we could see any more of it, but while we were still some way from the summit it appeared again. This time, it disappeared after only about 30 seconds".

"When we arrived at the top, there was not a sign of it."

"That is the true full account of what we saw. No one believed us, but four people saw it."[cxcix]

Ponte de Itabapoana: Brazil

Fishing | September 1, 1957, a newspaper picked up a wire story from Mimosa do Sul.

Here are the details which tell of: "an intensely illuminated object flying at very high speed... [That]..was seen last Sunday by residents of Ponte de Itabapoana. Several farms in the area confirmed the fact."

At the same time, a group of persons fishing near Mimosa do Sul at the Itabapoana river saw a similar object.

According to one witness, Mr. Alcebiades Moura, he was fishing at night and was perhaps sleeping when he became wide awake by the intense light coming from a speedy cigar-shaped object. The craft 'buzzed' the place where Mr. Moura was fishing, several times and disappeared flying very low over the mountains. No sound was reported, but the light was intensely strong and green. At the same time truck-drivers near Cachoeiro do Itapemirim, on the road from Rio to Vitoria, reported seeing the same strange craft."

The same paper that carried the news from Ponte de Itabapoana, Rio's Ultima Hora, carried word from Air Brigadier Melo Correia, Minister of Aeronautics (Brazilian Air Force). He said he didn't believe in flying saucers and called the recent alleged appearances are due to publicity stunts. The Brazilian Air Force, he had better things to do than to investigate the supposed objects.[cc]

8 witnessed a 40-foot long Cigar shaped ship
Interview by Gary Barker

Hunting | In November 1957 around 4:30 to 5:00 pm Hank Holloman and other hunters observed a UFO while looking up at one of the nearby mountains at Sutton, West Virginia.

Gary Barker, a columnist, drove to Sutton West Virginia to obtain the story of several hunters who observed a large UFO. The story was then relayed on Radio Station WCHS in Charleston (WV). Here is the story as he interviewed Hank Holloman.

Mr. Holloman reported the object appeared "to be 40 feet long, more or less in the shape of a hot dog bun. It had portholes around each side – I'd say half a dozen on each side. And there was fire coming out of these portholes. It would swing kind of (note he used the word "Kinda") like it was trying to get in under the timber, then it would back up. At times I could see both sides of it.

Barker: "Did it appear to be cigar-shaped?"

Holloman: "That right, similar to a cigar."

Mr. Holloman stated they were on the porch with a telescope and viewed the object with his hunting companions. He said looking at it, "It looked to me just like it was pointed off like a cigar at both ends, and it looked like there was a division right through the middle of it, with as much white down here as there was above. And I couldn't see no wings, myself".

Mr. Holloman stated: "Yes, smoke and fire. Kind of blue smoke looked to me like – the best I could tell, and, then like a red blaze of fire would fly-like they were having trouble with it or something. And it backed up, and it backed out, and he came back again like he was trying to get down in there, and he made a third attempt to come down in the woods right on top of that ridge. It was coming to a storm".

Barker: "Did you hear any noise?"

Holloman: "No, I didn't hear any noise."

Barker: "Could you see anything after it landed?

Holloman: "We could see movement, and it looked like people were working around it. It was getting dark then, and the shade was coming over it, and we couldn't see very good."

Barker: "When you saw this thing land, what was your impression that it was?

Holloman: "I thought it was something from the United States, maybe Army or Navy. There are so many experimental things.

When asked if he called the police, they said no they did not as people would think they were crazy. But then stated they thought about it and drove to Gassaway to report the incident to a State Policeman and another man called Rodney Belknap.

When asked how many witnesses saw this craft he mentioned eight names: Himself, His son and his son's wife, Walter Knicely, Ora Moats, Eddie Mollohan and his wife and another man on Gibson Ridge.

Mr. Holloman mentioned Aberdeen Maryland proving ground is not too far away. Finally the last few points:

Barker: "Did it seem to glow?"

Holloman: "No, only when the sun glinted on it."

Barker: "Did it appear metallic?"

Holloman: "Yes"[cci]

Hunting: Papua, New Guinea
Two separate hunting parties observe Lights within 30 minutes of each other

Hunting | On June 16, 1959, around 6:30 pm a party of hunters was encamped at a place called Maigwarip at about 7,000 feet on a high mountainside.

The witnesses saw a dazzling flash like lightning, which blinded them for a moment. Then they saw an object moving in the sky from north to south. They describe it as 'like a cricket ball,' smaller than the moon, but much brighter. It started green, changed to white and later to red. The color changes were slow, and it remained for a long period at the one color. It was dazzlingly bright and lit up the whole countryside, and the top of the forest with its alternating, green, white and red light. It stayed 'a long time' in the sky and moved slowly. It appeared to rotate as it went (they indicated an anti-clockwise rotation, but I do not know if that was correct), the rays of light which seemed to radiate from it rotating with the object.

"The narrator of the sighting, Birioudo, who was one of the eye-witnesses, said that they were all very frightened, but assumed that it must be one of the fantastic new inventions of the white man. It will be noticed that they never attributed them to magic or spirit phenomena. They seem convinced of their objective reality.

Around 7:00 pm 16 mountain people, men, boys, and girls, were camping out in the high mountain country, hunting for cuscus, tree kangaroos and rock wallabies.

They were 6,000 feet up in a high valley called Dumura, on the south side of the range. At about 7:00 pm they saw a brilliant light 'like a Tilley lamp' but yellow in color. It lit up the whole countryside 'brighter than the moon --more like the sun.'

It did not seem to be very high. It came from the southeast and traveled straight overhead until it disappeared in the north-west.   It appeared to travel 'at the speed of a firefly.'[ccii]

Pigeon Hunting: Diamond Rock, Oregon

Hunting | September 30, 1959 "About 3:30 or 4:00 pm these two men were hunting wild pigeons on the northern slope of the Tiller Trail Divide, and while looking for them in the sky, they noticed three rather round and bright silvery objects apparently hanging motionless high up in the sky toward the northwest. They were estimated to be at least five miles away and at a 45-degree angle of sight.

"While the men stood watching and wondering about them, a regularly scheduled passenger plane came in from the south, headed north and at a lower altitude than that of the UFOs. The three objects then headed towards the wrest at terrific speed and disappeared from view.

A few minutes after the plane had gone out of sight the three UFOs were seen to come in swiftly from the west, increase their altitude at a sharp angle and hover over the same area as before. All during the sighting they made very little motion, kept a close formation and were level with each other.

"As long as the men were in the area the bright objects remained in the same place. Total observation time would have been close to an hour."[cciii]

Hunting Kangaroos and Wallabies: Dumura
June 16 and June 17

Hunting | On June 16, 1961, around 6:30 pm hunters encamped at a place call Maigwarip at 7,000 feet on a high mountainside reported a UFO.

The hunters saw a dazzling flash like lightning, which blinded them for a moment. Then they saw an object moving in the sky from north to south. They describe it as 'like a cricket ball,' smaller than the moon, but much brighter. It started green, changed to white and later to red.

The color changes were slow, and it remained for a long period at the one color. It was dazzlingly bright and lit up the whole countryside, and the top of the forest with its alternating, green, white and red light. It stayed 'a long time' in the sky and moved slowly. It appeared to rotate as it went (they indicated an anticlockwise rotation, but I do not know if that was correct),- the rays of light which seemed to radiate from it rotating with the object.

At 7:00 pm 16 mountain people, men, boys, and girls, were camping out in the high mountain country, hunting for cuscus, tree kangaroos and rock wallabies. They were 6,000 feet up in a high valley called Dumura, on the south side of the range. At about 7:00 pm they saw a brilliant light 'like a Tilley Lamp' but yellow in color. It lit up the whole countryside 'brighter than the moon-more like the sun.' It did not seem to be very high.

It came from the southwest and traveled straight overhead until it disappeared in the northwest. It appeared to travel at the speed of a firefly.

On the night of June 17th, another hunting party on Mt. Manaman at 8,000 feet observed a UFO at 8:00 pm. The object colored red and white shot across the sky and appeared to be in the clouds.[cciv]

Fishing in New Hampshire

Fishing | May 27, 1962, during the evening an object was seen over the hill called "gap" at Troy, New Hampshire.

The next day in school another witness came forward to say while outside an object was seen over "Gap" hill moving up and down and sideways. It then went slowly out of sight. It later came back, and now 6 more objects were seen and went out of sight.

Then on May 29th, the group was fishing and got to the top of the hill and saw the objects. Calling his parents and a neighbor they observed the thing move around then disappeared.

The Air Force did not come to a final conclusion but marked this as probable "astronomical – Venus or Jupiter being the prime culprit."[ccv]

Famous Case: ET Robot attempts to capture Hunter
3 Unidentified Flying Objects

Hunter | September 4, 1964, around dusk three hunters became separated in a location known as Cisco Grove. One of the hunters became separated and spent the night in a tree on a high branch overlooking the Valley floor.

According to the Air Force Files. Three round flat glowing objects came into view. One of the objects landed on a nearby hill. According to the lead observer, these three objects were equipped with a protruding and rotating light that emitting cooing noises in the Loch Leven lake area from dusk to late in the evening.

The observer first thoughts these lights were helicopters looking for him figuring his buddies called for help looking for him.

In response, he threw three signal fires to bring attention to his location. It was then three silvery craft approached his location emitted no sound. One craft landed on a nearby hill, and it was that point he observed two humanoids approaching his location. He could see the humanoids coming through the brush.

He then took refuge in a low branch of a pine tree seeing if he could locate these people (beings). He observed the humanoids had a silver like a suit. He decided to move up the tree branches to get higher and better observation point.

It was then he could see these beings had a strange facial feature with protruding eyes. He commented that there appeared to be the absence of a neck. The files do not indicate a helmet at this point, but later in his testimony, it seems all three entities had some helmet with light showing facial features.

These "beings" tried to dislodge him from the tree. It was then he used his belt (army belt) to fix his weight to the tree limb to stay put. During this time, the observer fires a few arrows at the beings to warn them off (note: this arrow was later collected during the investigation). The robot emitted a vapor from his helmet which made the observer blacked out. The belt fixed to the branch kept the observer from falling to the ground.

Upon waking up six hours later the entities and the craft had left the scene. He then climbed down and was reunited with his buddies. His buddies after hearing the story believed he observed government helicopters looking for a fallen meteorite. His father suggested he report the story to authorities which he did which were relayed to Mather AFB.

A Teletype message was sent to ADC ENT AFB (CO), 28 AIR DIV Hamilton AFB (CA), AFSC, CSAF and OSAF, Washington (DC).

The Air Force concluded the case was "Psychological." The report further stated the encounter with "beings" attributed to psychological causes. It also stated see Specimen 7-3745-422 and a voice recording of the account. It is this voice recording that later became a book of the event.[ccvi]

Comments | I have heard the recording of the interview of this hunter's story. He seemed completely sincere and honest with what transpired. The event appears to be some sort of a robot with two extraterrestrials that attempted to capture the hunter.

For the record, this case should have been labeled "Unknown" or "Unidentified" as it involves three glowing objects and three entities, two of which appear human-like and the other being a robot.

In 1964, the US had not perfected walking robots. It was not until 2010 that MIT studies and Honda?

That produced the first walking hydraulic, mechanical robot. If you have the chance to listen to this recording, you will find the story very intriguing. A YouTube exists called" "Aliens in the Forest: The Cisco Grove UFO Encounter" with Noe Torres. The witness was Donald Schrum.[ccvii]

Chapter 19: Shooting UFOs

Perhaps no better way of saying get off my property to a visitor from another planet is to shoot their spacecraft.

Believe me, when I say, humans with guns, have no problem firing 6 to 12 rounds at the side of a disc or cigar ship. The only message these visitors get is "humans are hostile." Why that surprises us should be as to no surprise as to why UFOs do not land on the white house lawn or in Red Square in the Kremlin or better yet, on the main roads at Piccadilly square London.

Many humans want to see these visitors while others are still working through the psychological adjustment needed to adjust they are real and lived just outside our planet.

This is not to say some species should be feared. However, the problem is the governments for Britain, the US, Russia, Japan, China, France, Italy, Chile, Brazil have yet to tell us which one we should shoot at. They keep this information to themselves.

Boys shoot UFO: Langley AFB: Virginia (A Hoax or Real?) Congressman Porter Hardy (VA) requested a report from AF

Hunting | October 19, 1959, two 14 and 15-year-old boys were hunting in swampland northwest of Plum Island Bomb range, Poquoson, Virginia (Near Langley AFB).

According to the boys they heard an odd whirring sound and upon looking up, observed a circular object, shaped like a disc about 4 feet in diameter. When first seen the UFO was 75 to 90 feet above the ground. There was a black dome in the center of the bottom of the object. The rest of the UFO was "self-luminous."

It was after sundown, just before dusk, causing the object to "glow." No windows, doors or other openings could be seen.

The object began to descend to 60 feet. The observer felt a light draft stirred up by the UFO. He then indicated he was frightened and fired at the object three times. The third round contained a lead slug, and he heard it strike the object. He stated it sounded like "metal scraping against metal."

After the third shot, he closed his eyes and rubbed them with his hand, at which time the object disappeared.

The object had no tail, trail or exhaust and very little noise. The observation lasted "one minute."

The files indicate Congressman Porter Hardy (VA) requested information on this incident from the Air Force. NASA and GCI confirmed no aircraft from their locations were responsible for the sighting.

A Very detailed report was located in the file on this event. The Air Force concluded they believed the case was a Hoax.[ccviii]

Updated information on the case:

Twenty-four years later reporter Larry Bonko of the Norfolk, Virginia, '*Ledger-Star*' tracked down Mark Muza to ask him about the Poquoson case.

If the incident had been a hoax, Mr. Muza could have admitted it without embarrassment after so many years. Why pretend otherwise at such a late date. A lot of people brag about their schoolboy pranks. Bonko found that Mr. Muza still took the incident seriously. Asked if he shot at a UFO, Mr. Muza was emphatic: "Yes, I did." Mr. Muza repeated his 1959 claim that the UFO had a black body with silver trim. The memory was so strong it seemed as if it had "happened yesterday," according to Mr. Muza.

Why would the man risk ridicule by claiming he shot at a UFO? Indeed his co-workers would wonder. When Bonko interviewed Mr. Muza in 1983, the 39- year-old man was well established in his career as a police detective.[ccix]

Duck Hunting: Meadows near Atlantic City: New Jersey Hunter Almost shoots 60-foot diameter saucer

Hunting | December 3, 1960, around 6:00 am two duck hunters a grandfather and grandson were at the Meadows near Atlantic City when they observed a flying saucer. According to the report, they spotted an object flying at them, about 300 feet above the ground. Loaded with his shotgun he was prepared to shot the thing down, but it rose vertically into the air and flew away.

The Atlantic City Press reported the strange machine measured 60 feet in diameter. It had a red glow that lit up the ground, and that changed to purple as the machine zoomed up into the air. According to Mr. Leeds, the "UFO traveled silently at all times, and moved with a jerky motion "like a bouncing ball."

According to the grandson who yelled at his grandfather the reply was " "Don't worry if it comes at us, I'll shoot it."[ccx]

Young Men Hunting: Shoot at UFO that Landed: Alabama

Hunting | October 17, 1973, according to the *'Daily Herald'* two 18-year-old boys, Ira Lundy, and Frank Pierce were hunting birds in a Mobile County (Alabama) field near their home in the Tanner Williams Community when a UFO Landed.

According to the witnesses, the object landed 50 to 75 yards from them. They described the UFO as being round and about the size of three cars and 10 to 12 feet tall. They said it sat down on four legs.

A band in the middle had a red and white flashing lights, and there was an antenna on top.

According to them: "A door slid open and closed quickly." "Then we started shooting. The craft took off toward Mississippi, making some whirring sound it had made when it landed".

The youths said they fired several shots with a 12-gauge shotgun and a 38 caliber pistol. The two estimated the UFO was on the ground about three to four minutes and they watched it for an additional seven minutes or so until it went out of sight.

The paper stated: A sister of Lundy, Diane Sweeting, 26 said she visited the site of the reported landing and was convinced the two had not made up the story. She said: "I saw the imprints of the legs and where the grass was pressed down."

Officials in Jackson County said they had received "five or six" reports on UFO's Tuesday night, but none had been confirmed.

The report continues with a sighting in Louisiana where Sheriffs stated two deputies observed an orange object swing like a pendulum. Then on Tuesday officers reported two triangular objects hovering over Springhill.[ccxi]

Comment | Another example of how "fear" drives a man to run or attack what one does not understand. The other point, what constitutes "confirmation" of a sighting when the other callers may have witnessed something over their heads?

CANADA: Libau, Manitoba,

Hunting | October 1, 1977, around 7:00 pm two men, Leo and John Girardeau, were hunting 3 miles west of Libau when they watched the form shown In the sketches approaching them from the west, silhouetted against the sunset sky, at an estimated altitude of 500 feet. The witnesses went into their truck when the object came within a half-mile of them and turned on their lights.

The object reversed its direction of travel in mid-air and proceeded westward. One of the witnesses fired his shotgun towards it to attract it back; when this failed, the men turned off the lights in the truck and drove after it, trying to sneak up on it.

Running out of the road a couple of miles later, they were forced to watch It depart slowly out of sight. The object guesses to be 75-100 feet wide and 25-30 feet high, was always observed 10-15- above the horizon. It made a steady humming noise which grew louder as the object approached and diminished as it moved away. The sky was cloudless, the area uninhabited.[ccxii]

Chapter 20: Near Ships and Boats

The U.S. Navy aircraft carrier USS Franklin D. Roosevelt (CVA-42) underway in the Mediterranean Sea. | [ccxiii]

UFOs have been approaching ships at sea for thousands of years. Some of the best sources of these UFO cases can be read at WaterUFO.net, Project1947, and nicap.org. Two excellent books on UFOs near water are:

1. Carl W. Feindt ' UFOs and Water"
2. Jacque Vallee's "Wonders of the Sky."

Both books are a must for any UFO aficionado.

UFO at Sea, 200 miles off Baja: California

Fishing | In July / August 1956 Mrs. Janice Sanford, a secretary, was with her husband aboard their 41-foot fishing boat about 200 miles off the coast of Baja.

It was a clear night with the stars visible. Around 1:30 am Mrs. Sanford was on sea traffic watch while her husband was asleep below deck. Looking up she noticed a very brilliant, shimmering, yellow-white spot in the heavens.

The light source had a definite shape and appeared brighter on the bottom portion. The thing then began to move in straight lines with no undulations. She said:

"The object performed very violent maneuvers. It would approach the boat, and hover and flicker. It would rise up entirely out of sight, descend extremely fast, and perform acute angle turns. The sighting was mentioned to other fishermen in the area-none seemed surprised. The object appeared to be about the same size as our boat.[ccxiv]

UFOs off Martha's Vineyard: Massachusetts
Sports Fishing: "AF Hidden Report"

Fishing | October 12, 1957, five witnesses aboard a sports fishing boat observed a UFO off Martha's Vineyard. The witnesses were three members of the Woods Hole Oceanographic Institution and two Pilots (one was an Air Force Jet Pilot).

The five men were aboard Ronald Veeder's boat, the Sports Fisherman. At 3:20 pm, a strange round object bearing southeast approached the ship at high speed. The members through binoculars observed the strange craft. The witnesses stated the UFO appeared to be a sphere with some sort of sensing elements or spikes protruding from it. The tips of the "spikes" were red.

Figure 16 - Sphere with sensors protruding

The object hovered for about two minutes then took off to the southwest at speed higher than any UFO the witnesses had ever seen. The sighting was reported to Otis AFB, Mass. The notes to this event are as follows:

1. October 22, 1957, Air Force Colonel G. Griffin sent a memo "Unidentified Flying Object" to the commander of the AF Cambridge Research Center at Bedford, Mass. The report suggested the five (5) citizens noted an object, which descended to 30,000 feet, which appeared to enlarge to the shape and size of a beer can. The object had fins or an antenna. It appeared aluminum like in color and reflected the sunlight. The object was traveling at a tremendous speed. Two people through binoculars observed it before it disappeared. The letter was classified "Confidential."

2. The witnesses were Ronald A. Veeder, Capt. Scott Bray, and Capt. Eugene Mysona with one an Air Force jet pilot.

3. The Air Force labeled this object a "Balloon." [ccxv]

Updated information on the case:

According to NICAP, this fishing story was a "Hidden Report," the above encounter was reported to Otis. The report said that several weeks later on November 4, an object described as a sphere with fins surrounding it was sighted from Cathedral City, California.[ccxvi]

Comment: A Balloon! Really?

The above case is one of a reality check for all of us readers. I have never heard of a balloon that would descend from 30,000 feet, approach a boat at high speed, stop to hover for two minutes, reveal having some sensing units protruding from it, then turn around and fly off "at speeds greater than the witness has ever seen."

Hammerfest, Norway
UFO Hovers over Ship

Ship | On August 31, 1959, a mysterious object which was cylindrical, approximately 10 feet in diameter and made no sound, hovered above the bows of the Norwegian vessel Aida near Hammerfest.

Captain Kaara Eakariassen reported the sighting to a Hammerfest radio station. The captain, who was alone on board the vessel at the time, said the object remained for five minutes before rising rapidly out of sight.[ccxvii]

Fishing: Spokane, Washington
People on house Boat at lake see two objects

Fishing | On August 21, 1961, a family on a houseboat near Spokane, Washington reported the following event:

"The sighting Monday night of a bright silver object that exploded over Pend Oreille Lake was reported by a Spokane resident today. James M. Wilson, 1606 Cuba [Street?], said he and his family were in a houseboat at the lake when they sighted the object and a second object at 10:35 pm.

He reported: 'Number one object was seen first. It was bright silver, traveling at terrific speed when first seen. It seemed to slow down as it exploded. Number two object was seen right after the explosion. It circled the spot where the first object exploded, stopped for about two minutes in one position, and then started up and completed a circle.

It then seemed to go straight up out of sight. 'My first thought was that the second object was a satellite, but due to its actions, it couldn't have been. 'Mr. Wilson said.

"Air Force officials at the Fairchild base operations section reported interest in the sighting but had no comment."[ccxviii]

Fishing in the Bahamas, 120 miles southeast of Miami
UFO: "Came down at them."

Fishing | On June 21, 1968, about 11:30 a, two Miami newspaper reporters, a photographer, and a captain and first mate of a pleasure boat were fishing in Bahamian waters when they reported a UFO.

At that time, "two strange objects" came straight down at them, low over the water and across their bow. The elliptical UFOs had "what appeared to be stubby, wing-like projections jutting out from with either side." The objects remained in sight for two minutes.[ccxix]

Comment | This was not to our knowledge reported to the Air Force, it was not located in the US Air Force Project Blue Book Files for 1968.

Fishing Boat "Felipe" off the Coast: Chile

Fishing | On May 1972 The Chilean trawler, "Doggenbank" and the fishing boat "Felipe" were allegedly paced for five hours by a UFO which changed colors from bright blue to light green to orange-red.

The object, according to Captain Morales of the fishing boat, suddenly "showed up" near them, and after fifteen minutes began changing colors. It then approached the ships at high speed making a "high-pitched hum" which terrified the crews, consisting of 35 men.

The trawler was towing the fishing boat, and the object kept them company at approximately 1,500 meters altitude (about 5,000 feet) until they reached the harbor, a period of about five hours. The report was made on May 2nd out of Valaparaiso, Chile.[ccxx]

Fishing Trawler off Novy Georgy Island
Two ships confirm hovering UFO

Fishing | On December 1977 the crew of the fishing trawler Vasily Kiselev also observed something quite extraordinary. Rising vertically from under the water was a doughnut-shaped object. Its diameter was between 300 and 500 meters.

The UFO hovered at the altitude of four to five kilometers. The trawler's radar station was immediately rendered inoperative. The object hung over the area for three hours and then disappeared instantly.

The testimony of Alexander G. Globa, a seaman from GORI, a Soviet tanker, was published in Zagadki Sfinksa magazine (Issue # 3, 1992) Odessa.

In June 1984, GORI was in the Mediterranean, twenty nautical miles from the Strait of Gibraltar. At 16:00, Globa was on duty. With him was Second-in-Command S. Bolotov. They were standing watch at the left bridge extension wing when both men observed a strange polychromatic object. When the UFO was astern, it stopped suddenly.

S. Bolotov was agog, shaking his binoculars and shouting: "It is a flying saucer, a real saucer, my God, hurry, hurry, look!"

Globa looked through his own binoculars and saw, at a distance over the stern, a flattened out looking object (it did remind him of an upside-down frying pan). The UFO was gleaming with a grayish metallic shine. The lower portion of the craft had a precise round shape, its diameter no more than twenty meters. Around the lower portion of it, Globa also observed "waves" of protuberances on the outside plating.

The base of the object's body consisted of two semi-discs, the smaller being on top; they slowly revolved in opposing directions. At the circumference of the lower disc, Globa saw numerous shining, bright, bead-like lights.

The seaman's attention was centered on the bottom portion of the UFO. It looked as if it was completely even and smooth, its color that of a yolk, and in the middle of it, Globa discerned a round, nucleus-like stain. At the edge of the UFO's bottom, which was easily visible, was something that looked like a pipe.

It glowed with an unnaturally bright rosy color, like a neon lamp. The top of the middle disc was crowned by a triangular-shaped something. It seemed that it moved in the same direction as the lower disc, but at a much slower pace.

Suddenly, the UFO jumped up several times, as if moved by an invisible wave. Many lights illuminated its bottom portion. The crew of GORI tried to attract the object's attention using a signal projector. By that time Captain Sokolovky was on the desk with his men. He and his Second-in-Command were watching the UFO intensely. However, the UFO's attention was distracted by another ship, approaching at the port side. It was an Arab dry cargo ship, on its way to Greece.

The Arabs confirmed that the object hovered over their ship. A minute and a half later the UFO changed its flight's trajectory, listed to the right, gained speed and ascended rapidly. The Soviet seamen observed that when it rose through the clouds, appearing and disappearing again, it would occasionally shine in the sun's rays. The craft then flared up, like a spark, and was gone instantly.[ccxxi]

Chapter 21: Submerged UFOs

UFOs fly in the sky and also can travel underwater. It is incredible to think that UFOs can enter the water without exploding and travel extreme speeds under the ocean surface.

It is not known if the pilot goes underwater to avoid radar detection or look at the creatures in the sea. A declassified DIA (Defense Intelligence Agency) document that revealed several Navy personnel and onlookers observed UFO crews from one ship assisting the crew of another ship in fixing their broken craft. This has occurred several times and at great depth (at least 100 to 200 feet).

UFO submerged: Rostov region, Russia

Fishing | In the summer of 1945 during the day, a 9-year old boy was alone fishing for his family's meal and was about to return home when he watched a "giant plate" descend from the sky. The boy was fishing at Taganrog Bay, Sea of Azov, Rostov Region in Russia.

The saucer smashed into the water causing a strong impact and creating a fountain of water spray all around the witness, which totally soaked him. The plate was about 5 meters in diameter; its hull was metallic reflecting the rays of the sun.

Incredibly the witness felt no fear. The disc had descended on a sandbar, slightly covered by water only several meters from which the boy had been fishing. Suddenly, bubbles appeared around the disc, and a "man" came out from the disc. The man was dressed in a silvery overall.

He "jumped" from the top of the disc and approached the witness. He stopped at about 6 meters from the boy. His head was completely hidden under a non-transparent, oval-shaped helmet, and he had something resembling a large "can" behind his shoulders made of a dark-toned material resembling tinted glass.

There was some communication and then the "man" waved goodbye and climbed into the disc and vanished inside. The object rose up, hovered briefly, and submerged into the water like a submarine. At this point, the witness took his bucket and went home.[ccxxii]

The Pacific Ocean off Fort Bragg, California
"UFO Hits the Ocean"

Fishing | On July 7, 1947, around 3:10 pm two witnesses were surf fishing and observed a flat, glistening object approach them from the ocean. The incident took place on the Pacific Ocean off Fort Bragg, California.

They could not estimate its height as it was dropping rapidly and finally hit the water approximately a quarter of a mile (400 yards) offshore with an enormous splash. It was traveling at a high rate of speed, and just before it hit the water, they heard a humming sound. The object floated for a few minutes and then appeared to have sunk. Estimated to be the size of a large truck tire.[ccxxiii]

UFO Crashes into the South Pacific Ocean: Japan

Fishing | On April 19, 1957, at 11:52 am of April 19, a Japanese fishing boat Kitsukawa Maru was en-route to Japan from the South Pacific Ocean. The bosun and four crew members spotted two metallic very silvery craft descending from the sky and suddenly dived into the sea. After the craft submerged, there occurred violent turbulence.

"The bosun thought at first the objects were jet planes, but they had no wings and were approximately 10 meters long. His ship searched in the water but did not find any wreckage."

According to reports – the objects were never identified.[ccxxiv]

Fishing off Catalina; California
Surfaced UFO with occupants repairing ship

Fishing | On July 28, 1962, According to the article, on July 28 the skipper of a chartered fishing boat spotted lights in the darkness just before dawn about six miles southeast of Avalon (On Catalina).

He noted the lights were low in the water and apparently stationary as he swung his 46-foot craft through a change of course toward the tip of San Clemente. The lights were almost dead ahead by then, and he trained his binoculars for a good look.

The fisherman was startled to see a squat, lighted structure in which several men were working, although the enclosure seemed empty of any object. The skipper and another member of the crew view the strange sight. They described it this way:

"It appeared to be the stern of a submarine. We could see five men, two in all-white garb, two in dark trousers and white shirts and one in a sky-blue jumpsuit. We passed abeam at about a quarter-mile, and I was certain it was a submarine low in the water, steel gray, no markings, decks almost awash, with only its tail and odd aft structure showing."

Then: "it startled toward us, and I turned hard to keep clear. The UFO swept past us at surprising speed and headed toward the open sea, still on the surface. There was no noise that I could discern, no trailing white wake, just a good size swell.

The skipper thought for a while it was just an American sub on the surface for a small repair, but the odd superstructure puzzled him, so he reported to Naval Intelligence. The Navy reacted fast, taking detailed statements, having the skipper study alien submarine silhouettes and carefully checked his log for course changes, times and distances involved.

The Los Angeles Times after hearing about the incident checked with the Navy, got a cryptic answer: "There's nothing to it," Washington DC public information reacted the same.

Mr. Miles feature went on to say that no identification was made.[ccxxv]

UFO emerges from Lake Hefner: Oklahoma

Fishing | On August 1965 around 1:30 pm a 55 – 56-year-old Oklahoma City man fishing at Lake Hefner, Oklahoma when he observed a larger UFO.

According to the observer, the object was "saucer-shaped" with a dome on top, and flat bottom rose out of the Lake. It then hovered and flew off. The observer was admitted into an Oklahoma City Hospital in a state of shock. According to the records the sighting took place on Saturday afternoon at 1:30 pm.

Another youth reported seeing it rise from Lake Heffner or its shoreline.[ccxxvi]

Comment | The interesting thing about this case was the fact was that Flying Objects over Oklahoma were being seen by the Oklahoma Highway Patrol as well as tracked on Radar from Tinker AFB in Oklahoma from July 31, 1965 (1:30 am) through August 4th at various times and locations.

The objects were described as round or triangular shaped ships. In one case on the 4th – Twenty-five churchgoers observed several UFOs moving through the air and standing still at Cushing. Then around 8:44 pm a green, white colored UFO landed in a field behind a person's home at Tulsa.

Fishing off La Guaira, Federal District: Venezuela
"UFO emerges from the Sea."

Fishing | On August 4, 1967, during the early morning hours Dr. Hugo Sierra Yepez was fishing from his boat north of Arrecife, near La Guaira, Federal District, Venezuela when he reported a UFO.

According to reports, Mr. Yepez felt a vibration, and the seas "began to boil in big bubbles." A gray-blue flat globe then emerged from the sea about six meters in diameter.

As the object hovered close to the surface, he noticed a revolving section with triangular windows. The UFO then ascended in a curve, then shot upward into space.

One report stated the object was "Saturn shaped" having a ring that was red and blue.[ccxxvii]

Comment | This was not to our knowledge reported to the Air Force, it was not located in the US Air Force Project Blue Book Files for 1967.

Fishing Schooner: Chile
"UFO sunk below water."

Fishing | On September 25, 1971, around 10:00 am the entire crew of a schooner, en route from Antofagasta to Iquique witnessed a UFO.

Mr. Dietrich Barz, manager of the Guanaye Fishing Co., received a radio message from Manuel Malatesta the captain of the Martir Pescador, describing the event. At 10:00 a.m., local time, the Guanaye Fishing Co. released the following press statement:

"Our schooner Martir Pescador, sailing from Antofagasta to Iquique observed today at 6:10 hours a red ball of light which hovered over them for several minutes. At that time, they were 20 miles south of the mouth of the river Loa, 5 miles from the coast."

Afterward, the unidentified body sunk in the water about 3 miles from the ship.

The phenomenon was observed by the entire crew, which sails under the command of Captain Manuel Malatesta.

This report concludes with other Chile sightings over the next few weeks.[ccxxviii]

Fishing at Gulf of San Matias: Argentina

Fishing | On March 2, 1975, a group of men on a fishing boat saw a bright light with a definite form behind it moved horizontally through the evening sky at a low altitude at Golfo San Matias, Argentina. The crew was north of the Valdez Peninsula.

The object came from the Patagonian mesa flying out to sea and made a loud buzzing sound. It stopped in the air and dived under the sea.[ccxxix]

Fishing near San Benedetto del Tronto: Italy

Fishing | On November 8, 1978, around 5:30 pm while fishing on board of the "Exodus," three fishermen (Flaviano Mattiucci, Gennaro Mattiucci, and Dino Focaracci) saw, at low altitude and for a few seconds, a red and yellow spherical light. After emerging from the sea, it seemed to return to it, after rising and falling from the sky.

About one hour later, the radar of another fishing boat, the "Andrea Padre," reported a moving submerged object, which appeared to follow the vessel.[ccxxx]

Chapter 22: Near Planes and Jets

UFOs have been approaching military planes since the 1940s. Initially, these sighting shocked our pilots as to what they were. Just imagine you stepped into a P-51 and took a ride.

And once you get to 10,000 feet, a UFO suddenly appears out of nowhere and sits off your right wingtip. How would you react? Would you think you would be calm and view the object? Would you panic and try to get away from whatever it is?

Figure 17 - P-51D-5NA "Mustang" |ccxxxi

There is an innate mistrust between UFO pilots and military pilots. This mistrust came about from the "shoot down" orders put in place by the United States, Britain, Russia, and other countries during the 1950s.

In response to UFOs being shot at, the extraterrestrials beings had only two options. They could "run away from the conflict" or "defend themselves." For UFOs – they lost pilots and craft, yet for human's, it was far worse.

Many top officials around the globe are now on record stating they lost hundreds of pilots and planes chasing UFOs. These countries include the United States, Russia, Spain, Britain, and Brazil.

Witnesses observe Dangling Lights while fishing: Kansas Air Force Jets sent to intercept objects
Pilot: "What I saw was no imagination."

Fishing | On July 19, 1956, a news release stated "several unidentified tear shaped objects that case weird lights in the sky caused a new mystery when they were reported seen floating over several Kansas communities early today.

Two of the strange objects, with lighted, dangling tentacles, were viewed for five hours this morning over Arkansas City by four people and three policemen while fishing. The mysterious "bulbs" cast a metallic blue or bluish green light and moved slowly, frequently changing positions. Witnesses in Wichita, Hutchinson, Eldorado, and Wellington, Kansas, also reported seeing what appeared to be huge blub dancing in the sky.

A state policeman first said seeing the objects moving east at a high rate of speed near Hutchinson. Later, McConnell Air Force Base at Wichita sent out a B-29 Bomber, and Smoky Hill AFB dispatched two jet planes to investigate. A mysterious object also was picked up on the Radar Screen at Hutchinson Kansas Naval Air Station.

News articles report that the Denver Post reported the Kansas highway patrol said the object was being tracked by Radar at the Naval Air Station in Hutchinson.

The UFO was described as a ball of light traveling east at high speed. The reported stated a B-47 was dispatched from Forbes AFB, Topeka. The pilot reported seeing "waste gas torches in an oil field: However, in another report, he added: "What I saw was no imagination."

According to the reports the objects remained until daybreak first being seen around 3:00 am. One emporium officer stated the light came on an off and if being turned "on and off."

These objects were reportedly moving vertically and horizontally. The head of the object was green or blue, and at times streams of light would be directed down toward the earth and then extend from the sides of the object. It was "tear-shaped" one observer stated.

The Air Force labeled the sighting a "balloon" as a few had been known to be released from Dodge City or Wichita. There was no evidence in the Air Force files to indicate the balloons were in fact in the sky at the time.[ccxxxii]

Squirrel Hunting: Vicksburg, Mississippi
(Disc dive at Commercial Airliner)

Hunting | On October 31, 1956, Mrs. Marion Love reported seeing a big silver object having dazzling brilliance.

Mrs. Love and her hunting companion, Mrs. Jewel Hawthorne were hunting squirrels in the woods east of Vicksburg. The two women became frightened when they saw the object.

According to the paper, she observed a similar object last Thursday in which another person from Vicksburg watched a Disc shoot toward a commercial airliner. The UFO was described as large and metallic looking disc.

The articles point out 4 aircraft crashes occurred on November 27th. [ccxxxiii]

Comment | For anyone who believes these objects are made by a man of earth, one has to answer the questions: "why would a military secret disc dive at commercial jets?"

Coon Hunting: Indiana

Hunting | On November 14, 1966, around 11:30 pm several men coon hunting at Connersville, Indiana observed a UFO at close range. The sighting location was 5 miles NE of Brownsville, Indiana.

About that time, a plane started circling slowly at an altitude of 1,000 feet. One observer then spotted a bright star to the east, which grew larger and appeared to be approaching the group. At times it stopped and hovered, glowing a yellowish color.

As the object got closer, the plane flew to the right of it. The plane's engines cut out when the UFO was near the plane. The round star light object then was the size of an orange at arm's length and flew nearby overhead by a tall walnut tree.

One hunter flashed light from his flashlight at the object, and at that moment it took off. It left at a 45-degree angle to the west. The person who shot the flashlight at the UFO said he "wanted to communicate" with it.[ccxxxiv]

Comment | On several occasions, I have myself flashed light from a high-powered flashlight at these objects. In some cases, they will approach. On other occasions, they will stop in midflight and watch. Finally, in other cases, they will continue to move on a suddenly "flare up" as if to communicate. In one instance, we exchanged flashes back and forth – 4 times. It seems they will communicate some form of a message which could be interpreted as: "I acknowledge – I see you."

Chapter 23: Windows and Occupants

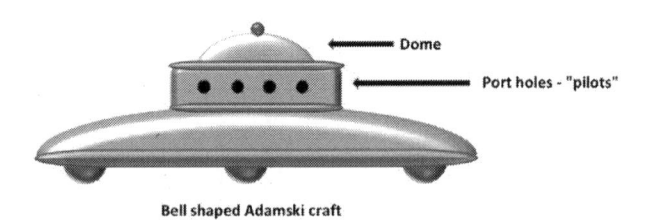

Bell shaped Adamski craft (Dome; Port holes - "pilots")

Whenever we see a UFO, there is a 60% to 80% chance the vehicle is operated by creatures (human type beings) from other worlds. The remaining 20% to 40% are remotely controlled drones, dispatched by mother ships to carry out routine assignments.

The size of the ship and the type of mission the vehicle is assigned will determine how many individuals will be on the spacecraft. If more routine, like checking stockpiles of nuclear weapons at the US and Global military bases, we can suspect the spaceship will carry only a few individuals. However, if on a major assignment such as the Aztec New Mexico crash in the past 70 years, we see the number of crew members reaching 100 extraterrestrials (e.g., persons).

Two discs at Sea: Eureka, California
"A row of Lighted windows seen."

Fishing | On March 29, 1950, two fishing boats at sea observed a UFO. Allan McVicar and Axel Johnson skipper and crew of the fishing boar Milmar, saw a light object passing overhead from their fishing boat about five miles out from the mouth of Klamath river at 7 o'clock Wednesday night.

Johnson who was standing by the wheelhouse first saw the brilliantly lighted object; He called it to the attention of the skipper who also saw it also.

The two men reported that the lighted object was traveling at a terrific speed and as they watched it, it zoomed along on a level plane and then shot suddenly upward and out of sight.

Frank and George Saubert, owner of the fishing vessel "Ethel S" also saw the object and reported it on a two-way radio. The Ethel S was in the vicinity of the other boat when it sighted the object. It was getting dark, so McVicar stated he is positive that it was not a celestial body, as it would not have shown so brilliantly.

It was traveling too rapidly for an airplane and appeared to be perhaps a row of lighted windows, according to the skipper and crew of Milmar.[ccxxxv]

UFO with windows at Otter Tail Lake, Minnesota
Fishing Trips ends up catching a UFO

Fishing | On July 14, 1955, around 7:48 pm a family reported seeing a UFO at Otter Tail Lake. According to the '*Daily Journal*,' a story was recently covered in the '*Wadena Pioneer Journal*' about a flying saucer seen at Otter Lake. As such the paper decided to pursue the story for more details. The family concerned about ridicule decided to keep quiet for some time, then came forward.

According to the observers, a summer resident was returning from the Lake on a fishing trip when something appeared in the sky, which drew their attention. Jokingly they said to one another: "They won't believe us." 15 minutes later after docking the boat, the object still being visible they decided to get the binoculars to observe the thing. The UFO was described at first as an elongated balloon, squashed together and seemed to be standing perpendicular.

They observed whatever it was, it was not affected by the winds – there was "no drift." According to one of the men: "It just stood there." With the binoculars, they made out windows, or portholes along its side – like a train coach.

According to them, the color was "whitish" or something like aluminum in the bright evening sun. They exclaimed the UFO was so bright you could not tell.

They believed the object was sitting at 25,000 feet and half the size of the moon. They then said it started to move against the clouds and in a sweeping arc disappeared to the south as it entered two layers of clouds.

His final words were: "I can't help but feel it was somebody up there making an observation, for it stayed there so long."[ccxxxvi]

Updated information on the case:

In a later publication, Loren E. Gross reported the staff of the local paper was told the story. They began the story with the following points:

"With the thought of being ridiculed by friends, and accused of suffering from hallucination, a summer resident at Ottertail Lake and his guest have kept silent on a story that the Mayor may not be important. The story, released by the parties this week, with the understanding that names be withheld.

The story started out: "I'm just as sure it was a flying saucer, as I am sitting here in your office." With this they tell of the following incident:

"While the resident and his guest were returning to the cottage from a fishing trip on Ottertail, their attention for unknown rational reason was attracted skyward, and they sighted a bright object suspended in the sky."

As they came along in the boat, they continued to watch the UFO, and jokingly remarked, 'they won't believe us, but we can say that on this night, at twelve minutes to eight, July 14--and--sighted their first flying saucer,' and continuing in lighter vein wondered if they would have their names in the second book when it was written on flying saucers.

"About fifteen minutes later when they docked their boat, the object was still visible but had moved to another quadrant. Calling to his family, the resident told one of his children to get his binoculars, as he wanted to get a better look at it. The entire group watched it for another possible fifteen or twenty minutes."

"In explaining the object, they state it appeared to be somewhat like an elongated balloon, squashed together, and seemed to be standing perpendicular. When it was first sighted, it was about 75 or 80 degrees to the east, and later moved into a south quadrant."

> "'Whatever it was, it wasn't affected by wind currents, for clouds moved around it, and there was no drift to it- it just stood still,' said one of the men."

'With the aid of the binoculars, they could make out what appeared to be a row of windows or portholes along the side of the object something like a train coach. On what they thought was the underside, was a 'V,' which appeared about the center off the craft to the front.

'It was whitish,' is the way the color was explained, 'maybe something like aluminum in the bright evening sun, but it was so bright it was hard to tell, it just looked 'whitish' is the best way to explain it.'

The object was estimated to have been at the height of 25,000 feet as near as they could determine from the cloud structure and it appeared to be about 'half the size of the moon.'

"When the object started its departure, they said it moved from the south slightly east, against the direction of the clouds, and then in a sort of sweeping arc started its vertical climb and disappeared into the south, passing through two thin layers of a cloud.

One witness stated; "I have never discounted the possibility of flying saucers, but I was always in hopes I could see one to verify it in my own mind and now I can,' and then went on, 'I can't help but feel it was somebody up there making an observation, for it stayed there so long.'[ccxxxvii]

A Cigar UFO with 4 porthole windows

Driving | On February 1957 around 10:00 to 10:30 pm, Mrs. Ina Salter from Ridgefield was visiting her daughter when she spotted an object while driving up a hill near a desolated area in Georgetown, Connecticut.

The trees obstructed the object until she came upon it. She took her foot off the accelerator, and the car came to a stop. The UFO was "cigar-shaped" without wings or fins of any kind.

The witness according to the APRO Bulletin stated, it "looked as if someone was holding a giant cigar in the air." The object was 10 to 15 feet to the left of the woods of the road and "hovering" not far off the ground. There were three to four portholes along the side of the object, and they were illuminated with a yellowish light.

Figure 18 - Giant Cigar ship with windows - Illustration

The portholes were approximately 18 to 20 inches in diameter. The observer then noticed movement inside the object through the portholes. In her words: "looked like shadows moving past the window."

The object had a large square bottom and was illuminated with a same yellowish light. I had the impression that the square was an opening because the light instead of going out, got smaller "as if a door was sliding along, the length of the square, scaling off the light."

She approached, and it suddenly rose straight up, staying parallel to the ground. It hovered for a second or two at just about tree top height than "sped away very purposely" still staying parallel to the ground.[ccxxxviii]

Communicating with Aliens

Saucer Hunting | On April 6, 1967, Mrs. Mary Hyre and reporter for the '*Ohio Messenger*" with another passenger (John A. Keel) was in an isolated spot on the Ohio River when a UFO appeared. The UFO was a pale red sphere about three hundred feet from their car at treetop levels.

One of the observers flashed his headlights on the UFO and to their surprise, the UFO returned the signal before shooting off into the night sky.[ccxxxix]

Comment | This indicated the occupants are intelligent and attempted to communicate with both witnesses before leaving the area. It shows the occupants are intelligent.

Hunting: Miami, Oklahoma

Hunting | On October 21, 1967, a retired Professor of Psychology a College Professor and his grown son observed a UAO at Miami, Oklahoma on the 21st of October. The four were on a hunting trip 18 miles west of the town, and when they reached their destination, it was daylight (6:15 am).

The men were just getting out of their cars when the sighting occurred. All were "rabid UFO disbelievers' and were stunned by the incident. The object, an elongated oval, appeared to be huge (all felt it was at least "a block long"), at tree-top level and no more than a half a mile away from the observers.

The object was soundless and gave off a brilliant white or blue-white light as it traveled at a very high speed. The Psychology Professor said he had the impression of windows along the side of the object and that he thought he could see vague figures moving behind the windows.[ccxl]

Hunting, Colorado – Disc with windows

Hunting | On October 31, 1967, five men hunting for deer in the desolate county of southwest Colorado stumbled upon a flying saucer. According to David Bernard:

> "I never had anything scare me so much in my life."
> "if I would have had to run, I just couldn't have."

David Bernard, brother in law, Jack Kerns, sons: Robert and Larry Bernard and Terry Kerns were witnesses to the phenomenon.

Bernard said they spotted the object near a dirt road, 12 miles south of Naturita, about 7:30 pm. Saturday it was a round disc with square windows and was 200 to 300 yards off the road.

Bernard said they took turns watching it through a scope on one of their rifles. He said seven or eight blue lights were flickering around the base of the object and it appeared they were moving. The UFO made no noise. He said he couldn't estimate how large it was except that it was a pretty good size. Bernard said he did not believe in flying saucers before the incident. He does now he said.[ccxli]

Fishing at Piney Creek Chews Ridge: California

UFOs with portholes

Fishing | On May 5, 1968, two ladies, both in their fifties and both married to prominent businessmen observed four objects while fishing on the morning of May 5 in the area of Piney Creek Chews Ridge Look-Out about 35 miles from Salinas and Monterey, California.

At 10:00 am the two observers were fishing at a reservoir on a private ranch. Their husbands were a few miles away herding cattle. The ladies heard the sound of a motor and thought the men were coming back in the pickup truck. Then they both spotted four metallic- appearing objects, oblong in shape and rather flat, with apparent size about that of the full moon. They were up Piney Creek Canyon and maneuvered in a manner that suggested that they could not possibly be conventional aircraft.

The women estimated the distance of the objects to be about four or five miles away, and they seemed to bob up and down incessantly. At one point one of the four objects left the others and appeared to approach the observers a short way, then rejoined the others. No details such as protuberances or portholes were observed. Most of the time the objects were seen against the background of the can' yon, and occasionally they would gain sufficient altitude so that they were observed against the clear sky.

Finally, two of the objects headed toward the west and disappeared from sight with a few seconds. The observers did not see the other two leave. The area where the observation was made is very isolated with no houses for at least seven miles. The Chews Ridge Lookout is the only building in the area.[ccxlii]

Comment | This was not to our knowledge reported to the Air Force, it was not located in the US Air Force Project Blue Book Files for 1968.

Chapter 24: Electromagnetic Effects

Electromagnetic interference with manmade equipment (having electric components) is a common occurrence when close to egg-shaped craft.

The egg-shaped craft propulsion system can impact the engines of cars, trucks, and plane. The effects can also extend to radios, television sets, clocks, watches, and lights. The interference is caused by the propulsion system of the egg-shaped craft to earth's gravitational field when near a manmade device.

If you want to know more about Electromagnetism, I have an article on my website at UFOETDOG.com on the subject matter. I also discuss this propulsion concept in my first book: "UFOs In U.S. AirSpace."

Lake of the Ozarks: Arkansas

Fishing | In 1953, the general manager and chief engineer of a St. Louis broadcasting station were fishing when they reported a UFO at Lake of the Ozarks.

Out some three or four hundred yards from shore, their outboard motor died. They were sitting there in the fog, listening for a passing boat, which might help them when they heard a heavy humming sound.

The two men could see nothing until the fog parted briefly; then about a hundred feet from them, and not more than five feet above the still waters of the lake, there was a shiny disc.

The unidentified flying disc was oscillating slowly, and both men noticed that directly behind it the water was dancing in thousands of tiny sharp-pointed waves.[ccxliii]

Comment| The Image of thousands of tiny sharp-pointed waves reminds me of playing a loud song causing vibrations on the waters surface.

Hunting: Conver, Georgia

Hunting | On November 17, 1968, a press report in the Atlanta Journal relates sketchy information about sightings in a swampy area near Conver, Georgia which is still under investigation.

Basic information is the following: Jim Beecham of Atlanta, who was coon hunting during the week of the 17th of November, saw a 70-80-foot object which hovered 300 to 400 feet above the ground in a swamp near Conyers.

The UFO was silent, whitish-orange in color and appeared to have "Zs" around its edge. Beecham and his brother were so frightened by the spectacle that they hurriedly left the area.

Other incidents involved a bank employee of Albany who claimed that his car's electrical system failed and the engine stopped when a UFO approached him while he was driving in a swampy area, and three coon hunters were frightened by a strange object bobbing in the air over some woods for about an hour.

Officials at Moody Air Force Base told the press that they would investigate reports of a UFO observed by several persons near Albany. One man described this one as a yellowish-orange oblong-shaped ball of fire, and others said it had blue and green lights, which upset their hunting dogs.

These incidents are under investigation and further pertinent details, when available, will be published if they merit the space.[ccxliv]

Night Hunting: Twin Falls, Idaho
"Electromagnetic Effects on Rabbits and Coyotes"

Hunting | On September 22, 1971, two boys, hunting at night, at Twin Falls, Idaho spotted an orange object with flashing lights that circled overhead for 45 minutes. The UFO initially approached them on a downward course, then momentarily disappeared.

After circling, it went out of sight over distant hills. The boys said they noticed rabbits running wildly in all directions while the object was in view, and coyotes could be heard yelping as though something was bothering them.[ccxlv]

Hunting Rabbits

Hunting | On September 1, 1978, Shortly after 8:00 pm in Llanerchymedd, Anglesey, Wales several villagers including a man hunting rabbits watched a bright white light descend slowly behind a new housing estate.

Other independent witnesses saw a large silvery sphere above a field and watched the cows panic, and neighborhood dogs start barking furiously. A woman and her young daughter looked out and saw three tall men in gray uniforms with caps or helmets attached to their suits walk across a field. She ran to the village to find some other witnesses.[ccxlvi]

UFOs while fishing at Somerset: England
"It was like all pandemonium let loose."

Fishing | On October 30, 1964, around midnight four businessmen on a night fishing trip reported an object described as a brilliant red light that lit the fields and the banks of a stream. The location was Somerset England.

A herd of about 50 cows made noise and ran when the object approached slowly at low altitude and hovered overhead.

According to NICAP: "The cattle were so terrified by the UFO that the men narrowly escaped being trampled. It was like all pandemonium let loose" said Sharman. "We hid behind a car, so the cows wouldn't sweep us into the water."

After a few minutes, the object accelerated and disappeared, and the cows quieted down. The presence or absence of sound from the Object is not addressed. No EM effects or physiological effects were reported. Fifty cows reacted to a low object.[ccxlvii]

Comment | This was not to our knowledge reported to the Air Force, it was not located in the US Air Force Project Blue Book Files for 1964.

Fishing Creek Valley: Pennsylvania
35 to 50-foot diameter Craft

Fishing | On April 1, 1967, around 6:30 pm three young children saw a sphere estimated to be 35-50 feet in diameter with two antennae and a varicolored halo at Fishing Creek Valley, PA.

The object approached at a low level, dropped to an estimated 40 feet altitude, and emitted a double-tapered light beam for 2 minutes that lit the ground 10 feet from the children. Two dogs barked wildly during the event (animal reaction). As they watched, the object suddenly disappeared.[ccxlviii]

Comment | This was not to our knowledge reported to the Air Force, it was not located in the US Air Force Project Blue Book Files for 1967.

Coming home from Fishing,
near Sargent Texas

Fishing | On July 5, 2005, around 8:50 pm near Sargent, Texas a man witnessed a UFO. The witness stated:

"I was coming home from a fishing trip in Sargent, Texas. I had just turned off FM587 onto FM2611 when, all of a sudden, the lights in my car blinked twice, and then the car went dead."

"I coasted to a stop at the top of a small hill that was a curve. I was frightened. For one, I am female and was traveling alone, and I was in the middle of nowhere. I thought that the reason for the power giving out in my car was because my brother had been using my car battery earlier in the day and may not have tightened the battery cables properly."

"I didn't have a flashlight on me, and I grabbed my cell phone to let someone know what had happened. Then I decided to get out of the car, knowing that my cell phone had a bright light on it, and I was going to check the battery cables."

"Before I could open my cell phone to turn it on, a bright bluish glow started to light up a wooded area across the highway from me. At first, I thought it was another vehicle coming up behind me, and I panicked for a moment because my car had stopped on top of the hill on a curve, and, if the vehicle were coming up the curve too fast, it would hit me."

"But I realized quickly that it was not another vehicle. I couldn't quite identify the light, but the woods got suddenly brighter. The light went bright like a blue-white light bulb. It was more like the light from a giant blue flashlight or helicopter [search] light."

"I watched it slowly start moving upward through the trees. I sat in complete silence while I watched it move up out of the trees until it was above the trees and clearly in the sky with the stars for a background. It was a huge bluish translucent ball of light, with the center of the ball much darker than the outer edges."

"The outer edges of the ball seemed to vibrate or tremble slightly. It continuously rose up into the sky, at first slowly, but, the higher it got, the faster it went. Which was straight up into the sky until it disappeared."

"I sat in the silent darkness for a few seconds and then turned my car keys, which I had never taken out of the ignition switch, and the car started right up."

"The UFO was about 30 to 40 feet up. It was huge, maybe 30 to 40 feet across, but I could be mistaken. It was much larger than my car-a Volvo DL wagon. I resumed my drive to Sweeny, Texas." [ccxlix]

Chapter 25: Near Industrial Centers

Figure 19 - Illustration of White Spheres over Nuclear Plant |[ccl]

Industrial plants have been visited by UFOs and their crews for over one hundred years across the globe. In several of my other books, I mention the crews most likely visit our production facilities to monitor smog (pollution) outputs as we manufacture cars, tires and other products.

The answers to these questions lay at the feet of the U.S. and other counties military establishments who have interviewed such extraterrestrial pilots.

Fishing | In the summer of 1933, Frank Van Keuren, an electronics assembler, and former Air Force veteran were fishing with his father in the land waterway complex between Tuckerton and Beach Haven, New Jersey when they reported a UFO.

"All of a sudden we were illuminated by a very bright floodlight from an object which couldn't have been more than a thousand feet... in the air".

The disc-shaped object was traveling slowly through the dark night sky. After displaying the bright light on the witnesses for several minutes, it crossed over and illuminated some radio tower in the distance.

According to Keuren, "it did not; have any running lights or make any sound."[ccli]

Circleville Waterworks: Ohio

Fishing | Last week of June 1955 two men had gone fishing witnessed a UFO near the Circleville Ohio waterworks. A local paper printed:

"Shrugging off with grins the good-natured jibes of their friends, two Circleville men today were standing firm in their story of a strange, 'square' light seen among the trees near Circleville waterworks."

"Chuck Rihl, confirmed how he and Dick Buskirk, had seen the light while in that area one night last week. They had gone there to fish. Rihl explained he and his companion, both employees of the local General Electric Company plant, had anticipated the ribbing their story would attract.

"'We just didn't say much about it,' Rihl laughed, 'because even as it was, they were kidding as plenty at the shop. Somebody said we had seen a flying saucer and boy, that did it!'"

"Rihl emphasized that he and Buskirk saw only a 'square and glowing light,' which otherwise had no particular details or pattern. Rihl added: 'It was a mighty bright light, though--brighter than anything I've ever seen before.'"

"Rihl said the light he and Buskirk saw glowed with an unusually brilliant 'bluish' glare. He said he and his companion first sighted the phenomenon after they had finished fishing and were walking back to their car, parked some distance away."

"It was about 10:15 pm, he said, and 'real dark.' The moon, he explained, was just beginning to rise and had yet to make an impression on the deep gloom around them. Buskirk carried a flashlight. The men said they are confident no other fishermen were in the area. And the moon, they recalled, was in a position where it could not possibly have been responsible for the mystery light."

"They first saw the light directly ahead of them while they were crossing a clearing and approaching the waterworks. It was well off to the right of the waterworks structure, motionless, and roughly at treetop level. Almost as soon as they noticed the light, Rihl said, it began to dim steadily and in a moment disappeared. The men, both able to claim more than average knowledge in the field of high-power lighting, stressed the fact that 'the light certainly didn't snap off suddenly---it dimmed, and very shortly went out altogether."

"When they first spotted the light, Rihl estimated, they were at a distance of approximately one-quarter mile. Made curious by what they had seen, they hurried forward but failed to find any sign of explanation for the light at the spot where they figured it had been. There was a dim light burning in the waterworks plant itself, Rihl recalled, but no sign of activity."

"Standing in the vicinity where they figured the light had appeared, Rihl said he and Buskirk were then puzzled by a noise in the trees overhead. He said: 'It's hard to describe that noise we heard. It was sort of like a big rustling of the trees, or like a whole flock of birds was fluttering around among the leaves. I honestly can't describe how it sounded. Believe me, it gave a fellow a strange feeling. As for Dick, he said: 'Let's get out of this place" And I certainly was willing to go.'

"Rihl said it would have been virtually impossible to have seen an object, even if of any great size if it had bee1 hovering overhead. The trees are fairly close together at the location he explained and the foliage is dense."[cclii]

Hunting: St Bernard Parish, Louisiana

January 21, 1977, two hunters had the scare of their life while hunting by boat in the Dyke Canal. At approximately 8:45 pm the two men spotted an extremely bright light which seemed to appear from nowhere.

The light moved over them and just hovered. There was no noise coming from the light source, but the men could feel heat emitting from it. The light moved slowly toward a fire station located close by and appeared to hover for about 30 minutes.

Finally, it moved over to the Shell Oil Plant for a while and then disappeared as quickly as it had come. The two hunters admitted that they had laughed about people reporting and believing such things. Now they feel differently.

When questioned as to what they thought the light source was they replied "We have no idea but would give anything to find out, All we know is that whatever it was it shouldn't have been there.[ccliii]

Chapter 26: Incredible Speeds

UFOs have been tracked on Radar speeding along the skies at 2,000 mph and above Mach 16. As unbelievable as it sounds, the visitors have the propulsion systems to overcome earth's gravitational forces easily exceeding what man-made crafts are unable to do presently.

Though many researchers have stated (including former Ben Rich, CEO Lockheed) that our government has retro-engineered alien technology, we are not able to view the progress made in black projects.

Moon shaped UFO, 3,400 miles per hour: Florida
Witnesses: Navigators
"Looking right at the spot and saw the damn thing lit up."

Fishing | On June 18, 1953, a group of individuals (two of which are Navigators) had been fishing off Key West at twilight (9:13 pm) when they saw a UFO.

They were sitting in the stern of skiff idly watching the course of bonefish his wife had hooked and was playing. He then said: "looking right at the spot and saw the damn thing lit up." They were anchored off the flats just east of Marathon, Florida.

According to the observers, everything was still, no clouds at all except a cumulonimbus piling up in the SW horizon at some 11 miles distance.

Suddenly, a half-moon shaped object "like a Quonset hut on its side", lit up out of nowhere, 20 degrees high and in the next 13 seconds traveled through approximately 100 degrees of arc, rising to 30 degrees when it was abeam, directly south, and then disappearing in the SW, behind a thunderhead.

In the 13 seconds under observation, the object lit up or went through 2 and ½ cycles, of illumination, of 3 seconds each, during which time it glowed a translucent, greenish –yellow, with dark splotches or markings on it. The drawing showing the half-moon shaped object had a "tapering tail" that was "dark and indistinguishable."

The outline of the object was still visible as it passed through the darkened phases, there was no sound associated with this phenomenon. All people saw it; one was wearing Polaroid sunglasses, another, prescription glasses, and the 3rd observer saw this with the unaided eye.

The estimated altitude of the object was 12-14,000 feet. The speed would have been 3,400 miles per hour. The incident was reported to the Department of Defense, Air Force Center, Pentagon (DC). The report was incredibly detailed information provided by the observer.

Further notes in the file stated: "To me, the most striking feature of the fantastic episode is the absolute and complete lack of noise that accompanied the phenomenon. There was not a sound of any kind, either before or after its appearance.... if you can exclude my exclamation "Jesus Christ, what's that's?"

In reviewing the drawing of the UFO in the file, it appears the reference to a Quonset hut would have been if someone were approaching it from the front. It is clearly a Half moon or half-circle shaped object on its side moving forward – horizontally.

The report was sent to 18th Air Force, Donaldson AFB (SC), TAC Air Command, Langley AFB (VA), ATIC WPAFB (OH) and to the Director of Intelligence Air Force, Washington (DC).

The Air Force did not come to a firm conclusion as a result of several factors:

1. the object changed direction sharply eliminating an Astro event,
2. winds aloft do not coincide with weather balloons.

The Air Force offered up the fact a TEW was equipped with a searchlight at the time pointing downward.

Written statements were located in the file including that of Paul M. Leino, Chief Radio Electrician, USN, Seaplane Base, Key West, Florida. The light being emitted from the thing reminded him of the 30-inch carbon arc searchlights used on Battleships.[ccliv]

Comment | There is "no confirmation in the file this is in fact what caused the sighting."

Crocodile Hunting: Australia
"It was something none of us had ever seen before."
"The thing was dead silent."

Hunting | On July 14, 1959, two prominent businessmen and two doctors who saw something while crocodile hunting near Karumba, Australia, made the front page; as did the "landing" on Prince of Wales Island with its story of terrified natives.

According to the article at 6:30 pm the men were 20 miles down the Norman River from Karumba when they observed the object. The object was described as being half the size of the full moon having an exhaust like tail.

The object was traveling twice the speed of a Canberra Jet Bomber. They said it stayed in the sky for five to eight seconds before disappearing. The men were Mr. J.H. Horn (director of General Motors-Holdens), Mr. W.A. Green (Managing Director of Eagers Holdings, LTD), Dr. Athol Qualye and Dr. C.A.M. Renou (Surgeon).

Mr. Green commented: "There are no shenanigans about this. It was something none of us had ever seen before".

According to them: "What impressed us most was that the object traveled parallel to the ground, It did not move down or up, as you would expect with something natural. And the thing was dead silent".[cclv]

Bow Hunting: Returning from Hunting: Minnesota
"it had such tremendous speed that it just disappeared into space."

October 21, 1965 at 6:10 pm, on the evening of 21 October 1965, Mr. Arthur Strauch, Deputy Sheriff of Sibley County, Minnesota in the company of four others, was returning from a bow hunting trip by car when he spotted a strange appearing object which appeared to be two thousand feet above the ground and one-fourth a mile distance in the northwest,

They were 2 miles west and 2 miles north of St. George. The group stopped the car and watched. Strauch got out of the car and watched the object with 7x35 binoculars, while the others watched from inside the vehicle.

After watching for about ten minutes, the group drove down the road about a half-mile and stopped. Strauch got out of the car and snapped the photo shown on this page, just as the object began to move.

The UFO moved into the wind (northeast) for what appeared to be several hundred feet, stopped for a few seconds, at which time its light changed from a bright white to a dull orange several times. It then moved toward the southeast at a high rate of speed and disappeared out of sight in the sky. As it passed over their heads, the observers heard an audible high-pitched whine, as made by an electric motor starting up.

The witnesses were: Arthur A. Strauch, 47, Deputy Sheriff of Sibley County, Minnesota, his wife, Mrs. Katherine Strauch, 44, housewife; Cary Martin Strauch, 16, high school student and son of Mr. and Mrs. Strauch; Donald Martin Grewe,26, a technician with Minnesota Valley Breeders Association, and his wife, Mrs. Retha Ann Grewe, 25, a registered nurse. All witnesses checkout as honest and reliable.

Mr. Strauch's description was most detailed as he viewed the object with the aid of binoculars. He said:

> **"I have no idea what it was.
> All I can report is that it was different from anything
> I had ever seen in the sky. I'm positive it was a machine
> driven by some inner power that has tremendous speed."**

"The outline was unmistakable through my binoculars, like that of a "flying saucer;" In a letter responding to our request for more detail, Strauch stated:

"The rounded top of the dome was a metallic silver gray that reflected the rays of the setting sun, turning it (the Rendition of a Strauch object as viewed through binoculars- Staff Artist Richard Beal) into a giant orange ball."

"Surrounding the dome were four small portholes that emitted a bright yellow light. Just below the windows or ports was an area that glowed a light blue. This light seemed to be a reflection of some inner light or perhaps exhaust."

"From the edge of the blue light's reflection to the edge of the flat saucer surface (outer edge) the outer ring was rotating counter-clockwise, causing it to throw off an aurora or halo of light that changed from orange to white with an overall tinge of blue and green. The extreme outer edge of the saucer glowed a bright orange, and this part did not move or rotate."

"To my left, or I assumed, the front of the machine was a black spot or perhaps an intake port for air. This indentation is visible on the picture but does not show up as clearly as I could see it through my binoculars. If there was another one on the other side, I do not know."

"The machine was not hanging or hovering parallel to the ground, but was at an angle, the front, as I assumed it to be, was tipped down about 15 degrees while it was hovering, and tipped even a little more as it left. I do not believe that the light went out in the machine, as it left and we lost sight of it, but rather that it had such tremendous speed that it just disappeared into space."[cclvi]

Fishing Camp: St Petersburg, Florida

Fishing | On April 4, 1965, several witnesses observed a UFO at St Petersburg, Florida. Observers were at a doorway of a post near 5 Guard offices observing the sky when a "tear-shaped object" appeared in the sky.

The UFO was said to be two feet wide and six feet wide. The object was traveling "far greater" than a jet and appeared as a falling star, giving off sparks. At one moment the object bounced up or rose in elevation. It was seen traveling from northwest to southeast. No sound was heard.

A Teletype message went to ADC ENT AFB (CO), 73 AIRDIV Tyndall AFB (FL), FTD Wright Patterson AFB (OH), CSAF, and OSAF Washington (DC).

The Air Force concluded the observance was caused by "satellite decay." Notes suggest decay object 1965-25B burned in or on April 4 at a later hour. They then said "possibly that this is the object seen. The "rise in elevation" was believed to be the entry into the atmosphere.[cclvii]

Chapter 27: Strange Lights and Noises

The shape and contents of a UFO is not always easy to see. At night when the sky is completely black, the most one can see is a bright light. This is, in fact, true if we are watching a UFO a half a mile away and is less than 20 feet in length. The only time such a ship would be visible clearly is if the ship was lit up and of extreme size (800 feet in length or more).

Seeing such smaller crafts in the black of the night skies is very frustrating as the details are difficult to pin down. In this case, only three things remain:

1. what color was the craft,
2. what shaped was the craft and
3. did it make any sounds or unusual movements?

Hitch Hiking | On July 8, 1947 *'The Hartford Courant'* ran a story of several local UFO sightings. In this next case; a "North End girl" and her parents witnessed a disc "zooming eastward" on Sunday evening.

Another individual hitchhiking home from Cherry Park in Avon witnessed three flying saucers about midnight. The report states he said: "they looked like big potato covers...and were traveling at great speed."

Another person seeing the same objects stated they "were like polished aluminum" and noted they were flying high.

On the next evening Monday around 8:40 pm, another witness stated they were "grayish" in color and did not appear to have a definite shape, but added more like a "tub." He noted it was traveling at an altitude between 8,000 to 9,000 feet. He stated it was going south.

Another person noted a similar object traveling in the same direction around 2:30 pm. Although his UFO was "black or brown" in color. Mrs. Carl Mueller of Berlin noted an object she thought was a plane, then she saw a real plane and noted this object began coming closer, "she believed it was a disc." Mrs. Mueller stated the object "seemed silvery" in color and was the size of a plane.

The final witness for Monday night came from Alton Hall on Laurel Street who said at 9:00 pm, the disc headed north, then flipped over and turned west. His sighting lasted 4 minutes and mentioned, "it looked more like the size of a teacup than a saucer." He stated the object was round, white and appeared "to shine with its own light." He believed it went faster than a plane. [cclviii]

Duck Hunting: Near Sacramento: California

Hunting | On November 13, 1952, around 6:05 am three duck hunters observed a blunt cylindrical object without wings at 5 miles south of the causeway on Highway 40 west of Sacramento.

The observers stated the UFO was seen for 15 to 30 seconds and had a blunt nose. The craft was cylindrical in shape and looked like a 1000-pound blockbuster. At a half, a mile distance the UFO appeared to be 20 feet in diameter. One observer, a former Air Force man, said it seemed not to have wings.

It was said to fly parallel to the ground in a straight line and was very fast. No sound was emitted from the object. No maneuvers were noted other than it appeared to waver or undulate slightly in flight.

The Davis Police department stated the observers who reported the incident were reliable businessmen and states he has no reason to doubt them.

The CAA could not confirm any flights in the area; however, the weather bureau was contacted, and the weather was clear. Both the Air Force and observers confirmed no unusual meteorological, natural or aeronautical phenomenon could account for the sighting. Travis AFB confirmed no flights were in the area at the time.

It was the opinion of Major Allan B, Newton (USAF) that the observers saw some definite object or phenomenon, which has not been otherwise identified.

The Air Force concluded the object seen was a "Meteor." Though no evidence to suggest, one landed in the state or adjoining state that day.[cclix]

Near the reservoir

Driving | On December 9, 1952, at 7:00 am near Derby Reservoir, Daniel Jones was driving to work when he saw suspended in the air above the reservoir what appeared to be three circles of fire, each about twenty feet in diameter.

After getting out of the car and staring at them for several minutes, they finally went off in a southerly direction. The UFO event happened at Derby, Connecticut. [cclx]

Cigar Ship: Brazil

Fishing | On September 3, 1954, a story of a wife from Mimoso do Sul and residents reported a Cigar Shaped Object of Ponte de Itabapoana.

According to the paper "Ultima Hora," Mr. Alcebia des Moura was fishing at night and was perhaps sleeping when he became wide awake by the intense light coming from a cigar-shaped speeding object.

The craft "buzzed" the place where Mr. Moura was fishing, several times and disappeared flying very low over the mountains. No sound was reported, but the light was powerful. At the same time, truck drivers near Cachoeiro do Itapemirin, on the road from Rio to Victoria, reported seeing the same strange craft.[cclxi]

UFO over a School

Ham radio Operator | On November 9, 1954, at 12:30 am a young couple at Damascus Ohio experienced a large UFO hovering over the local high school. The wife of a local ham radio operator was contacting her husband when the house began to shake, and dishes rattled. Throughout the house, she could hear a strange sound.

Looking out the front window of her home she could see a large ufo sitting over the local high school across the street. According to the witness, the UFO appeared to be 100 feet long, with a silver color and giving off a pale glow. She could determine its size by the area in which it covered the high school.

Then she heard the engines of a jet approaching heading for the location. This was then that the UFO disappeared. As soon as the jet circled the area several times, it left, and then the UFO reappeared.

She expressed the sighting of the strange craft dropping a small sparkling object on the roof or behind the school. The husband came back home and found his wife in a state of shock.[cclxii]

Hunting: Venezuela

Hunting | On August 18, 1966, Euclides Bencomo, Jesus Zapata, and Juan Ramos reported to authorities that on the 18th of August, while hunting in the Bum-Bum forests in Barinas, Venezuela they observed a strange luminosity behind some bushes.

The men approached the bushes and saw a huge egg-shaped object hovering some six feet off the ground. They said the strange object was giving off multi-colored lights which emanated from large round windows.

The UFO made a whistling sound. The three men became frightened, dropped their guns and ran. The *'APRO Bulletin'* shared; a posse was formed by those to whom the hunters reported the incident, to investigate the area. [cclxiii]

A dozen people report 300-foot diameter saucer

Motorcycling | On April 19, 1968, two boys on motorcycles near the Alleghany River near Pittsburgh observed a UFO within 50 feet of them on Friday. According to them the UFO was 300 feet in diameter and had a glass dome.

The UFO made a humming and whining sound, then swooped out of sight. They also mentioned stationary lights were along the circumference, and a red flashing light appeared on the bottom of the craft.[cclxiv]

UFO lights up Fishing Area

Fishing | On October 17, 1973, around 11:00 pm two young men were fishing when a UFO appeared over their favorite watering hole at Fort Walton, Florida. According to the men they were dishing in Santa Rosa Sound behind "Bacon's By The Sea" when a large orange UFO suddenly appeared.

The UFO lighted up the whole are and made no sound before it moved off out to sea. The case was reported to the military.[cclxv]

Comment | I do not know what's worse, being visited by a UFO when not expecting one or a UFO disturbing the quiet fishing hole with major lights and unusual sounds!

UFO at 500 feet

Golf course | At approximately 11:00 pm Ed Mulholland pulled off Interstate 84 to have a closer look at some lights over a golf course in Danbury Connecticut.

"I parked near the fairgrounds and got out of my car, it was 500 feet above me. It was huge, like a spaceship, and it had seven lights. They weren't extremely bright."

"Then all of a sudden all seven went out and these blue lights came on, but they didn't come on like you'd flip a switch. The came on very low, like a dimmer, and then all of a sudden they got to its brightest points and stayed on."

" The object was very low, and there was no noise. It was moving at a very slow speed, like ten tor fifteen miles per hour. I got a good look at it. The strange things is, it looked transparent. I could see the sky above it because it was a clear night. I didn't see any real shape. It didn't have any matter to it. [cclxvi]

Chapter 28: Attracted to Dams

Figure 20 - Chief Joseph Hydroelectric Dam, Washington [cclxvii]

It is believed that UFOs are attracted to our Hydroelectric dams to see how we generate electricity. It is also thought they visit these locations to recharge their engines.

Two sightings at Salmon Dam Twin Falls: Idaho
20 foot and 6-foot diameter Crafts

Fishing | On August 13, 1947, around 9:30 am County Commissioner L. W. Hawkins, and Mr. Brown observed 2 disc-shaped objects while fishing at Salmon Dam, 40 miles SW of Twin Falls, Idaho.

These objects were reported at 300 feet in altitude and appeared to be six feet in diameter. The object reportedly was reflecting light and making the echo of a motor, at 4,000-6,000 ft flying at high speed.[cclxviii]

Around 1:00 pm at Twin Falls 3 male civilians (a farmer and his sons) spotted an object at 75 feet in altitude traveling at 1,000 miles per hour. The disc was 20 feet in diameter and 10 feet thick. The UFO was seen 300 feet from the observer just above the Canyon Floor. Heading east to west along Snake River the thing traveled up and down over hills and hollows of the canyon.

The object was said to look like an oblong broad-rimmed type hat with low crown inverted pie plate.

A slight exhaust was seen at the side of the top or hood, which appeared to be a red tubular fiery glow. It emitted a swishing sound.

The notes in the file state: "As the machine went by the place, the trees over which it almost directly passed (Mormon Poplars) did not bend with the wind as if a plane had gone by, but "spun around on top as if they were in a vacuum."

The *'Times-News'* reporter who furnished the information to Special Agents stated that the observer appeared completely sincere about the machine. The names were kept out of the paper as the observers were fishing at Salmon Dam when they should have been working in Twin Falls.

The story becomes more complicated as the two observers watched two objects at a higher altitude several miles away. They were doubtful these objects were planes. According to the observers, the father of the two boys was sent to the river for some tops from his boat. As they were overdue, he wanted to look for them, when he noticed some 300 feet away some 75 feet in the air a sky blue object silhouetted against the steep walls of the canyon on the far side.

The canyon is nearly 400 feet deep and 1,200 feet across at that location. The object was traveling 75 feet in the air some 300 feet below the Canyon Wall.

The Air Force concluded this was an "atmospheric eddy." This theory was put forth by Dr. J Allen Hynek's deduction. The Times-News carried a drawing of the object on the front cover.[cclxix]

Comment | Dr. J Allen Hynek was a skeptic until the 1960's when he finally came to a conclusion, something was happening. At the beginning of project blue book, he was the chief Investigator scientist for the Air Force. As he became a believer, he kept his thoughts to himself or a few close friends to continue access to military sighting reports.

5 Discs were seen near San Acacia Dam: New Mexico

Fishing | July 17, 1948, around 4:50 pm two Kirtland AFB Sergeants on a fishing trip with their families saw a group of 7 aluminum circular possibly spherical objects approach from the S at 20,000 ft pass overhead at 1,500 mph. The location of the event was 5 miles south of San Acacia Dam, New Mexico.

The Air Force files were limited in content; however, a researcher after filing an FOIA was able to determine the following information.

At first, the objects appeared looking like snub-nosed jet fighters of unknown type. These objects then shifted from V formation to L formation to circular formation to no regular formation.

The objects did not emit any noise or trail.[cclxx]

Fishing at Blue Lake: Washington Dam gets UFO visitor

Fishing | On April 22, 1967, on or about the 22nd of April, Carey Lee Walt, and his wife and another couple of Ephrata, Washington, were enrooting to Blue Lake for early morning fishing. At about 1:00 am, he spotted a brilliant light in the sky ahead of him between George and Naylor Junction.

The object seemed to stay in the distance for a while, then the car began to gain on it, and at times the engine sputtered and seemed to lose power. The light at that time seemed to be only about 10 feet in front of the car, and he stopped the car, afraid that he was going to hit it. The light then moved off across a field, disappeared in the distance and then reappeared behind the vehicle. Walt and his passengers said the light stayed behind, turning to an amber color as it pursued the car for about 5 miles. As the fishing party approached Ephrata and other traffic the object disappeared.

When the party arrived in Ephrata, a report was made to the sheriff's officer. Sheriff Fletcher said the people were visibly shaken and still terrified days after the experience.

Mrs. Adella Scott, who reported the incident, included the following information: Ephrata is approximately 30 miles from the Grand Coulee Dam and is surrounded by several others: Rock Island, Dry Falls, Priest Rapid, and Wanapum. An AFB is located near the town also, and the Hanford AEC Project is south of Ephrata. Mossyrock Dam, third highest in the U. S., is near completion, is primarily a power project and massive power lines are. [cclxxi]

Comment | The Hanford AEC plant had UFO visits several times, and AF jets chased off the craft. This was not to our knowledge reported to the Air Force, it was not located in the US Air Force Project Blue Book Files for 1967.

UFO at Cowan's Ford Dam: North Carolina

Fishing | July 1972 around 9:30 pm businessman Robert P. Sartin, who lives near the Lake Norman Airport and Duke Power Plant's 150 high Cowan's Ford Dam spotted a UFO.

His attention to the UFO came when he heard children fishing from a nearby pier, who were shouting about an object in the sky. Four other persons became eyewitnesses to the UFO, which was seen about four miles East of the Marshall Steam Plant near Terrell.

The UFO appeared to be about the size of a basketball court and had a thickness, one-half its width. The object looked like "one saucer inverted on top of another and had a row of flashing windows through its middle."

The object had red, white and yellow-lighted windows and hovered in the area overhead for about 10 minutes, before it flew sideways, then moved up and away at an unbelievable speed as it disappeared in the sky. [cclxxii]

Chapter 29: Conclusion

In this book, we learned many things about UFOs appearing near sportsmen and sportswomen from 1947 to 1970.

How many believe in UFOs in the United States

As we discussed earlier; In 1966 a Public Opinion Poll by George Gallup shared: "More than five million Americans claims to have seen a flying saucer."

"About half the US adult civilian population believe these frequently reported flying saucers, while not necessarily saucers are real and not just a figment of the imagination." [cclxxiii]

By 1973, the number of Americans who have claimed to see a real UFO jumped to 15 Million. This again comes from a Gallop Poll. [cclxxiv]

Today as of 2018, over 50% of the U.S. population has either seen a UFO or know of someone who has seen the strange crafts from other worlds. The United States falls behind Europe where 80% of the population believes in UFOs.

What can we say about UFOs

They are "silent":

UFOs are crafts from other worlds

We now have much evidence, comprised of 1) radar records, 2) eyewitness testimonials, 3) deathbed confessions and 4) photographic, motion picture and video film records. This evidence is now available to civilians, scientists, and government agencies around the world. The most compelling evidence to date has been those cases documented at civilian airports, military bases, and nuclear and atomic storage sites.

UFOs travel through U.S. Air Space

Regardless of government protocols and procedures, these visitors in their advanced craft routinely violate restricted airspace around the world. The most significant concern we face as world citizens is the potential for midair collisions between these visitor spacecraft(s) and our civilian or military airplanes.

UFOs appear in all shapes and sizes

It is evident these ships display themselves in all shapes and sizes. To that end, the smaller vessels have been deploying from, the more massive ships (e.g., "Motherships"). This method of using smaller reconnaissance craft from larger vessels is very similar to how jets launch from modern aircraft carriers.

UFOs are attracted to sensitive military installations

Though we discuss U.S. UFO cases in this book, the same phenomenon is happening in Russia, China, England, Japan, France, and Belgium. These flying objects appear to perform surveillance of our capabilities as they hover over AEC plants, atomic weapons storage areas, power plants, uranium mines, and missile sites. One would assume the visitors appear to be monitoring what humans are doing with advanced explosive devices.

UFOs affect the electrical systems in our planes and cars

The very fact these flying objects can impact human-made navigational systems, engine performance can be a threat to humans in airplanes or fast-moving vehicles. Catastrophic failures in our modes of transportation could injure human beings.

UFOs have shut down the launch capabilities of U.S. and Russian Nuclear Missile sites

Military men at U.S. and Russian Missile bases have confirmed UFOs shut down nuclear silos in the 1960's and 1970's. We do not have the reason for doing so; however, deductive reasoning would suggest that these visitors are concerned "man is being told not to use such weapons" or that they "fear our weapons."

Scientists confirm UFOs are not manufactured on this planet

It has established by several government leaders around the world that the materials used in the construction of these flying objects do not appear in our periodic tables. This conclusion came from scientific studies at labs from early 1950's and 1960's. It suggests humans could not have built the flying craft we are discussing in this book.

UFOs when confronted, display flight characteristics similar to cat and mouse games

As far back as the 1940's the mission of these visitors appeared to be one of observance and non-hostile engagement. However, after the U.S. and other world leaders approved shoot down orders in 1952, we learned they would reciprocate if we fired on their craft and crew. After years of air battles and the loss of human pilots and planes, we can only assume the strategy changed from "shoot down" orders to that of "chase and escort them out of the area." We can expect this became a more appropriate practice when civilian passenger planes, around the world, were now being approached by these flying ships.

Testimonies confirm UFO occupants usually avoid human contact

There are UFO cases in Russia, France, England, Norway and other countries where these extraterrestrials beings (pilots) have attempted to communicate with men, women, and children.

When you read these stories, some appear to be friendly encounters while others seem to have hostile consequences. The part of our government obligation to educating humanity is to reveal to its citizens which species are friendly and which ones are hostile. If we engage a snake in the grass, we learn through the Boy Scouts of America, which snakes are friendly and which ones are poisonous. Not all people become Boy Scouts, so they have to learn these facts from other sources.

Should not the governments around the world put out a joint pamphlet on what species we should fear and which one to accept?

Regardless of whether the governments around the globe fulfill such obligation, reports reveal some extraterrestrials are afraid of man. After all, we shoot at them as they hover over our barns and cars.

If they have been studying us, they know more about us than we know about them. Most assuredly, UFO pilots fear our reaction when in close proximity to man. Man is unpredictable – we flee (flight) or fight!

No world power had the aerial dynamics of these extraterrestrial spacecraft

During the 1940's the power plants of the flying devices were beyond man's technology (sciences). The sheer number of sightings from 1945 to 1949, suggests these ships were built in mass far from earth.

Why Government Secrecy?

There were many reasons to keep the UFO information under wraps in the beginning. The CIA and other agencies gave UFOs a "Top Secret" level for National Security reasons. You can read more about this in my book "UFOs In U.S. AirSpace: Hard Evidence" chapters 1 and 2.

Today the only reason to keep this phenomenon a secret is to guard against the "extreme embarrassment" facing the very government agencies that established the public debunking campaigns. This could occur as the truth continues to be revealed. I believe none of us want our government agencies to face embarrassment for past acts. However, it is time to inform the people.

How to see a UFO in your backyard

The best way to spot a UFO is to;

1. Go outside after 8:00 pm when its dark.
2. Make sure your house lights are dimmed – take a flashlight.
3. Grab a blanket or lawn chair, lay in the middle of your backyard and stare at one star. If you look at the entire sky, you will miss the UFO. While staring at the one star, at some point, you may see out of the corner of your eye an object moving against all the other stationary stars.
4. At his point shift your eye to that object.

Now, the first thing you need to do is determine if this object is a satellite, the space station, a high flying plane or meteorite. Satellites and the space station continue across the sky "glowing."

Planes fly across the sky at high levels with usually white and red blinking lights. If they remain in on a constant path, these object may just be a satellite, space station or plane.

Meteorites do glow and have a short tail. Remember they usually have a downward trajectory and could burn out or hit the ground. They are typically brief sightings in terms of seconds.

However, if you suddenly see the object – "zig, then zag, or take a 90-degree turn, you have something that is not one of the above potential natural explanations.

If you have a video camera, I learned through experience it's great to have a tripod but its impractical for such quick UFO videos. Just try to keep the video camera on it as still and long as you can.

What to do when you see a UFO?

Report your UFO sightings to the following organizations. Make sure you jot down the time, your location, which direction the object was flying. Explain the description the best you can. If you have a clip of the craft, send it along with your online write up one of the following organizations. I recommend the following reporting centers.

FOR: NATIONAL UFO REPORTING CENTER (NUFORC)
Click: http://www.ufocenter.com
or
FOR: MUTUAL UFO NETWORK (MUFON)
Click: http://www.mufon.com/report-a-ufo.html

If you report your sighting, congratulations you just joined millions of individuals around the globe who also came forward to tell their story. Insert chapter ten text here. Insert chapter ten text here.

About the Author

John Scott Chace is the author of "UFOs In U.S. AIRSPACE" and several others books on the unique phenomena. He is the son of Colonel Chaplain Alston R. Chace (USAF Retired) and Nephew of Colonel Frank C. Chace (U.S.M.C.).

A Christian and military brat, he lived on many of the U.S. Air Force bases where the better known UFO incidents have taken place Langley (US), Lakenheath (UK) and others.

John became a witness to his own UFO sightings in Connecticut from 2011 to 2013. He then became a researcher, and historian to educate the public on the UFO reality and paradigm shift needed to understand this worldwide phenomenon.

John is the author of many UFO books at Amazon;

"UFOs In U.S. AirSpace: Hard Evidence"
"UFOs in European AirSpace: More Evidence"
"UFOs in Central and South America"

"The Invasion of Earth: UFO & Extraterrestrial Contact
"Project Blue Book: The Untold Truth"
"God, Extraterrestrials and Man: For Clergy, Counselors and Parishioners"

"UFOs In The Sky: Celebrities, Politicians and Military Officers"

"UFOs In The Sky: The Upper Midwest States
"UFOs In The Sky: The Southwestern States
"UFOs In The Sky: The Med-Atlantic States
"UFOs In The Sky: The Southeastern States

Addendum 1: The Ships "Illustrations"

This Addendum comes from one of my other books is dedicated to helping you to identify the type of UFO ships you have seen or may see in the future. It is segmented into shapes and then flight configurations.

Types of Ships

Motherships | Like aircraft carriers, motherships are larger vessels that transport occupants, equipment and smaller ships to various locations. Motherships come in multiple shapes. On earth, researchers have identified, Boomerang or "V" shaped motherships, Cigar ship formed motherships, Massive Disc motherships and Saturn shaped motherships. Some of these ships have been said to be miles long.

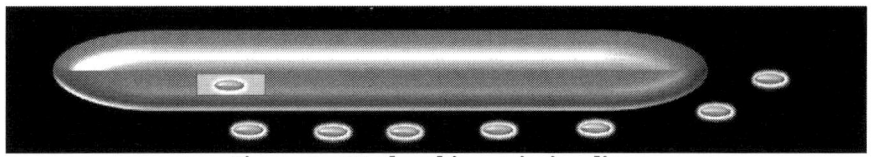

Figure 21 - Mothership retrieving discs

Sphere (Ball) | Sphere or Ball-shaped crafts are usually smaller in size from several feet to 20 or more feet. However, we have case files showing they can be hundreds of feet in diameter. The sphere comes in usually a silver color, but against the case, histories show us other colors are readily seen – white/yellow, green, blue, black and red.

Figure 22 - The Sphere UFO (seen frequently)

Disc (Disk) | The disc is usually from 12 feet to several hundred feet in diameter. They sometimes come with a dome and windows, but not always. The disc usually comes in silver color; however, it has been known to show other colors such as blue, black and red.

Figure 23 - The Disc (Seen Frequently)

Egg | The Egg is a ship that sort of looks like a squashed egg while in flight or more like a less elongated egg when landing. The egg is usually seen as silver at rest, white/yellowish in flight. Sometimes other colors red and green are displayed.

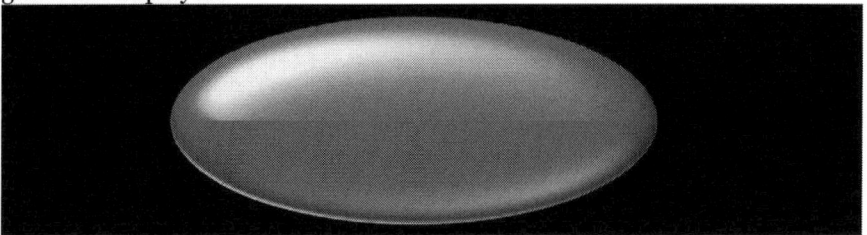

Figure 24 - The Egg shaped UFO (Seen Frequently)

Cigar | The Cigar ship can come in all sizes from several feet to several hundred feet in length excluding the motherships which are much more significant. Some of the Cigar ships come with windows / or ports. A few cases reflect the cigar may or may not have a dome. Some people have stated this dome looks like a conning tower (on a submarine but rounder). The cigar comes in many colors, black, silver, brown, white, copper (gold), red, etc.

Figure 25 - The Cigar ship (supercarrier)

Triangle | The Triangle can come in all sizes from several feet to several hundred feet in length excluding the motherships which are much more significant. The triangle is usually determined by its shape and size. Much like the Boomerang below, lights are stationed equidistant along the craft in the form of a triangle.

Figure 26 - The Boomerang or Triangle (Rare sightings)

And then at night – us usually cannot see the structure in the black sky – if the ship is black.

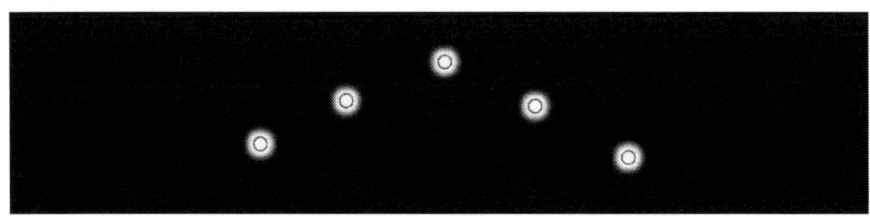

Figure 27 - Illustration of Boomerang (At night)

Boomerang | The boomerang is a massive ship, again, much like a mothership which can carry occupants, equipment and vessels. The Boomerang was the large ship seen in the 1997 Phoenix lights case as well as the mid to late 1980's cases in New York and Connecticut Hudson Valley sightings. Usually, with these ships, they are so vast we often just see the lights reflecting downward or to the front. Most of the Boomerangs in the Hudson Valley cases were darker colors – Mat Black, Dark Blues, etc.

Rectangle | The rectangle is a box-shaped craft that carries occupants to desired locations. I have seen these ships on numerous occasions in Connecticut. It is one of the most bizarre vessels as they are no round features or sharp nose or tail. It is an elongated box. The box I saw was dark blue with light blue windows.

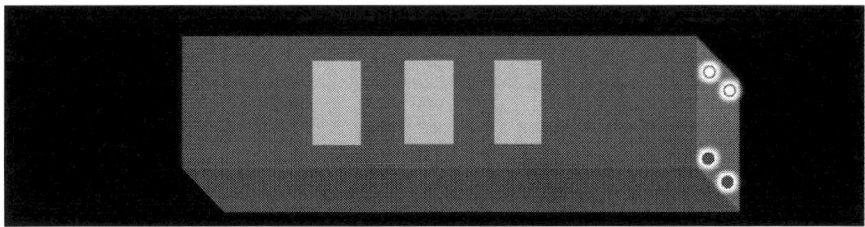

Figure 28 - The Rectangular UFO "The Box" - (Rare sightings)

Octagon / Hexagon | I have only seen one Octagon in my life, and it was silver with red and white lights. I have only heard of a few other cases being shared at NUFORC and MUFON. I share this case in one of my other books.

Figure 29 - The Hexagon or Octagon UFO (Very Rare)

Rocket Ship | I have only seen one rocket ship – a fuselage with no tail and wings over my home in Connecticut. The ship was silver/white in color with a canopy and windows down the sides that were black. I share this case in one of my other books.

Flight Configurations

Fleet | A fleet of UFOs usually consists (as far as I am concerned) with 5 or more ships. The ships can be of any type (sphere, egg, disc, cigar, etc.). If we use 5 as the number comprising a fleet, case histories tell us each of the above ships just described have flown over the US and European soil over the last 70 years.

Waves of 3, 4 of 5 objects (smaller fleets) | In many UFO cases, we will not see a fleet, but one or several. In some cases, reports have indicated several weaves of disc, egg or sphere ships traveling in pairs of 3 to 5 ships. This being followed by a second grouping of 3 to 5 ships and then followed by a third grouping of similar objects.

Figure 30 - Illustration of Discs in V formation - A Fleet of them

Solo | As it sounds, 1 disc or 1 of some type of craft traveling by itself.

Pairs | As it sounds, 2 discs or 2 of some type of craft traveling together

Pairs   **Solo**

Formations/configurations | Case histories show us the ships can arrange themselves in different formations. In Italy, about 25 ships flew in two V formations forming an X (cross) over the Vatican in the past. In the United States, many cases on file show many "V" formations or "L" Line formations. In a few cases "S" formations were noted as well as "Box" formations.

Box Formation   "V" Formation   Line Formation   "L" Formation

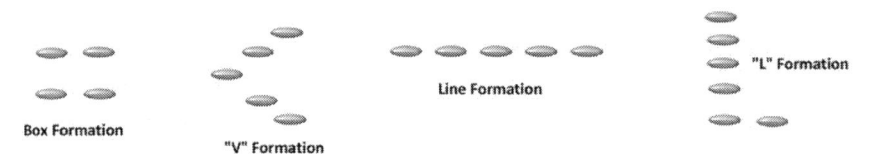

Figure 31 - Illustration of flight configurations

Tilted | Discs and Cigar ships have noted to "tilt" while hovering or moving in flight. This is not always the case. The "tilt" formation is observed in more of the disc cases than cigar ships.

Tilted Forward   Tilted sideways

Figure 32 - Discs in Various Positions - Illustration

Hovering | All UFO, extraterrestrial craft are able to hover (hang in the air). I have seen most if not all of the above ships come to a halt and hang. While hovering, the UFOs may be totally silent or give off a humming sound.

"Hovering"   "Tilting"   "Erratic"

Figure 33 - Discs in other positions - Illustration

Windows / Portholes | Not all UFOs have windows or Portholes. In fact, in my own case, I only noted windows on several discs and the rectangular (box) ships as well as a rocket.

Viewing Ports
Windows

Figure 34 - Typical Disc with windows

Plasma Emission | In all my own sightings, I have never seen any plasma discharge, yet many cases on file suggest it does happen. In my personal UFO cases, the objects were hovering or moving extremely slow. In the case studies across America, the plasma discharge is usually seen when the object is moving at a faster speed.

Plasma Emission

Figure 35 - Illustration of Yellow Sphere "glowing"

Domes / Canopies | Many ships (not all) come with some type of dome or canopy.

In a rocket ship, the canopy is more like a cockpit you would see on any plane.

The dome is a different feature. Most of the time seen on discs, the dome is at the top in the center of the craft.

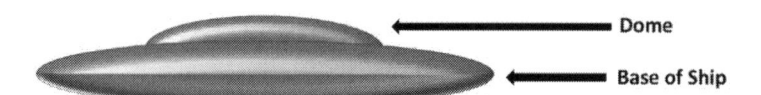

Figure 36 - Illustration of Disc with dome on top

Legs / Girders | I have yet to see a landed craft. All my sightings were close hovering several feet off the ground. However, case history tells us if a craft lands most of the ships, eggs, discs, and cigars have some form of legs that extend from the fuselage. Much like the Apollo Lunar Lander, the legs continue to provide support to keep the body of the ship off the ground.

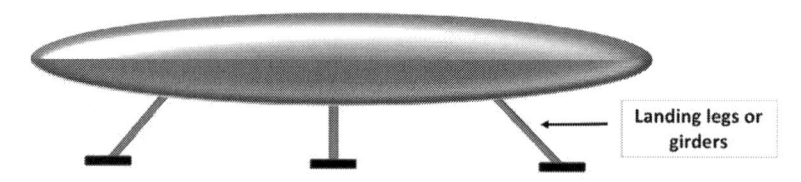

Figure 37 - Illustration of Landed UFO disc on landing pads

Addendum 2 : My Book and other Authors

My Books

"UFOs In U.S. AIRSPACE: Hard Evidence" | 2018

Provides a view of UFO activity in the United States from 1945 through 1970. The first two chapter specifically discuss the reasons for the U.S. government secrecy of UFOs as a reason for National Security.
This book covers UFOs following passenger planes, cars. Arriving at airports, people's homes, military bases, industrial and nuclear plants. The book also discusses fleets, motherships and electromagnetic effects on vehicles, people and animals.

"The Invasion of Earth: UFO & Extraterrestrial Contact" | 2018

Provides a view of UFO activity around the World from 1945 through 1970. This book is the be the European and South American version of UFOs in US AirSpace. The book focuses on UFO activity around the world with minimal US cases. The book covers UFOs and occupants at Airports, following trains, cars, bicycles, and motorcycles. Also discussed, UFOs landing at farms and other locations. As well as fleets, motherships and electromagnetic effects on vehicles, people and animals.

"Project Blue Book: The Untold Truth" | 2018

This book is an analysis of UFO cases covered in the U.S. Air Force Project Bluebook files. Examples are presented with the author's comments or counter-points to the findings or government conclusions of specific UFO cases in America. This book focuses on UFO cases from 1945 through 1970.

"God, Extraterrestrials, and Man: For Clergy, Counselors and Parishioners" |
2018

This book is specially written with counselors and clergy in mind to assist them as they engage parishioners who have seen UFOs. It is a Christian centered book to support all members of the Protestant and Catholic Church by providing basic answers to tough questions on Extraterrestrial origin versus man and how each relates to God. The book includes over 100 sightings by Protestant and Catholic Clergymen and Parishioners as a basis of reference. This book covers the emotional impact of the UFO sighting on Parishioners, worshippers, pastors and priests and provides ideas on coping skills.

"UFOs In The Sky: Celebrities, Politicians and Military Officers" | 2018

This book provides proof that beyond the citizen and military personnel who have seen UFOs so do celebrities like Jackie Gleason and Mayors, Congressmen and Presidents. The book provides evidence of UFO visitation as well as what UFOs are, why the UFOs were covered up. What politicians knew what when. Finally, the book goes into why some Congressman wanted to the truth out, while others did not.

"UFOs In The Sky: The Upper Midwest States | 2018

In this book, we provide many UFO sightings in the Upper Midwest six states including Indiana, Illinois, Ohio, Minnesota, Michigan and Wisconsin from 1947- 1970. This book covers cases such as UFOs following passenger planes and cars. UFO arriving at airports, industrial plants and Hospitals as well as many other exciting places.

Other Authors Books

The following are some of my favorite books on UFOs. I have provided links to Amazon. Please check to see if there are new updated versions more recent.

FRANK EDWARDS (TV AND RADIO COMMENTATOR)

1. "Flying Saucers - Serious Business" – 1966
2. "Flying saucers, here and now!" – 1968

Both of the above books are must-read. If you are on vacation, take one of these with you. You will not regret it.

DONALD E. KEYHOE (UNITED STATES MARINE CORPS; MAJOR)

1. "The Flying Saucers are Real"- Jun 1, 2011
2. "Flying Saucers: Top Secret" (Revised Edition) - Nov 22, 2016

Like Frank Edwards, Both of the above books are a must-read. If you are on vacation, take one of these with you. You will not regret it.

EDWARD J. RUPPELT (USAF, PROJECT BLUE BOOK)
1. "The Report on Unidentified Flying Objects": The Original 1956 Edition - Mar 1, 2011

JOHN G. FULLER

1. "Incident at Exeter, the Interrupted Journey: Two Landmark Investigations of UFO Encounters Together in One Volume" - Jul 1, 1997

A great book on the UFOs in New Hampshire during the 1960's.

Dr. J Allen Hynek (Astronomer and chief Scientist for project Blue Book USAF)

UFOs In The Sky: The Upper Midwest States
1. "Night Siege: The Hudson Valley UFO Sightings" - May 8, 1998
2. "The Hynek UFO Report" - Dec 1, 1977

"**Night siege**" is a must-read. If you want heavy details on UFO activity in New York and Connecticut during the 1980's – this book is it. The number of businessmen and women, scientists, physicians as well as ordinary citizens observed colossal boomerang ships over the two states during this time. Police were called in and confirmed the sightings.

Raymond E. Fowler (Historian)

1. "UFOs: Interplanetary Visitors" - May 29, 2001

Dr. Leonard H. Stringfield (Psychologist)

1. "Situation Red: The UFO Siege: An Update on Strange and Frequently Frightening Encounters" 1977
A great book on ufo activity in Ohio, in the 1950's and 1960's

Lawrence Fawcett (Former policeman) and Barry J. Greenwood

1. "Clear Intent: The Government Coverup of the UFO Experience" - Jun 1, 1984
2. "The UFO Cover-up - What the Government Won't Say" - Jul 1, 1990

"**Clear Intent**" is a must read – you will come away shocked at how much work these two men did with FOIA requests to share secret ufo cases in the military. "**clear intent**" is one of the books of the ufo bible.

Timothy Good (Researcher and Historian)

1. "Earth: An Alien Enterprise: The Shocking Truth Behind the Greatest Cover-Up in Human History" - Nov 15, 2014
2. "Above Top Secret: The Worldwide U.F.O. Cover-Up" - Sep 1989
3. "Need to Know: UFOs, the Military, and Intelligence" - Nov 15, 2007
4. "Unearthly Disclosure" - Jan 22, 2002

The books above are a great source of historical ufo activity in Europe and us. Timothy has done an excellent job on resourcing his material. "**Above Top Secret**" and "**Need to Know**: are must reads."

DONALD R. SCHMITT AND THOMAS J. CAREY (RESEARCHERS)

1. "Witness to Roswell: Unmasking the Government's Biggest Cover-up (Revised and Expanded Edition)" - May 15, 2009
2. "Inside the Real Area 51: The Secret History of Wright Patterson" - Aug 20, 2013
3. "The Children of Roswell: A Seven-Decade Legacy of Fear, Intimidation, and Cover-Ups" -

Feb 22, 2016

The books are the best books on the market for the many witnesses (over 600) on the Roswell crash in
1947 in New Mexico. "**Witness to Roswell**" and "**The Children of Roswell**" must read.

DR. STEVEN M. GREER (MEDICAL, MD)

1. "Hidden Truth: Forbidden Knowledge" - Apr 28, 2006
Great book on the Government cover-up and Politicians, CIA and other agencies.

LESLIE KEAN (JOURNALIST)

1. "UFOs: Generals, Pilots, and Government Officials Go on the Record" - Aug 2, 2011

TERRY HANSEN (HISTORIAN)

1. "The Missing Times" - Feb 10, 2001

RICHARD M. DOLAN (HISTORIAN)

1. "UFOs and the National Security State: The Cover-Up Exposed", 1973-1991 - Sep 1, 2009
2. "UFOs and the National Security State: Chronology of a Coverup", 1941-1973 - Jun 1, 2002

PAUL R. HILL (HISTORIAN)

1. "Unconventional Flying Objects: A Scientific Analysis" - Dec 1, 1995

ROBERT HASTINGS (HISTORIAN)

1. "UFOs & Nukes: Extraordinary Encounters at Nuclear Weapons Sites" - May 12, 2017

STANTON T. FRIEDMAN (NUCLEAR PHYSICIST) AND KATHLEEN MARDEN

1. "Captured! The Betty and Barney Hill UFO Experience: The True Story of the World's First Documented Alien Abduction" - Aug 15, 2007

Great book on the barney and bill hill abduction case

STANTON T. FRIEDMAN (NUCLEAR PHYSICIST)

1. "Flying Saucers and Science: A Scientist Investigates the Mysteries of UFOs: Interstellar Travel, Crashes, and Government Cover-Ups" - Jun 15, 2008
2. "Top Secret/Majic: Operation Majestic-12 and the United States Government's UFO Cover-up" - Aug 19, 2005
3. "Science Was Wrong: Startling Truths About Cures, Theories, and Inventions "They" Declared Impossible" - Jun 20, 2010

References and Sources

Introduction

[i] Source: Psychology Today, September 17, 2017, Shahram Heshmat Ph.D.
[ii] https://www.merriam-webster.com/dictionary/denial

Chapter 1

[iii] "Over 5 Million American Say They've Seen UFOs", By George Gallup, Ogden Standard Examiner, Ogden, Utah, May 8, 1966, Sunday, Page 4A.
[iv] 51% in Gallup Poll Believe in UFOs; 11% Note Sightings, November 29, 1973; the New York Times
[v] Why are people starting to believe in UFOs again? Joseph P. Laycock, AP News, Texas State University, July 5, 2016
[vi] 48 Percent of Americans Believe UFOs Could Be ET Visitations, Weird News, The Huffington Post, September 11, 2013, and updated December 6, 2017
[vii] Majorities across Britain, Germany, and the USA believe that extra-terrestrial life exists, YouGovUk by Will Dahlgreen September 24, 2015

Chapter 2

[viii] The US Capital Building – West View; By Martin Falbisoner - Own work, CC BY-SA 3.0, commons.wikimedia.org; curid=28359031
[ix] "Senator Barry Goldwater Joins NICAP Board of Governors," The UFO Investigator, May 1974, Page 1
[x] Columbia, South Carolina, "The State," 30 December 49 and Greenwood, South Carolina, "Index-Journal," 29 December 49; "UFO's: A History," Loren E. Gross, 1949 Revision, Page 69
[xi] Sulphur Springs, Texas, News-Telegram, August 31, "UFO's: A History" 1952, August, Loren E. Gross, Page 35
[xii] The APRO Bulletin, November 1955, Page 7
[xiii] "UFO's: A History, Loren E. Gross, 1956, November-December-SN, Pages 25, 28, original source: Mitchell, South Dakota. The Republic, November 30, 1956
[xiv] US Air Force Project Blue Book Files: NARA T1206, Roll 0086, 1961, January
[xv] Newspaper article: "Flying Saucers Above, Mooseburgers Below," Luce Press Clipping Bureau, New York, Patchogue, NY, Advance, February 16, 1961; "UFO's: A History," Loren E. Gross, January-June, Page 17
[xvi] US Air Force Project Blue Book Files: NARA T1206, Roll 0044, 1962, Presque Isle, Wisconsin, reported four years after the event, letter dated April 3, 1966, from Lombard, Illinois
[xvii] "Forbidden Science, Journals 1957-1969", Jacques, Vallee, North Atlantic Books, 1992, Page 133, found in Blue Book

Chapter 3

[xviii] "It's Happened-Flying Disc Sighted By Sergeant Bethea!" by Marshall L. Reed., Florence Morning News, Florence, South Carolina, January 8, 1950, Sunday, Page 4-B
[xix] "Chameleon Globe In Michigan," The APRO Bulletin, November 1961, Page 8
[xx] The UFO Investigator, July-August 1961, Page 7
[xxi] "UFO's: A History," Loren E. Gross, 1961, July-September, Page 10, original source: Mt. Clemens, Michigan, July 10, 1961, United Press International (UPI))
[xxii] U.S. Air Force Project Blue Book, NARA T1206m Roll 0056, Cocoa Florida, August 1965, "Colorful Objects Seen in Cocoa Sky," Miami Herald, August 5, 1965
[xxiii] The Unreal World of UFOs, Bob Pratt
[xxiv] "Police Chase Mysterious Flying Object," Aiken Standard, Aiken, South Carolina, February 15, 1989, Wednesday, Page 2

Chapter 4

[xxv] The APRO Bulletin, November 1956, Page 6, original source: St Paul Pioneer Press, Chicago Daily News, Omaha World-Herald, St. Paul Dispatch, Cr: J. Myers, Mrs. C. Brunes, E.O. Dahl, and H.J. Muenchen
[xxvi] "UFO's: A History," Loren E. Gross, 1957, March 23-May 25-SN, Page 7-8, original source: Shreveport, Louisiana. The Times. 14 November 57
[xxvii] "Smoke Trailing Disc Reported Over New Zealand", April 27, 1957, The UFO Investigator, Page 12, 1957, Statement by Samuel E. Rix, Director, Tauranga Big Game Fishing Club, for sighting of Ronald L. Matheson, retrieved at US Air Force Project Blue Book Files, NARA T1206, Roll 0027, 1957, May, Randall, Iowa file. (Note in the UFO Investigator the name of the boat was "Rosa" not Rose)
[xxviii] "Florida Official Seeing Is Believing," The UFO Investigator, January 4, 1974, Page 3
[xxix] International UFO Report, 1980, Volume 5, Page 7, original source: UPI; various newspapers via Edwin Gatia
[xxx] International UFO Report, 1995, Volume 20, May-June Page 21, original source: "UFO Flap in Zimbabwe," By Cynthia Hind
[xxxi] International UFO Report, 2000, Volume 25, Summer 2000 Page 14-15, original source: Mark Cashman a professional software developer, custodian of the Project 1947EM Effects Catalog, he is also a senior investigator for MUFON CT

Chapter 5

[xxxii] US Air Force Project Blue Book Files: NARA T1206, Roll 0002, 1948, Fielding Lake, Washington, Incident Number 145, the Checklist states location was Fielding Lake: Alaska, however, the file card states: Fielding Lake, Washington
[xxxiii] U.S. Air Force Project Blue Book Files: T1206, Roll 0005, 1949, April, Springer, New Mexico
[xxxiv] Baltimore, Maryland) News-Post, 20 August 49. "The Riddle of 'Monstrator" written by Norman Markham, Doubt. #25, pp. 385-387; "UFO's: A History," Loren E. Gross, 1949-Revision, Page 63
[xxxv] US Air Force Project Blue Book Files: NARA T1206, Roll 0006, 1949, August, San Francisco, California
[xxxvi] US Air Force Project Blue Book Files: NARA T1206, Roll 0007, 1950, March, Marrowbone Lake, Tennessee, an article found in AF file titled: "2 Marrowbone Fishermen See Saucers Fly by – Noise, Speed Cause Scare."
[xxxvii] "UFO's: A History," Loren E. Gross, 1953, March-July-SN, Page 36, original source: Letter: To Mr. Richard C. Olson c/o Hon. Morris K. Udall, United States Congress, Washington D.C., 20515. From: Dr. James McDonald, The University of Arizona, Tucson, Arizona. 10 March 70. Dr. McDonald's personal papers, Special Collections Division, University of Arizona Library, Tucson, Arizona. Photocopy in author's files, pages 2-3, also Prescott Evening Courier, "Flying Saucers Return To Prescott."

Chapter 6

[xxxviii] Flying Saucer Review May 1959 also Jacques Vallee, Passport to Magonia Case number 53
[xxxix] International UFO Reporter, January/February 1994, Vol 14, No. 4, Pages 4-12 original source: "The Continuing Search for the Roswell Archaeologists" Closing the Circle, by Thomas K. Carey
[xl] "Monguzzi Takes Saucer Photos of the Century," by Lou Zinstag, FSR, 1958, September-October, Volume 4, Number 5, Pages 2-6
[xli] HumCat #340. Mesnard and Bigome. "Les Humanoides en France," p.24. Quoting I'Union (Reims?). 23/24 October 54; "UFO's: A History," Loren E Gross, 1954, October-SN, Page 59
[xlii] US Air Force Project Blue Book Files: NARA-PBB89-877, original source, APRO Bulletin, Page 9, note another note in the file states the name is Pardo River near Pontal Brazil.
[xliii] US Air Force Project Blue Book Files: NARA T1206, Roll 0022, 1954, December, Porto Alegre, Brazil"
[xliv] APRO Bulletin. September 1960, page 5 from Fortaleza Gazeta de Noticias, Brazilian Newspaper, May 24; Salvador A Tarde, May 25, "Two beings of human appearance"; "UFO's: A History, Loren E. Gross, 1960, January-June, Page 93

[xlv] The APRO Bulletin, September 1960, Page 5, original source "Gazeta De Noticias, May 24, Rio de Janeiro A Noticia, O Jornal, Ultima Hora, O Globo, etc., May 25, Sao Paulo Folha De Sao Paulo, Ultima Hora, etc., May 25

[xlvi] "UFO's: A History," Loren E. Gross, 1960, January-June, Page 123, original source: Flying Saucer Review, January-February 1961. Volume 7, Number 1, page 29 (News quote from The Eastern Province Herald, June 30, 1960

[xlvii] Albert S. Rosales, Humanoid Contact Database 1979, citing Dr. Libirajara Franco Rodriguez & Maria Jose Pereira, Nicaop.org 1979 Chronology

[xlviii] "Impressive Evidence in N.J. Landing Case", The UFO Investigator, September-October, 1964, Volume 11, No. 12, Page 1 and 3

[xlix] US Air Force Project Blue Book Files: NARA T1206, Roll 0056, 1965, August, San Mateo, California, Saucer News, Volume 12, No 4. December 1965, information only

[l] US Air Force Project Blue Book Files: NARA T1206, Roll 0075, 1967, September, this 1965 case was in a 1967 file, according to the witness he observed on several occasions phenomena throughout 1965 and 1967 at this location

[li] Albert S. Rosales, Humanoid Contact Database 2006, citing National UFO Reporting Center. NICAP 2006 Chronology

Chapter 7

[lii] "UFO's: A History," Loren E. Gross, 1957, August-September, Page 31, original source: Letter: To Leonard Stringfield. From: Ted Bloecher. 2 September 57, Copy in author's files

[liii] "UFO's: A History," Loren E. Gross, 1957-November 7-12-SN, Page 11, original source: The APRO Bulletin. November 1957, Page 8

[liv] "UFO's: A History," Loren E. Gross, 1958, May-July, Page 36 original source: Moore, William L. "Red Skies: A History of UFOs in Russia." UFO Report. Vol.8, No.2. April 1980. pp.2-3. The Chimbay case-was one of those collected by Russian engineer Turi Aleksandrovitch Fomin of the Department of Automatic Devices of the Moscow Technological Institute. Fomin might be considered Russia's first Ufologist

[lv] "UFO's: A History," Loren E. Gross, 1958, November-December, Page 51, original source: News article: "Lampasas Couple Victims of Mysterious Fast- Flying Lights," Lampasas, Texas, Record, January 29, 1959

[lvi] The APRO Bulletin, July 1963, Page 6 and 7, original source: The Lampasas, Texas Record, Thursday, January 29, 1959

[lvii] Reno, Nevada, Gazette, November 17, 1959; "UFO's: A History," Loren E. Gross, 1959, October-December, Page 18,

[lviii] "UFO's: A History, Loren E. Gross, 1960, July-December, Page 76-78, original source: Page, Tom. "Coming Out of the Closet." MUFON UFO Journal. # 226. February 1987. pp.8-9. Page was not a believer in UFOs, but his Oregon experience haunted him. Years later he finally took a serious interest in the UFO mystery hoping to find a rational answer. (See drawings on pages 79-80

[lix] (Source: SL-71, page 5)

Chapter 8

[lx] US Air Force Project Blue Book Files: NARA –PBB89-116, also NARA PBB88-1242; retrieved at bluebookarchive.org

[lxi] US Air Force Project Blue Book Files: NARA T1206, Roll 0013, 1952, July, Albuquerque, New Mexico, this Montana story was in a "New Mexico File."

[lxii] "Argentina. Galpan, Salta. 1956-11-?" APRO files, Photocopy in author's files; "UFO's: A History," Loren E. Gross, 1956-November-December-SN, Page 1-2,

[lxiii] "World round-up." Flying Saucer Review, Vol. 6, No. 1, January-February 1960, page 17; "UFO's: A History," Loren E. Gross, 1959-SN, Page 10,11

[lxiv] Houston, Missouri. Republican. 13 July 61; "UFO's: A History," Loren E. Gross, 1961, July-September, Page 5,8

[lxv] "Blue Flash Goes Spat," The APRO Bulletin, September 1961, Page 3

[lxvi] Flying Saucer Review, September-October 1963. Vol. 9, Number 5, pages 21- 22; " UFO's: A History," Loren E. Gross, 1963- January-June, Pages 64-64,

[lxvii] "Sighting Advisory," The UFO Investigator, December 1972, Page 3

Chapter 9

[lxviii] "Area Has Share of UFOs"; Lubbock Avalanche-Journal. Lubbock Texas, March 22, 1969; Saturday, Page A-11
[lxix] Milwaukee, Wisconsin. Milwaukee Journal. 27 August 56, Page 25; "UFO's: A History," Loren E. Gross, 1956-August-SN, Page 7
[lxx] The APRO Bulletin, September 15, 1956, Page 25, credit: J.E. Turner
[lxxi] US Air Force Project Blue Book Files: NARA T1206, Roll 0030, 1957, November, Albuquerque, New Mexico, this Ottawa case was information only buried in a New Mexico file.
[lxxii] "Police Chief Views UAO," US Air Force Project Blue Book Files, NARA T1206, Roll 0052, 1964, Fall, Lansing, Michigan, original source: APRO Bulletin, November 1964, note this "Montana sighting was an article buried in a Michigan file
[lxxiii] "Hunters Sight Dozen UFO's." The APRO Bulletin, 1966, January-February, Page 7
[lxxiv] US Air Force Project Blue Book Files: NARA T1206, Roll 0058, 1965, October, Lone-Prairie, Minnesota, the story also appeared in the St. Paul Pioneer Press on 10/25/65 and the Minneapolis Star on 10/25/65, further reported in Saucer News, Vol 13, #1, March 1966 also "Little, Little Men in Minn.", The APRO Bulletin, November- December, 1965, Page 8
[lxxv] The Flying Saucer Review, May-June, 1966, Volume 12, Number 3, Page 14, original source, St. Paul Pioneer Press, 10/15/65 and Minneapolis Starr, 10/25/65, found in US Air Force Project Blue Book File: NARA T1206, Roll 0058, 1965, October, Lone-Prairie, Minnesota
[lxxvi] US Air Force Project Blue Book Files: NARA T1206, Roll 0070, 1967, March, Dayton, Ohio, "Flying Saucers Seen By Fishermen At Plevna," The Tweed News," Wednesday, March 8, 1967

[lxxvii] "Saucer Sighting Puzzles Officials," Manchester Journal Inquirer, Manchester, Connecticut, July 30, 1976, Friday, Page 8
[lxxviii] International UFO Reporter, November 1976, p. 6 and "Campers View Flying Saucer," The Hartford Courant, July 30, 1976, Page 23
[lxxix] Submitted by Mike Swords. Sources: Cotile Lake file, CUFOS, [contains correspondence and a photo of Hynek with the witnesses, and two of the site; "Is there something out there watching?", Alexandria LA Daily Town Talk, April 20, 1980; article contains a drawing of the event
[lxxx] "UFO Mystery Grows As Countians Continue To Sight Strange Objects"; Santa Ana Orange County Register, Santa Ana, California, April

Chapter 10

[lxxxi] NICAP.org, Edwards, FSSB, pages 99-100; Randle/Estes, FOV, page 273
[lxxxii] "UFO's: A History: Loren E. Gross: 1954, November-December-SN, Page 50, original source: "Venezuela Carora," APRO files. Translation by "Joe." Photocopy in author's files, the story also in the "Hunters Clawed and Beaten," APRO Bulletin, 1955, January 15, 1955, Volume 3, Page 2
[lxxxiii] "UFO's: A History," Loren E. Gross, 1961, July-September, Page 40-41, original source: Cameron, Vicki, UFO Experiences in Canada, General Store Publishing House: Burnstown, Ontario, Canada, 1995. pp.29-31. Unfortunately, the name of the witness to these events was omitted. Vicki Cameron is merely the editor
[lxxxiv] International UFO Reporter, July/August 1989, Vol 14, No. 4, Page 13 original source: "The abduction phenomenon in Australia, by Keith Basterfield, Vladimir Godic and Pony Godic report by Mark Moravec
[lxxxv] "Miss, Contact Case Remains Puzzle," The UFO Investigator, November 1973, Page 2
[lxxxvi] "Twinkle, Twinkle, little what? Reports of UFO spotting sprinkle regions of the country", by Craig Ammerman, Associated Press Writer, Winona Daily News, Winona Minnesota, Wednesday, October 17, 1973., Page 13a
[lxxxvii] "Coast Guardsmen Said Chasing Underwater UFO," Monroe News-Star," Wednesday, November 8, 1973, page 42, this story was also in the Biloxi Daily Herald, Thursday, November 8, 1973
[lxxxviii] "UFOs: Believe In Them or Not, Evidence Mounts They're Real" by Jack Mabley, Chicago Tribune.; Colorado Springs Gazette, Colorado Springs, Colorado, March 27, 1977, Sunday.
[lxxxix] The Encyclopedia of Extraterrestrial Encounters, edited by Ronald D. Story. New

American Library, a division of Penguin Putnam Inc., 375 Hudson Street, New York, N.Y. 10014. 2001. Feature submitted by researcher Billy J. Rachels. (mysterious-america.net)
[xc] ufosightingsdaily.com

Chapter 11

[xci] "Monitoring and Scanning Discs," The APRO Bulletin, January 1963, Page 5, original source: The Amarillo Texas, Sunday, News-Globe, April 9, 1950, "So You Saw A Flying Disc? - This boy Touched One!" also found in the (Los Angeles, California) Herald-Express: April 10, 1950, Page A-7, United Press)
[xcii] US Air Force Project Blue Book Files: NARA T1206, Roll 0055, 1965, July, Dayton, Ohio, original source: Flying Saucer Review, November-December 1965, "The Valensole Affair written by Aime Michel, this story was buried in a Dayton Ohio file
[xciii] "UFO's: A History," Loren E. Gross, 1954, October - SN, Page 59, original source: Vallee, Jacques. Passport to Magonia. Chicago, Illinois: Henry Regnery Company, 1969. p.232, note this information stated the event occurred on October 17th
[xciv] "UFO's: A History", Loren E. Gross, 1961, July-September, Page 90, original source: news clipping: "UFO's Cause Panic, One Death", paper source found at US Air Force Blue Book Files NARA T1206, Roll 0044, 1961, October, Las Vegas, New Mexico, also The UFO Investigator, January-February, 1962, Page 1
[xcv] "Man Reported Injured by UFO," The UFO Investigator, 1965, March – April, Page 6

Chapter 12

[xcvi] "Spotted UFO in 1930, but kept mum for 35 years", The Hawke Eye, Sunday, October 28, 1973, Page 2, Burlington Hawk-Eye, Burlington, Iowa, October 28, 1973
[xcvii] US Air Force Project Blue Book Files: NARA T1206, Roll 0002, 1948, July, 20 miles south of Montgomery, Alabama, Incident Number 144, original source: "Hunter Support Airmen's Story Of Flame-Shooting Wingless Craft", The Atlanta Constitution, Monday, July 25, 1948, this was located in the Captain Chiles and Whitted UFO case file
[xcviii] US Air Force Project Blue Book Files: Investigation by S/A Thomas H. Kelly, 19th District OSI, point #3., 2 August 49, US Air Force Project Blue Book File #367, retrieved at US Air Force Project Blue Book Files, NARA T1206, Roll 0004, 1949, March, Bend Oregon, also found in NARA T1206, Roll 0005, May, Rogue River, Oregon; "UFO's: A History", Loren E. Gross, 1949, Revision, Page 77
[xcix] US Air Force Project Blue Book Files: NARA T1206, Roll 0006, 1949, July, Yellowstone National Park, Wyoming; "UFO's: A History," Loren E. Gross, 1949 Rev, Pages 5-6
[c] Graystone, Regina. "Immense UFO Over Maura Lake." Flying Saucer Review Case Histories. No.3. Pages 14-15; "UFO's a History", Loren E. Gross, 1951- SN, Page 28
[ci] US Air Force Project Blue Book Files: NARA T1206, Roll 0009, 1952, April, Lake Meade, Nevada
[cii] US Air Force Project Blue Book Files: NARA T1206, Roll 0010, June, Benedict, Maryland
[ciii] Crookston, Minnesota. Times. 23 July 52; "UFO's: A History," Loren E Gross, 1947-1959-SN, Page 64
[civ] San Luis Obispo, California, Telegram-Tribune, 22 July 52; "UFO's: A History," Loren E Gross, 1952, June to July 20-SN, Page 77
[cv] "UFO's: A History, 1952, August, Loren E. Gross, Page 45, original source: "Tentative Observers Questionnaire, August 15, 1952, US Air Force Project Blue Book Files, White Cloud
[cvi] "UFO's: A History, Loren E. Gross, 1952, August - SN, Page 146, original source: Mt. Sterling, Kentucky, Advocate, "Flying Saucers have visited Montgomery County?" dated 28 August 52
[cvii] "UFO's: A History," Loren E. Gross, 1953, August-December-SN, Page 14, original source: Letter: To Civilian Saucer Investigation Committee (CSI Los Angeles), Box 1971, Main Post Office, Los Angeles, 53, California. From: Richard Clapper, Derby, Vermont. Date of report: 26 January 54. CUFOS archives
[cviii] Melbourne, Australia. Melbourne Herald. 7 January 54; "UFO's: A History," Loren E. Gross, 1954, January-May-SN, Page 1
[cix] "UFO's: A History," Loren E. Gross, 1954, June-August-SN, Page 21, original source: APRO files. Photocopy in author's files, a drawing in the file is that of a typical disk-shaped UFO.

cx "UFO's: A History," Loren E. Gross, 1954, November-December –SN, Page 47-48, original source: "Islade Francis 54-11-7." APRO files. Translation: probably by "Joe." Photocopy in author's files. Newspaper: La Tribuna Popular. 8 January 55
cxi The APRO Bulletin, January 1958, Page 3, original source" Pacific Stars and Stripes."
cxii Letter: To Dr. J. Allen Hynek. From: (name censored) Date: 28 February 78; "UFO's: A History," Loren E. Gross, 1958-SN, Page 31, 33
cxiii US Air Force Project Blue Book Files: NARA T1206, Roll 0039, 1960, August, Pontiac Michigan
cxiv "UFO's: A History," Loren E. Gross, 1962, July-December, Page 21, original source: Lorenzen, Coral. Flying Saucers: The Startling Evidence of the Invasion from Outer Space. The New American Library: New York, N.Y., 1962, Page 215 and The ARO Bulletin, September 1962. Page 4
cxv US Air Force Project Blue Book Files: NARA T1206, Roll 0051, 1964, June, Dale, Indiana, news clipping, Information from American UFO Committee Review, Volume 1, No 2, September 1964, Dale City, Indiana June 14, 1964
cxvi US Air Force Project Blue Book Files: NARA T1206, Roll 0052, 1964, July, Binghampton, New York, attached to the file was "The Sun-Bulletin" and Binghampton Evening News," note there are a lot of UFO reports from the papers in this file
cxvii US Air Force Project Blue Book NARA T1206, Roll 0071, Green Lake, Wisconsin
cxviii "Flickering Lights Take Hunters By Surprise," The UFO Investigator, 1974, January, page 3
cxix US Air Force Project Blue Book Files: NARA T1206, Roll 0055, 1965, July, Lake Michigan
cxx US Air Force Project Blue Book Files: NARA T1206, Roll 0072, Ontario, Oregon
cxxi "Two From Wisconsin," The APRO Bulletin, September-October 1970, Page 6
cxxii International UFO Report, 1986, Volume 11, Page 14-15, March-April, original source: TBD
cxxiii U.S. Air Force Project Blue Book Files: NARA T1206, Roll 0002, 1957, July, Incident number 26, Pan American Airways, Harmon Field, Newfoundland (Illegible) also found at USAF-SIGN8-209-210
cxxiv Project Blue Book Air Force Files Numbers 27, 26, 27A, 60; "UFO's: A History", Loren E. Gross, 1947-Revision, Pages 44-45
cxxv Avalanche-Journal, Lubbock Texas, 26 August 51; "UFO's: A History," Loren E. Gross, 1951, Page 44, 45
cxxvi Avalanche-Journal, Lubbock Texas, 26 August 51; "UFO's: A History," Loren E. Gross, 1951, Page 44, 45
cxxvii "Special Inquiry," by S/A Howard Bosseat. DO#23. Carswell AFB, Dayton, Ohio. 7 November 51. OSI Records, Blue Book Files; "UFO's: A History," Loren E. Gross, 1951, Page 56
cxxviii Bloecher, Ted. "Casebook." UFO Investigator. Published by the National Investigations Committee on Aerial Phenomenon, May 1972, pp. 3-4. and "Special Inquiry," by S/A Howard Bosseat, DO#23, Carswell AFB, Lubbock, Texas. 23 October 51. OSI Records, Blue Book Files; "UFO's: A History," Loren E. Gross, 1951, Page 71 and 72
cxxix "Jet Bombers Bring Saucer Reports, Lansing Residents Spot Objects Near Onaway," July 28, 1952; "UFO's: A History," Loren E. Gross, 1952, July 21-31-SN, Page 51
cxxx "UFO's: A History," Loren E Gross, 1952, July 21-31-SN, Page 50, original source: Detroit, Michigan. News. 30 July 52
cxxxi Pampa, Texas. News. 18 August 52; "UFO's: A History," Loren E. Gross, 1952-Aug-SN, Page 107
cxxxii "UFO's: A History," Loren E. Gross, 1952, September-October-SN, Page 32, original source: San Angelo, Texas, "Standard-Times," 15 September 52
cxxxiii US Air Force Project Blue Book Files: NARA T1206, Roll 0016, 1952, October, Hickman Canyon, Utah, letters from both witnesses in the file
cxxxiv "UFO's: A History," Loren E. Gross, 1954, January-May-SN, Page 31, original source: Sighting report typed on Civilian Saucer Investigation, New Zealand, stationary. Date report submitted not given. The drawing indicates the witness, W.R.F. Johnson, typed report. Murray Bott, Auckland, New Zealand, files
cxxxv US Air Force Project Blue Book Files: NARA-PBB90-826-828
cxxxvi US Air Force Project Blue Book Files: NARA T1206, Roll 0021, 1954, September, New Baden, Illinois
cxxxvii "UFO's: A History," Loren E. Gross, 1955, January-June–SN, Page 22, original source:

Letter: New Zealand Herald, "Mystery light paces aircraft," 11 February 55

[cxxxviii] "UFO's: A History", Loren E. Gross, 1955, July-September 15, Page 14, original sources: "Flying Saucer Hovers Over Boat in Channel" July 10, 1955, Los Angeles, California, Times, July 10, 1955, and "Saucer Skims Channel, So Say Fishermen", July 11, 1955, Santa Ana, California. Santa Ana Register, July 11, 1955, and the San Bernardino, California "Sun," July 12, 1955

[cxxxix] Raymond L. Boyd, 1827 West 17th Avenue, Albany, Oregon 97321. NICAP UFO report form, Date form filled out: 20 January 67, CUFOS archives. Photocopy in author's files; "UFO's: A History," Loren E. Gross, 1956, January-April-SN, Page 9

[cxl] The APRO Bulletin, September 15, 1956, Page 31, credit: El Universal, Joe Rolas

[cxli] "R.A.F. Radar Picks Up UFO Over S.W. Scotland", Flying Saucer Review, 1957, May-June, Volume 3, Number 3, Page 2

[cxlii] "UFO's: A History," Loren E. Gross, 1957-November 7-12-SN, Page 12, original source: "The Wichita Beacon," Wichita, Kansas, November 11, 1957, Page 1

[cxliii] "UFO's: A History," Loren E. Gross, 1958, May-July, Page 13, original source: news clipping: "Odd Light A Mystery," Ft Lauderdale News, Florida, May 18, 1958

[cxliv] "UFO's: A History," Loren E. Gross, 1959, January-March, Page 98, original source: Flying Saucer Review, September-October, 1959, Page 8

[cxlv] US Air Force Project Blue Book Files, Air Force BLUE BOOK Files, 10 January 61) – also found at "UFO's: A History, Loren E. Gross, 1961, January-June, Page 9

[cxlvi] "UFO's: A History," Loren E. Gross, July-September, Page 108, original source: UFO Investigator. Vol. II, No.3. January-February 1962, Page 6, also in The UFO Investigator 1962 January-February, Page 6

[cxlvii] "UFO's: A History," Loren E. Gross, July-September, Page 112, original source: US Air Force Project Blue Book Files: November 23, 1961

[cxlviii] "UFO's: A History," Loren E. Gross, 1962, July-December Page 1, original source: Flying Saucer Review. September-October 1962. Volume 8, Number 5. Page 21

[cxlix] "Maybe saucer- spotters tell it like it is' by Frank Bowers, The Hawke Eye, Sunday, October 28, 1973, Page 2, Burlington Hawk-Eye, Burlington, Iowa, October 28, 1973

[cl] "Sighting Advisory," The UFO Investigator," March 1975, Page 3

Chapter 14

[cli] The APRO Bulletin, January 1956, Page 14

[clii] Florence, South Carolina, News, November 6, 1957, also in the Gross 1957, October 1- November 2nd, Page 83 monograph; "UFO's: A History," Loren E. Gross, 1957, October- November 2- SN, Page 20

[cliii] "UFO's: A History," Loren E. Gross, 1958, May-July, Page 65 original source: Schwarz, Berthold Eric, "UFO-Dynamics." (Moore Haven, Florida: Rainbow Books, 1983, Pages 61-62

[cliv] "UFO's: A History," Loren E. Gross, 1963, July-December, Page 1-2, original source: Biesele, Mildred. "Two Sightings in British Columbia." MUFON UFO Journal. No. 194. April l984, pages 12-13

[clv] "More USA November Reports" The APRO Bulletin, 1968, January-February, Page 6

[clvi] US Air Force Project Blue Book Files: NARA T1206, Roll 0053, 1964, November, 33.58N 164.14E (Pacific), APRO, "Three View UFO In Canada," APRO Bulletin, May & June 1965)

[clvii] "Black Disc Sighted in Massachusetts," The UFO Investigator / July 1971, page 3, a drawing of the disc can be seen in the UFO Investigator of August 1971, Page 2

[clviii] "Colebrook Resident Sees 'Bright Light'," by David Bergmann, The Hartford Courant, April 24, 1977, Page 38A1

Chapter 15

[clix] The APRO Bulletin, May 1958, Page 1, 3, original source – local papers no names given

[clx] Flying Saucer Review, Supplement 14, April 1973, Pages 13-14; "UFO's: A History," Loren E. Gross, 1958, May-July, Page 40

[clxi] From Here and There", The APRO Bulletin, January 1959, Page 7

[clxii] "UFO's: A History," Loren E. Gross, 1959, July-September, Page 9-10, original source: Unidentified Flying Object Report." 1958, July (8-14?), CUFOS archives

The Sportsman Guide to UFOs: Around the World

clxiii US Air Force Project Blue Book Files: NARA T1206, Roll 0040, 1960, October, Point Lookout, Long Island, New York
clxiv "Personal Story at Nuforc.org, Report Number 045-S45492
clxv UFO's: A History", Loren E. Gross, 1963- January-June, Pages 64-64, original source: Flying Saucer Review. Vol. 9, Number 5, September-October 1963, page 21
clxvi "UFO's: A History," Loren E. Gross, 1962, January-June, Page 43-44, original source: Flying Saucer Review. September-October 1962. Vol. 8, Number 5, page 23
clxvii "UFO's: A History," Loren E. Gross, 1962, January-June, Page 74, original source: U.S. Air Force Project Blue Book Files: June 9, 1962
clxviii US Air Force Project Blue Book Files: NARA T1206, Roll 0045, 1962, June, Biloxi, Mississippi
clxix "UFO's: A History," Loren E. Gross, 1963, January-June, Page 67-68, original source: Ledger, Don, "Maritime UFO Files," Nimbus Publishing Limited: Halifax, Nova Scotia, Canada, 1998. pp.46-47. (Ledger gives his source as the "Shelburne weekly newspaper Coast Guard. Date: May 1963."
clxx "UFO's: A History," Loren E. Gross, 1963, July-December, Page 61, original source: BUFORA Journal, published by the British U.F.O. Research Association. Spring/Summer 1971
clxxi Ledger and Styles, 2001, pp. 14-17, 21-44
clxxii International UFO Reporter, 2011, 34-1, Page 9
clxxiii "Canadian Diver Search for UFO," The UFO Investigator, November to December 1967, Page 4
clxxiv "UFOs and the National Security State, Chronology of a Cover-up 1941-1973, Richard M. Dolan, 2002, Pages 337-338, original sources: Gillmor 1969, 351-353; Sanderson 1970, 38-39; Keyhoe 1973, 150; Lorenzen and Lorenzen 1968, 56 and Clark 1996, 135-136
clxxv International UFO Reporter, 2010-2012, Volume 33, Page 23, original source: "I See by the Papers," Fate, April 1971, pp. 19–20

Chapter 16

clxxvi US Air Force Project Blue Book Files: NARA T1206, Roll 0007, 1950, August, Ernest Harmon AFB, Newfoundland, BBU 790 and MAXW-PBB8-178
clxxvii US Air Force Project Blue Book Files: NARA T1206, Roll 0015, 1952, October, York, Pennsylvania, this Massachusetts case was buried in Pennsylvania file
clxxviii US Air Force Project Blue Book Files: NARA T1206, Roll 0017, 1953, January, Bataan, Philippines, Air Intelligence Information ~art, by Capt. Charles Malven, ATIL Office, May 1, 1953, Page 4
clxxix "UFO's: A History, Loren E Gross, 1953- January-February
clxxx US Air Force Project Blue Book Files: NARA T1206, Roll 0021, 1954, July, 15 Miles SE Ocean City, Maryland
clxxxi To: APRO. From: W.L. Powell, P.O. Box 217, Tualatin, Oregon. 97062. Date: 30 July 68. APRO files. Photocopy in author's files; "UFO's: A History," Loren E. Gross, 1955, January–June–SN, Page 1
clxxxii "UFO's: A History," Loren E. Gross, 1955, July-September 15- SN, Page 5,; Seattle, Washington. Seattle Daily Times, 6 July 55
clxxxiii "UFO's: A History," Loren E. Gross, 1957, August-September, Page 15, original source: Flying Saucer Review. January-February 1959. Vol.5, No.1. Page 7, also found in The APRO Bulletin, January 1959, Page 4
clxxxiv US Air Force Project Blue Book Files: NARA T1206, Roll 0032, 1958, January, Albuquerque, New Mexico, original source The APRO Bulletin, March 1960, Page 1
clxxxv UFO-Critical Bulletin. Vol. III, #4. July-August 1959, Page 3; "UFO's: A History," Loren E. Gross, 1959, July-September, Page 32
clxxxvi The Reference for Outstanding UFO Sighting Reports. Ed.: Thomas M. Olsen. UFO Information Retrieval Center, Inc.: Riderwood, Maryland, 1967, pages 3-73; "UFO's: A History," Loren E. Gross, 1961, January-June, Page 50.
clxxxvii US Air Force Project Blue Book Files: NARA T1206, Roll 0046, 1962, September, WSW Biloxi, Mississippi, BBU 8133, also Mary Castner/CUFOS; Berliner
clxxxviii "Flying Saucer Review, Vol 16, No 4, July-August 1970, Pages 18, 24, "A Norwegian UFO Experience in 1963", Nils J. Jacobsen"; "UFO's: A History," Loren E. Gross, 1963, July-December, Page 45

clxxxix International UFO Report, 1979, Volume 4, Page 18, original source: Oggi magazine (December 2, 1978), Gente magazine (same date)
cxc International UFO Report, 1979, Volume 4, Page 18, original source: Gente magazine dated December 2, 1978
cxci International UFO Report, 1979, Volume 4, Page 18, original source: Gente, Oggi, and Il Messagero Magazine
cxcii The APRO Bulletin

Chapter 17

cxciii F-18A Super Hornet; By Photographer's Name: Sgt. Robert Reeve - This media is available in the holdings of the National Archives and Records Administration, cataloged under the National Archives Identifier (NAID) 6401113., Public Domain, commons.wikimedia.org; curid=5996016
cxciv "The First Papuan Sightings," The APRO Bulletin, July 1961, Page 6
cxcv "AF Rejects NY Photos, NICAP Dissents", The UFO Investigator, May-June 1967, Page 5 also in UFO Investigator Vol III, No 11, Page 7, the edition shows two pictures of the disc-like object hovering over the lake, photographs of the object at the lake are found at US Air Force Project Blue Book files: NARA T1206, Roll 0094, 1966, December, Bear Mountain State Park, New York, Incident Number 11229
cxcvi "Fisherman's Photos Authentic," The UFO Investigator, March-April 1967, Page 6
cxcvii International UFO Reporter, July 1979, p. 6; The APRO Bulletin, May 1980, p. 2
cxcviii "Flying Saucer Review," 1981, Volume 26, Number 5, original source: Teletype received Tokyo, dated November 5, 1980

Chapter 18

cxcix "Europe, Great Britain, FSR, 1956, November – December, Volume 2, Number 6, Page 8
cc "UFO's: A History", Loren E. Gross, 1957, August-September, Page 63, original source: Ultima Hora, Rio de Janeiro, Brazil, 3 September 57
cci US Air Force Project Blue Book Files: NARA T1206, Roll 0033, 1958, May, West of North Africa file, original source: "The Holly River Sighting" by Hank Mollohan as told to Gary Barker, Flying Saucer, May 1958. Note this story was buried in a North Africa file
ccii "UFO's: A History," Loren E. Gross, 1959, April-June, Page 54 original source: Cruttwell, The Reverend, E.G. "Flying Saucers Over Papua." Flying Saucer Review, Special Issue No.4. August 1971, Pages 11-12
cciii "UFO's: A History," Loren E. Gross, 1959, July-September, Page 90,92, original source: Typed report on plain paper. Witnesses are anonymous. Copy in author's files: "#15 Report on UFOs: Addresses: Tiller Trail Highway No.42.
cciv The APRO Bulletin, September 1961, Page 8
ccv US Air Force Project Blue Book Files: NARA T1206, Roll 0045, 1962, May, Troy, New Hampshire
ccvi US Air Force Project Blue Book Files: NARA T1206, Roll 0062, 1964, September, Sacto Area, California
ccvii Also not the APRO Bulleting places the date in September 1963; however most books and AF, place this in September 1964.
See - More information in the International UFO Reporter 1995, Winter Volume 20, page 16-22

Chapter 19

ccviii US Air Force Project Blue Book Files: NARA T1206, Roll 0037, 1959, October, N of Langley AFB, Virginia
ccix Bonko, Larry. "A Chilling Secret at Langley?" Norfolk, VA. Ledger-Star. 28 December 83, also see original newspaper "Tenth Grader Sees Saucer In The Sky," October 21, 1959, this was also noted in the APRO Bulletin May 1963, page 5; "UFO's: A History," Loren E. Gross, 1959, October-December, Page 18
ccx US Air Force Project Blue Book files: NARA T1206, Roll 0041, 1960, December, Spokane, Washington, original source: "New Jersey Hunter Almost Shoots Saucer", Atlantic City Press,

December 2, note this New Jersey case was buried in a "Washington state file", the same story "Saucer Shaped Aircraft Is Sighted By 2 Hunters", Atlantic City NJ Press, December 14, 1960, retrieved at "UFO's: A History", Loren E. Gross, 1960, July-Dec, Page 129

ccxi "UFO's stay away Tuesday Night," The Daily Herald, Biloxi-Gulfport, Mississippi, Wednesday, October 17, 1973, Page 20

ccxii International UFO Reporter, Dec 1977, Vol 2, No. 12, Page 2 original source: Manitoba Centre for UFO Studies

Chapter 20

ccxiii USS FDR Aircraft Carrier; commons.wikimedia.org/wiki/File:USS_Franklin_D._Roosevelt_(CVA-42)_Sep_1967.jpeg#

ccxiv "UFO's: A History," Loren E. Gross, 1956, May-July-SN, Page 57, original source: NICAP UFO report form. Mrs. Janice H. Sanford, 16300 Harwood Road, Los Gatos, California. 95030. Date form filled out: 27 January 67. NICAP files. CUFOS archives. Photocopy in author's files

ccxv The UFO Investigator / JULY - AUG 1960, page 6 retrieved at CUFOS.org and Project Blue Book file number NARA-PBB1-173

ccxvi US Air Force Project Blue Book Files: NARA T1206, Roll 0026, 1957, October, Martha's Vineyard, Massachusetts

ccxvii "Mystery Cylinder Hovers Over Ship," The APRO Bulletin, September 1959, Page 8

ccxviii Spokane, Washington. Chronicle, 24 August 61; "UFO's: A History," Loren E. Gross, 1961, July-September, Page 32

ccxix "Ocean Sightings," The UFO Investigator, July-August 1968, Page 7

ccxx "Press Reports," The UFO Investigator, November-December 1972, Page 5

ccxxi "Amazing Soviet-Era UFO Sightings in & Over Water Bodies" by Paul Stone Hill found at ufoevidence.org, doc743

Chapter 21

ccxxii Rullan; Not in Blue Book

ccxxiii San Rafael, California, "Independent," July 10, 1947, page 14; retrieved at "UFO's: A History," Loren E Gross, 1947 Revision, Page 18

ccxxiv S.P.A.C.E. May 1957. Bulletin #6; "UFO's: A History," Loren E. Gross, 1957, March 23-May 25, Page 45

ccxxv "Submarine Saucers," The APRO Bulletin, May 1963, Page 2, original Source: Soviet Subs" by Marvin Miles, Los Angeles Time Writer

ccxxvi US Air Force Project Blue Book Files: NARA T1206, Roll 0058, 1965, September, Carson City, Nevada, this sighting was found in an article called "Now Its Saucers By the Squadron," found in a Nevada file, note this file is full of Oklahoma sightings from newspapers

ccxxvii El Universal, Caracas, 8/20/67, 8/28/67 copies in NICAP files; The UFO Investigator, March 1968, page 5

ccxxviii "UFO Wave Over Chile," The UFO Investigator, May-June 1972. Page 5

ccxxix Wendelle C. Stevens, Saga UFO Report, March 1977, page 39

ccxxx NICAP.org, 1978 Chronology, Carl Feindt, found at the Italian Center for UFO Studies

Chapter 22

ccxxxi P-51D Mustang; Autor: USAAF/361st FG Association (via Al Richards) —-gallery-albums-U-S-Air-Force/361st-fg-p-51.jpg, Voľné dielo, commons.wikimedia.org; curid=13361630

ccxxxii US Air Force Project Blue Book Files: NARA T1206, Roll 0025, 1956, July, Arkansas City, Kansas

ccxxxiii The APRO Bulletin, November 1956, Page 5, original source: The New Orleans Times-Picayune and Baton Rouge Morning Advocate, Cr: James E. Turner

ccxxxiv US Air Force Project Blue Book Files: NARA T1206, Roll 0066, 1966, October, Hazlet, New Jersey, note this "Indiana case was buried in a New Jersey case file

Chapter 23

ccxxxv "Flying Saucers Sighted Here On Wednesday" Humboldt Times, Eureka, California, March 31, 1950; "UFO's a History," Loren E. Gross, 1950, January- March, Page 52
ccxxxvi "UFO's: A History," Loren E. Gross, 1947-1959-SN, Page 92, original source: "Wow, Here's A Flying Saucer Story From Otter Tail Lake," Daily Journal, Fergus Falls, Minnesota, August 20, 1955
ccxxxvii Staples, Minnesota, "World," August 25, 1955; "UFO's: A History," Loren E. Gross, 1955, July-Sept-15, Page 20-21
ccxxxviii "Connecticut Landing 1957", The APRO Bulletin, March 1962, Page 1., this report was submitted by Harvey B. Courtney who interviewed the witness
ccxxxix "UFO's: What's Really Going On? Public and Air Force Figures on UFO's Create A Rather Large Math Gap"; By John A. Keel, North American Newspaper Alliance; Burlington Daily Times-News, Burlington, North Carolina, June 19, 1967, Monday, Page 1
ccxl The APRO Bulletin, 1967, November – December, Page 8
ccxli "Deer Hunters Say They Find Flying Saucer," (UPI), The Amarillo Globe-Times, Amarillo, Texas, Tuesday, October 31, 1967, Page 24)
ccxlii "Daylight Sighting in California," The APRO Bulletin, May-June 1968, Page 7

Chapter 24

ccxliii "Flying Saucers –Serious Business" By Frank Edwards, Tenth Installment, Ironwood Daily Globe, Friday, July 21, 1967
ccxliv "Spate of Reports in Georgia, The APRO Bulletin, 1968, November-December, Page 7
ccxlv "Sighting Advisory," The UFO Investigator, September 1971, Page 3
ccxlvi Richard Hall, The UFO Evidence, Volume 2: A Thirty Year Report, pp. 281, 491; David F. Webb & Ted Bloecher, HUMCAT: Catalogue of Humanoid Reports, case A1961; Robert Gribble, MUFON UFO Journal, issue # 245).
(Source: UFO Chronology 1978
ccxlvii The UFO Investigator, Volume III, No 3, June-July 1965, Page 5
ccxlviii The UFO Investigator, Vol. IV, No. 1, May-June 1967, p. 1; Pennsylvania NICAP Subcommittee report
ccxlix International UFO Reporter, 2010-2012, Volume 33, Page 23, original source: UFO Roundup, Vol. 10, no. 28, July 13, 2005

Chapter 25

ccl Nuclear Power Plant - Public Domain, commons.wikimedia.org; curid=363064
ccli The UFO Investigator, March 1968, Page 8
cclii "UFO's: A History, Loren E. Gross, 1955, July-September 15, Page 11, original source: Circleville, Ohio. Herald, July 6, 1955
ccliii "Sighting Advisory," The UFO Investigator, February 1977, Page 4

Chapter 26

ccliv US Air Force Project Blue Book Files: NARA T1206, Roll 0018, 1953, Key West Florida
cclv "UFO's: A History," Loren E. Gross, 1959, July-September, Page 30, original source: "UFO's: A History," Loren E. Gross, 1959 –SN, Page 6, "'Terror in Gulf Country," the Courier Mail, Brisbane
cclvi "Deputy Snaps UAO Color Photo," The APRO Bulletin, 1965, November- December 1965, Page 1 and 3 also at US Air Force Project Blue Book Files: NARA T1206, Roll 0058, 1965, October, St. George, Minnesota
cclvii US Air Force Project Blue Book Files: NARA T1206, Roll 0054, 1965, April, Illegible

Chapter 27

cclviii "Discs Vary From Tub to Cup in Size, Increase Noted in Reports of Objects Seen in Local Area," The Hartford Courant, July 8, 1947, Page 17
cclix US Air Force Project Blue Book Files: NARA T1206, Roll 0016, 1952, November, note the first card is illegible
cclx Haven Evening Register, Tuesday, Dec 9, 1952, found by Jan Aldrich, Project 1947

cclxi US Air Force Project Blue Book Files: NARA T1206, Roll 0022, 1954, December, Houston, Texas. The following account was published in the "Ultima Hora" on September 3, 1954, stated the above Brazil encounter

cclxii The APRO Bulletin April 15, 1955, Page 7, Walter Webb provided the story to APRO.

cclxiii "Hunter See UAO On ground In Venezuela, The APRO Bulletin, 1966, September, Page 8

cclxiv "UFO seen North Of Pittsburgh," Oil City Derrick, Oil City, Pennsylvania, April 20, 1968, Saturday, Page 1

cclxv "Tis the Season UFOs Abundant"; Fort Walton Beach Playground Daily News, Fort Walton Beach, Florida, October 18, 1973, Thursday, Page 1

cclxvi Bob Pratt and Dr. J. Allen Hynek; "Night Siege", Page 104-105.

Chapter 28

cclxvii Chief Joseph Hydroelectric Dam; By U.S. Army Corps of Engineers, photographer unknown - U.S. Army Corps of Engineers Digital Visual Library Image Visual Library home page, Public Domain, commons.wikimedia.org; curid=1896635

cclxviii US Air Force Project Blue Book File; 40 miles SW of Twin Falls [at Salmon Dam]. Idaho (BBU), McDonald list; FOIA; FUFOR Index

cclxix US Air Force Project Blue Book Files: NARA T1206, Roll 0002, 1947, August, Twin Falls, Idaho, Incident Number 75, the case was also sighted by Major Donald E. Keyhoe in one of his books, page 80, account found in the "Times News" entitled "Heads Up, Folks! The Discs are Flying Again", published on August 15, 1947, at Twin Falls, Idaho, also found in the UFO Investigator, January 1958, Page 17, also found at NARA-PBB86-630, Case IX (Serial 0066.00)

cclxx US Air Force Project Blue Book Records: NARA T1206, Roll 0002, 1948, July, San Acacia Dam, New Mexico, also MAXW-PBB3-1155, NARA-PBB2-1246, NARA-PBB3-1102, incident number 146; retrieved at bluebookarchive.org and archives.gov

cclxxi "Car and UAO in Near Collision Near Grand Coulee," The APRO Bulletin, 1967, Page 10

cclxxii NICAP – Lake Norman, NC, Personal Files of George D. Fawcett (1974)

Chapter 29

cclxxiii Over 5 Million American Say They've Seen UFOs", By George Gallup, Ogden Standard Examiner, Ogden, Utah, May 8, 1966, Sunday, Page 4A.

cclxxiv "Resident Tell UFO Sightings," Ogden Standard Examiner, Ogden, Utah, Saturday Evening, December 1, 1973, Page 1B

John Scott Chace

Made in the
USA
Middletown, DE